AFGHAN R

MW00365033

"Part memoir, part journalism and part storytelling, the book is a heady ride into the craziness that is Afghan life … [Arbabzadah's] deep affection for Afghanistan is as obvious as is her amusement about the absurdity of life there … For a look into an often misunderstood country from a woman who is both an outsider and an insider, *Afghan Rumour Bazaar* is a must read."

— Jyotsna Nambiar, *PostNoon*

"Nushin Arbabzadah's Afghanistan is a wonderful and terrible place, a land of heart-stopping beauty and unspeakable horrors … The book is chaotic, and wonderfully so. Its great strength as a national portrait is that the jumble of anecdote and analysis, with serious scholarship and pithy observation and trivial detail all thrown in together, feels three-dimensional and complete."

— Cordelia Jenkins, *Mint*

"*Afghan Rumour Bazaar* … takes the reader deep into the Afghan culture … The book offers an almost-irreverent, splendidly revealing take on Afghanistan."

— *The Telegraph (Calcutta)*

"A brilliant narrative of the often-overlooked emerging threads and subcultures in Afghanistan."

— *Outlook Magazine*

NUSHIN ARBABZADAH

Afghan Rumour Bazaar

*Secret Sub-Cultures, Hidden Worlds
and the Everyday Life of the Absurd*

HURST & COMPANY, LONDON

First published in the United Kingdom in 2013 by
C. Hurst & Co. (Publishers) Ltd.,
41 Great Russell Street, London, WC1B 3PL
© Nushin Arbabzadah, 2013
All rights reserved.

Printed in India

Distributed in the United States, Canada and Latin America by
Oxford University Press, 198 Madison Avenue, New York, NY 10016,
United States of America.

A Cataloguing-in-Publication data record for this book
is available from the British Library.

ISBN: 978-1-84904-231-4

www.hurstpublishers.com

This book is printed using paper from registered sustainable
and managed sources.

Dedicated to the accidental victims of Afghanistan.

CONTENTS

CONTENTS

CONTENTS

PROLOGUE

A Health and Safety Warning

After throwing up into a rose bush, the drunk Afghan communist staggered, just about avoiding a head over heels, face down, fall. Mini-disaster avoided, he recovered his balance and looked at the footprint left behind in the soil. He stared at it as if it were a work of art and blurted out, "The footprint of a dog!"

My twelve year-old brother and my eight year-old self put the man into our father's car and asked for directions to his home. It was a dark night, and the bribery party my father had thrown for the communist regime's minor leaders was ending. Dad called himself a businessman and you could not do business in Afghanistan unless you paid what basically amounted to extortion money to the regime. This sharing-the-turf mentality has always been part of our political culture. We Afghans are an economically unproductive people—life is all about sharing the few resources we have. It's about grabbing, shifting and sharing economic resources with brute force. This thievery is dressed up as ideology and served to the nation as socialism, Islam or democracy. The bottom line is robbery disguised as politics, religion and culture.

My brother and I had a hard time keeping a straight face. "The dog's footprint" became our favorite phrase for a long time, making us burst into laughter each time we remembered it. Looking back, I realize that we were traumatized and the dark humor was our method of coping with an otherwise unbearable reality. We drove the drunk communist home because many more drunk communists were still in our house, needing post-intoxication care. Like all young boys, my brother was obsessed with cars so he used the urgency of the situation, offering our father his services as a driver. Under normal circumstances our father would not have allowed my brother to drive because he was a child. But that night, he was overwhelmed and caved in.

It was midnight. My brother was driving and I, his moral support, was sitting on the passenger seat next to him. We both kept an eye on the regime's representative, making sure he got home alright. At the time, scenes like this seemed perfectly normal to me. I didn't know that I was living in an exceptional country where collective irrationality reigned supreme, the madness served to us as "our distinct way of life."

"Have you ever met this kind of people? Do they exist any-where else in the world?" I asked my Afghan friend in LA. She and I meet up for breakfast every week and exchange our Afghan stories. I guzzle down coffee, she keeps to her healthier herbal teas. We are both academics teaching in the United States and we both admit that our qualification does not equip us to understand the craziness of our own people. "Nope, I don't know any people like that among other communities," my friend shakes her head every time we exchange another bizarre story. Like the one about the recently dead soothsayer of the San Fernando Valley whose expertise it was to solve Afghan office workers' social anxiety problems by giving them magic spells. My Afghan friends reassure me that my experiences are pretty normal by Afghan standards—they are just a bit on the extreme side. But everyone who has been to Afghanistan and dealt with Afghans knows about the madness and absurdity that is inevita-bly mixed up in Afghans' heartrendingly tragic stories. Maybe adopting absurdity as a way of life is itself a collective survival strategy. Over centuries we have left our problems unresolved so they grew, becoming super complicated. Little wonder, then, that many Afghans believe that it would take a miracle, a proper divine intervention complete with thunder and lightening, to sort us out.

In 2008, when I first started writing about Afghanistan, I was obsessed about finding out the truth. But the deeper I dug, the more confusing the stories became. Even simple stories had many layers to them and by the end of my research I would have to admit to myself that the truth was exceptionally elusive to us Afghans. Ours is an oral culture. We are a people of warrior poets and warlord balladeers. We routinely embellish these stories for dramatic effect, inventing new angles, adding new "facts". I was too deep in the Afghan morass to see that what I was dealing with was basically numerous tales that may or may not be true. I understood the plausibility of this assessment when the Afghan government launched one of its famous anti-corruption drives in 2008. My inbox was soon filled with offers of "proofs" that this or that minister was corrupt. The evidence came with a price tag, "If you can't afford to pay for this evidence, then I'll sell it to the Australian journalist who can actually afford it," said a source. I told him that the fact that the evidence was on sale made it useless. He laughed, understanding the absurdity of the endeavor.

Ultimately, I gave up on the idea of finding the truth. After all, we were a nation of fakers. If you looked at statistics, you would find numerous employees on payrolls, school teachers, for example, or new school buildings, but few of them actually existed in the real world. They existed on paper and few people tried to check whether they were actually there. Rather conveniently, the schools were often in officially dangerous places so only suicidal people dared to check out whether the buildings listed on official documents were made of bricks and mortar. Whether the female teachers, the cooks and cleaners listed on payrolls were actual beings of flesh and blood. In reality, somebody somewhere pocketed the money intended for such ghost institutions and staff. An Afghan warlord summed up the situation neatly. He was asked on television about his activities as a factional commander during the wars of the early 1990s. The journalist was rigorous and wouldn't cave in, "Do you or do you not admit that you gave orders for rockets to be fired which ultimately killed civilians?" The warlord kept shifting on his sofa and finally blurted out, "Look, this is Afghanistan. Somebody fires a rocket; it hits somewhere and kills someone. Who fired the rocket or why? No-one knows!" Earlier, the television program had shown footage of civilians cowering under a bridge, trying to avoid being hit by stray rockets thrown around the city. A tiny, terrified girl little girl burst into hysterical crying, holding on to her mother's burqa. But who were the people firing the rockets? The warlord's statement neatly summed up Afghan politics—nobody knew; nobody cared.

We don't know what to do with our warlords. We pretend that like poisonous mushroom, they grew in the wild or that they were parachuted onto Afghan soil by evil enemies. The truth that they are products of our own society is too painful to accept so we resort to fantasy. There is a spooky story about a young woman who was shot dead by a warlord in the 1990s. The story goes that after killing the girl, God took revenge on behalf of the innocent female by producing a lightning bolt which hit and killed the warlord on the spot. The girl's grave subsequently became a shrine. What is creepy about this story is that the warlord is still alive. He drives around the town in his well-recognized land cruiser just as people tell the story of his having been killed through divine intervention. The line separating reality from fantasy is often blurred in Afghanistan, perhaps as a collective coping mechanism. From the inception in the 1980s, the fog of war has been a useful smokescreen for covering up crimes as politically-motivated action. The tradition continues with the new official enemy: the Taliban. A father may kill his daughter for reasons of "honor" and then blame it on the Taliban. The Taliban usually happily admit to the killings they haven't actually committed (after all, it enhances their reputation for brutality). Local journalists then write up a story about the Taliban murdering a young woman in such-and-such district. There are no checks or balances—there is no way of finding out the actual truth. Afghanistan is the land where even the truth has become ghostlike.

When my uncle disappeared in the early days of the communist regime, my family was told that he had been killed by the regime's secret service. Looking back, I am no longer certain it was the regime. It could have been anyone, a business rival, a friend or maybe, someone from his own extended family. I have given up on finding out the truth in Afghanistan. All I can offer to readers of this book is how Afghans understand their personal truths. If you, the reader, are looking for concrete answers, for solutions fitting neat academic models or political theories, then, this book is not for you. We are too chaotic, complex and unknowing of ourselves to fit theories and categories. To describe Afghanistan other than the absurdity and chaos that it mostly is would amount to fantasy, if not a lie. This, the reflection of people's thoughts, is the closest I could get to the truth as perceived by Afghans. That is why this prologue is a health and safety warning. This books reflects the chaos that we are.

To simplify the disorder, I have divided the book into three parts. Part One is the typically Afghan-tragicomedy that has been my life. A personal story, after all, is a fragment of a nation's story. This is my official excuse but the truth is that I didn't know how to write an introduction that was not sleep-inducing. That is why when the Afghan inner rebel in me came to my rescue I was more than happy to oblige and listen to her. This inner voice told me to improvise and tell my own story instead of writing a conventional introduction. "No introduction can be as interesting as my life story"; I rationalized my decision the way we always rationalize our failures. But there's more to the biography part than the story of my life. I offer you, the reader, the "buy one get one free" option. Through my own story, I reflect on and compare Afghanistan under the Soviet occupation to the present society under US occupation. After all, the Soviets were a homogeneous dictatorial power with a clear vision for the countries under their occupation. The international community, by contrast, is democratic and divided with contradictory visions for Afghanistan. Dictatorship and aerial bombing are logical companions while drones and democracy don't go well together, creating confusion among Afghans.

The confusion is exacerbated by Afghans' own unpredictability. We Afghans are not used to order, planning and foresight and this makes us good at improvisation, at coming up with unorthodox, if not crazy, solutions that we can always justify this or that way. The world has been both kind and brutal to us—so I hope that kindness prevails when readers realize that replacing the introduction with my mini-biography is yet another Afghan trick. I learned the gimmick in Afghanistan. We were stuck on the other side of the iron-curtain with no access to the West. Every time my father's Fiat car broke down, he couldn't get replacement parts from the car's producers in Italy, Brazil and Argentine. They were forbidden places. But with the help of his creative car mechanic, he learned to replace the car's original Italian tires with Japanese ones and so forth. Over time, the car became a curiosity. The small international community of Kabul at the time would often stare at the car, wondering at the way it was put together with a mishmash of exotic parts that did not match but somehow still worked. "You have to make do with whatever you have," my Afghan friends told me, and I followed their advice.

If part one is me and my homeland under the Soviet leadership versus me and my country under American leadership, then, Parts Two and Three have little to do with me and all to do with Afghanistan. They are about culture, politics and war. They are neat and coherent and make more sense than the story of my life. The book, in a way, is written in the style of classical Afghan literature. Each part and each essay is a stand-alone piece that can be read and understood by itself, without the need to have read the previous pages. This is how Afghans used to read classical Persian literature. You opened a book at a random page and you read a stand-alone story. The only difference is that unlike classical Afghan literature, my essays often do not entail a moral lesson at the end. I have decided that the moral lesson is the job of Afghan mullahs (shifting unpleasant responsibilities is yet another favorite Afghan pastime).

The reader will be pleased to know that we have reached the end of this health and safety warning. If the book turns out not to be to your taste, then, please accept my apologies and picture me shame-faced, hiding under the black dining table on which it was written. Add to the image a purring, Himalayan Seal Point cat (a mountain Persian, like me) and you might find it in your heart to forgive me. Enough of Afghan melodrama (another national characteristic), get on with reading and if you don't like what you read, skip it and go to the next story. There is something for everyone in here. Or so I hope.

PART ONE

A Backstory by Way of Introduction

Booze Bribes and Illegal Exits

If the Coen brothers were to make a film about Afghanistan, it would be called *No Country for Nice Men*. My father was a nice man, sensitive and incapable of standing up for himself against brutes. One of his earliest childhood experiences was of sectarian violence. A bunch of kids started to play "let's stone the infidels," beginning with throwing stones at Shi'ite-owned stores. When they figured out that my father was a Shi'ite, they started to throw stones at him, too. He went home upset but instead of comforting him, his older brothers beat him.

The beating was in fact terror in disguise. His brothers were alarmed that my father's protest against injustice would turn the majority community of Sunnis against the minorities, setting off a violent sectarian uprising, targeting Jews and Shi'ites. Bloodshed had to be avoided and through the terror of physical abuse, my father was taught a lesson to shut up. The fault lines of Afghans' unresolved conflicts were encapsulated in that childhood experience and my father's fighting spirit was broken as a child. In theory, in Afghan culture kindness is encouraged because it's the way of Islam but in reality, brutes reign supreme. The whole nation is hostage to psychopaths, leaving healthy minds with three options: to fight back, to submit but keep one's option open or to numb one's senses with drugs or insanity. It was only natural that my father had zero chance of surviving in Afghanistan, especially during the war when the brutes became leaders. He decided to flee and in 1988, put his small family on a flight from Kabul to Delhi.

Standing at the top of the plane stairs, already nostalgic, he turned his head and threw one last glance at Kabul's mountains. He was also a romantic and Afghanistan was no country for romantics either. The truth was that over the previous three years, the not-so-beautiful mountains of Kabul had lost their virginity. The mujahedin had penetrated them as their frontline. From the heights of the mountains the Moojs fired rockets into Kabul, often shooting blanks. The bearded men were sloppy. It was the poor quality of their fighting that made them dangerous. One time, they aimed at a government office nearby but hit our neighbor's home instead. When the couple returned in the evening, they found their matrimonial bed chopped neatly in half. The cut may not have been a perfect split as the neighborhood rumour merchants said. But still, the rocket landing inside the bedroom was a fact. We met them afterwards and saw terror in their eyes. They fled and Afghanistan lost two highly-trained specialist doctors. The country was quickly becoming no land for educated people.

No-one, least of all the Moojs themselves, could guarantee that their explosives would kill their intended targets of Soviet and Afghan soldiers and officials. Little wonder, then, that the war was doomed from the outset, with the Soviet interest in Afghanistan dwindling fast. After all, how could Moscow draw up a strategy against an enemy that could not know its own immediate actions? Having lived for centuries in conditions of uncertainty, Afghans had lost their capacity for planning and foresight (unless they planned an escape) becoming masters of improvisation and living in the moment. It was precisely this unpredictability that made the Moojs unconquerable, proving the truth of the Afghan saying that there is no winning against the insane. As the number of accidental martyrs killed in sloppy Mooj attacks exploded, a mass exodus of those who were not suicidal took place. My family was part of this collective flight.

When I lived in Kabul, I was a run of the mill "good Afghan girl"—shy and submissive, with only the vaguest sense of self. School, society and family had all made an effort to fulfill their collective duty of turning me into a non-person. They were doing me a favor—a non-person, after all, was the closest thing to the ideal Afghan girl. It was the nearest proximate to the perfect girl but not its embodiment. The perfect girl would have pale skin, green eyes, and yellow hair. She would be fourteen years old, and her bones would be covered with just one pound of fat. This teenager would be so secluded that, as a saying went, she would not have seen the sun or the moon in her entire life. She would be, as another pearl of Afghan wisdom went, a "*cheshm va goosh basta*," a girl who had, metaphorically speaking, her eyes and ears closed. Such was the glorification of female ignorance in Afghan society. If you were a girl, you aspired to becoming the human equivalent of a baby rabbit—a mammal born with closed ears and eyes.

I later realized that at the core of this ideal lay a basic misunderstanding, a confusing of ignorance with innocence. Such mix-ups were common on the list of desirable Afghan qualities. In their "wisdom" the folks had confused recklessness with bravery, militant dogmatism with religious devotion and banditry with politics. My family raised me typically Afghan because I was a girl and otherwise I would have been in danger. But in all other aspects, they were too different from the ideals of the common man to stand a chance against them, be they in the seats of power, on the streets, or the mountains of Kabul. Our escape was politically caused but it also had cultural reasons. "You are Muslim so why don't you have more kids when you can feed them? Why don't you come to the mosque to pray together with us? Why does your wife sit in the front seat of the car?" Random neighborhood people, a class of conspicuously pious new rich merchants who had made money in the war economy, kept pestering my father with these questions. They had no respect for privacy and individual choices. As Hamid Nilofar, the first openly gay Afghan man, puts in his memoirs *Passing Through a Nightmare*, many of us are cultural refugees. In his time in Turkish and Iranian exile, Hamid had met young Afghan boys who had escaped arranged marriages with the cousins they had never met. He met married gay men who had fled their wife and kids and single gay men who had escaped the fate of having to marry a woman, impregnate her and give her sons. He encountered families who had escaped because their daughter had fled with a boy and the community would not leave them in peace even in exile, mocking and harassing them constantly because of the dishonor. These cultural refugees would rather do hard, physical work on construction sites in Iranian towns than live with mainstream Afghans. Ours was an oppressive, dictatorial culture where the common man dictated life for everybody else.

Violating the Borders of Our Own Country

When Afghan communists and mujahedin and their international backers turned Afghanistan into a warzone in the 1980s, we became a nation of smugglers. We smuggled each other and ourselves out of our own country and into other countries. Our borders had been violated by the Red Army from the north and we violated our own borders and the borders of other people in return. This is the problem of illegal action like military invasion—it triggers a spin-off of endless other illegal actions, with illegality ultimately becoming legitimized.

On the day of our exit in 1988, we smuggled ourselves illegally out of Afghanistan. My family had ended up on the communist regime's "black list," with my father finding himself under house arrest. His "crime" was to have rented his house to the Japanese embassy (he couldn't compete with the bearded meat-and-vegetable mafia that monopolized the food industry, owing to their good relations with the Moojs, so he rented his house to make a living). This was sufficient reason for the authorities to regard my father as a spy for the West. But the Afghans' famous corruption came to our rescue and my father paid a considerable bribe to get us out of our dangerous homeland.

At the airport, we went through eight baggage searches before reaching the departure lounge. In each bag, my father had hidden a bottle of vodka. At every search spot, the mustached airport officials would rummage the bags and discover a bottle of Russia's favorite drink. Feigning surprise, they confiscated the alcohol in the name of Muslim piety but knew that the booze was a bribe intended for them. The airport officials, after all, had a reputation for regularly downing vodka is if it were their last day on earth—given the risks, every day could indeed have been their last. As if it was not bad enough that we had to flee our own country, to reach this goal, we had to intoxicate our own people. For an officially dry country, the frequency of booze bribes was quite remarkable. The airport staff knew their part in this comedy and dutifully held up the bottle, pulling a disgusted face before winking and breaking into a happy grin. "*Boro bakhair*," go with god, they said. For a long time I had the misconception that the communist regime's guards were the only ones to be bribed with booze. I stood corrected when a friend told me that his family had bribed the Mooj guards at the Pakistani border with Scottish whiskey. Vodka for communist guards, whisky for their Mooj nemesis; to each their own international backers' favorite drink.

After a hard day of rummaging the bags of escapees, the airport officials went on all-night booze benders in *Shahr-e Naw* neighborhoods' restaurants. Just like in New York, these eateries stayed open throughout the night, filled with drunk Afghan and Soviet spies and security officials. Kabul's nights belonged to these men who knew the post-curfew security code and roamed the streets freely. The rest of us cowered in the corners of our rooms, dodging rocket attacks. Looking back, I hope that the airport guards enjoyed the vodka, and celebrated our escape from our own people. After all, we all were together in this game of deception and corruption, intoxication and exit.

Mission Accomplished

We arrived in Delhi at night. The distinct smell of India, a mixture of gasoline, excrement and spice, was in the air. At the baggage reclaim section, we met other Afghan families on the run and immediately lied to each other, "Of course we are going to go back to Kabul. This is just a little holiday." India at the time was a Soviet ally, and Kabul's secret police were operating in Delhi. We were told back in Kabul that the spies were keeping an eye on Afghan families who intended to go to the West. This story might have been just a rumour but it was still terrifying, prompting everyone to lie. We had left Afghanistan physically but the emotional scars of persecution had traveled with us.

My favorite Afghan folktale is a story about invisible wounds. The folktale's hero is a bear who loves and trusts his human companion, wanting to sit by his side day and night. The need for constant companionship is typically Afghan, driving foreign visitors, who are used to having their privacy and space, to distraction. (The constant companionship is also a reaction to the widespread thuggery that is politely referred to as "insecurity." After all, two people are better-equipped at tackling thieves than solitary travellers.) The bear is a constant friend and companion of the human but one day, the human becomes irritated and tells the bear to move away by a meter or so. Puzzled, the bear asks, "Why?" The human says, "Because you stink." Displaying a typically-Afghan flair for all things melodramatic, the bear stands up full length, pulls a knife (yes, even our bears carry knives) and cuts a wound across his chest. He makes the human watch the blood stream down his fur. With this startling gesture of self-mutilation (martyrdom, after all, is big in Afghanistan), the bear leaves the human, marching off into distant wilderness. Some years pass with no sight of the bear. But one day, out of the blue, the bear re-appears. Standing on his hind legs, he points at his chest and says, "As you can see, the knife scar is no longer visible. But inside I am still bleeding." With this, the bear is gone again, heading back to the dark woods that separate humans from beasts.

We had left Afghanistan but, like the bear, we carried our invisible wounds with us. In Delhi, my father kept looking over his shoulders, expecting to be arrested at any moment. One time we walked past a group of Russians and were about to make a run for it when we realized that not only were they peace activists, one of them even played the accordion.

The World is Our Oyster (or Not)

In the Indian capital, with a vicious war behind and an uncertain future ahead of us, we sought out a reliable human smuggler. The Indian capital was home to thousands of Afghan and Iranian refugees, waiting for visas to take them to Australia, Europe and North America. A thriving black market of second-hand goods had emerged, catering for the needs of new arrivals and those about to depart for the West. Finding a reliable smuggler was a terrifying prospect. Stories abounded of conmen who took large sums, promising a safe passage to the free world only to disappear, leaving families stranded and penniless. My father sought out a trusted family from our original hometown of Herat, an Afghan patriarch who was the envy of Delhi's Afghan community. He was father to three young, obedient sons. "They have THREE healthy, grown-up, SONS!" the community women hissed, green with envy. The family also had some fine daughters who, needless to say, were overshadowed by their brothers. No matter where in this world we went, we took our misogyny with us, protecting it as if it were our highest achievement. It was the girls who brought us tea while the patriarch bragged that his sons were at our disposal, ready to help with anything. (In a way, every large Afghan family, my family included, is a mini-mafia clan run by a Don Corleone and a host of cousin co-conspirators. It is the position of the godfather that everyone contests in internal clan struggles that go on for generations. This is the secret domestic war of Afghans that is not globally known). The patriarch told us about our savior, a trusted human smuggler. "I give you my word. He is trustworthy," he said, sipping at his tea on a hot Indian afternoon.

In Comes the Savior

The smuggler's name was Sharif—and this was ironic given that his name meant "he who is noble and respectable." He was a tall, mustached man in his thirties and always dressed in jeans and trainers. His face was tanned, his teeth bright and his eyes flashing. There was too much sparkling going on across his face. And then there was the permanent wolf-like smirk. He was a morally ambivalent man, an ex-sheep that had become a wolf. Over a lunch of Iranian rice and kebab in Bombay, Sharif told us that back in the early 1980s when he was a communist bureaucrat in Kabul, he had an epiphany one day. He looked out of his office window, watching the filthy road outside. It was clogged with dirty cars, skinny mules, burqa-clad women, and a bunch of beggars, all of them vying for space. It was at this instant of sudden lucidity that he realized that communism had little chance in Afghanistan. The former idealist said, "I liked the communist ideology, the dream of equality and progress. But it had no chance in *Afghanistan*!" He stressed the last word as if to say, "You get my meaning, right?"

My father knew what Sharif was on about. In his own time, my father had seen the same stubborn opposition to change. He had offered the people of his ancestral village his own money to build schools, but the pious folks were uninterested. They said, "If you want to do something good, Nasir jaan, build us a mosque." Later in life, when my father tried to regain the land illegally confiscated from the family, he once again promised to build a girls' school in the village; the villagers had told him that the only girls' school in the region was too far away and for security reasons, they couldn't afford to send their daughters, for fear of abduction and rape. But my father lost the land to pious folks in our own family who had joined the land mafia. They built the villagers a mosque. The battle against the pious criminal common man was once again lost in the last years of my father's life. He died, defeated.

In encounters with educated Afghans, the common man is not exactly modest. The dictatorship of Afghan folk wisdom means that he usually knows better and makes no secret of his superior knowledge. Generations of egalitarian movements, from Communism, Socialism and Maoism to all sorts of Islamisms had played their role in sustaining the common man's cultural power as "the only rightful representative of authentic Afghanistan," legitimizing hostility towards progressives and intellectuals. Lazy thinkers that we were, few people had dared to challenge the holy cow of traditional Afghan wisdom. There were avant-garde circles of progressive cultural critics in the 1920s and later the 1960s and 1970s but they all lost the cultural battle to the common man. Owing to representing the majority of Afghans, the common man had a solid sense of entitlement. He had God on his side and centuries of traditional wisdom. In our age of dogmatic obsession with cultural authenticity—a spin-off of minority rights in the United States—the common man has new allies among liberal Westerners who dismiss intellectual Afghans as "not authentic enough." The common man is glorified abroad (clue, Ghaith Abdul-Ahad's articles about the Taliban published in *The Guardian*) and on the ground. In Afghanistan, the common man's wisdom is dictatorial, handed down as it is by our ancestors. Religion among Afghans, after all, is nothing but ancestor worship. That is why at the beginning of every new year, the political pillars of society gather together to pray and pay their respects to the founding fathers, *Baba*s, of Afghanistan.

I got a taste of this attitude during a debate panel with Afghan and American audiences. Hearing me speak, an Afghan exile and devotee of the common's man's wisdom ideology stood up and shouted, "Oh yes, you experts with your international degrees! Throw around your fancy ideas. But we all know that the common man knows best." The liberal Americans in the audience nodded in agreement, throwing him glances that said, "Well done for standing up for your people against these westernized lackeys of US cultural imperialism!" I tested the common man theory in Kabul and it went like this. I would be driving around the city in a taxi and every time we passed a historical landmark, I would ask the representative of the common man par-excellence, the cab driver, "So what's this building?" The common man would look, shrug and say, "It's an old building." Wanting to give the theory another chance, I would inquire further, "Who built it?" And the answer I would get was, "An old king."

But back to Sharif, our smuggler and savior. On the day of his epiphany, Sharif decided to ditch communism and seek his fortunes abroad, smuggling illegal Afghan immigrants for around US$1,500 per head. At the time, this was a considerable sum, allowing only for wealthy families to leave chaotic and dangerous Asia for the order and safety of the West. Taking a sip from his coke, Sharif told us what happened next, "I put my communist membership card into my drawer, closed it and left the building, and never, even once, looked back." He was happy now, an independent bachelor entrepreneur with dollars in his pocket and a pistol in his sock. The only thing missing in his life was a wife, a girl from a good family. In Asia, a good family is a euphemism for a wealthy clan and it doesn't matter how the wealth has been acquired. The idea that good equals money is widespread throughout Asia and people use the attribute without a hint of irony. Sharif proceeded to offer his views of the community in Delhi, "Afghan girls in Delhi have all gone astray. You see them walk in public parks, listening to music on their Walkman and chewing gum in public!" He found the girls' behavior bordering on prostitution. Getting excited, he blurted out, "There's even an Afghan prostitute in Delhi. I have seen her." He then noticed my father's discomfort (after all, we were a "good family") and dropped the subject.

Sharif was an aspirational Afghan, and with money no longer an issue, he was seeking social prestige through marriage to a rich family. He wanted to stride up the social ladder, making sure that his name, "the respectable one," matched his social position. My father nodded politely to this plea, knowing that Sharif's dream was practically impossible. If Afghanistan's media image was one of homogeneous masses of uniformly poor-looking people, the reality could not have been more different. The truth was and still is that just like gender, class, too, was destiny in Afghanistan. The rich only married each other. When love marriages took place between a rich girl and a poor boy (or the other way around), the result was often an unhappy family haunted by the ghosts of class inequality. My grandmother, for example, who came from provincial aristocracy, referred to her husband of poor origins as, "that pitiful orphan." It was this sharp inequality in wealth and opportunities that first radicalized the Kabul university campus in the 1960s and 70s, creating two proletarian-based political fronts, the communists and the mujahedin. Sharif had been part of the former but now, he wanted to join the very elite he used to fight in his left-wing days.

Spot the First World

Bombay was our next destination after the Afghan patriarch had introduced us to Sharif in Delhi. Sharif said Bombay's airport was better suited than Delhi for smuggling illegals out of India. He was in our hotel room and ordered a round of tea, relaxing in a chair and waiting for the Indian waiter to leave the room. For some reason, Indian waiters liked to stare at customers in a manner that can only be described as disconcerting. Exactly what went through their minds as they stared was a mystery because their faces remained blank. When the waiter left, Sharif posed the key question, "Where in the world do you want to go to?" He paused, unfolding a map of the world on the table. I stared at the map. Most of the countries depicted there were miserable, full of wars, poverty and conflict—just like our own homeland. We opted for Germany because we already had family there.

The next step was to choose the right nationality for our fake passports so that we could pass through the airport without getting caught. Stealing legitimate passports and faking them was the key task of human smugglers. We were a small family of four which made things easy for Sharif. He was a seasoned professional, having already smuggled to the free world typically large Afghan families of twelve or more people. Imagination and creativity were crucial in the smuggling business. To avoid drawing attention to themselves, large families had to be split into smaller units, with brothers and sisters presented as married couples and parents to their younger siblings. Some men had two wives and with polygamy banned in refugee destinations of the West, they had to present one of the wives as their sister. When the sister/ wife inevitably became pregnant at some point, the situation could only be described as *awkward* (pronounced with a Californian accent). The husband either had to come clear or face incest charges. It felt like deception was just an inevitable part of survival if one happened to be born Afghan. My family, too,

PART ONE

joined this circus of pretense as our smuggler introduced us to the ways of the Europeans. The goal was to observe their manner of dress, walking and talking and to copycat all three.

Our amateur ethnographic study of the people of the free world took place on the streets of Bombay. The enterprise was undignified as it involved stalking European tourists, as if we were a bunch of bird enthusiasts and they, exotic birds. The aim was to watch, understand and imitate them. This, in turn, would help us pretend to be free worlders and pass through the airport without our "developing world" identity sticking out like a sore thumb. Sharif, who was quite enjoying this part of his job, summed up the key difference in eastern and western esthetics, "As you can see, unlike us Asians, Europeans don't bejewel themselves. They don't walk about covered in gold, looking like wedding camels." We started stalking a group of pale, emaciated, sweaty Europeans. "They are all heroin addicts," Sharif explained (in hindsight, I realized that the tourists must have been suffering from Indian heat and Bombay belly). I noticed that something curious had happened to the people we were stalking. The men had long hair while the women sported closely cropped hair cuts—though not without also wearing hoop earrings. I had been raised in a society where the only men with long hair were Sufis and mountain rebels. Respectable men kept their hair short while respectable women kept theirs long. The tourists in front of me confused me. I was timid but was also dying to walk up and ask the men, "Are you really men?" and ask the women, "Are you really women?" Sharif noticed my curiosity and warned my parents, "Your daughter is too inquisitive. Keep an eye on her or she'll get you all caught and imprisoned."

He was right. I had developed an obsession with authentic versus fake. I always checked the roots of women's hair, acting like a self-appointed fashion police. In a post-office with a long line of Iranians waiting to call their relatives in Canada, for example, I blurted out, "This one is Iranian pretending to be Canadian." The woman was mortified.

13

After some more preparatory lunch meetings where we were stared at by Indian waiters, Sharif made a decision. He said what we needed was Israeli passports. My parents were taken aback but Sharif gave them a look that said, "Have a look at yourselves in the mirror. Do you seriously think I can pass you as Norwegians?" Israel was the perfect country because its people typically had our complexion and hair color. He explained that the people whose passports he stole would encounter little problem. All they needed to do was to turn up at their embassy and report the passports stolen. Watching the look of dismay on my father's face (we were from a "good family"), Sharif changed track, "I don't steal them, I was joking. I buy them with the money you give me and trust me, they are more than happy to oblige. Everybody wins in this game, you see. Everybody gets money and they can get extended holidays while waiting for their new passports."

A week later, we held our fake Israeli passports, complete with Jewish names and the city of Tel Aviv as our hometown. On the night of departure, the former Leninist turned smuggler rushed to a bar famous for its whisky. "If they catch you, tell them that the smuggler was Indian," he shouted before disappearing into the crowds.

Becoming Professionally Afghan

In 2004, I applied for a job as a chief sub-editor for BBC Monitoring's Afghan desk and was asked for an interview. Needless to say, given that Afghans were involved in this enterprise, a surreal scenario was bound to unfold. The unfolding occurred during the second interview stage which involved a team-building exercise dreamed up by the HR office. Personifying the UK's equal opportunity laws, HR included two people of Asian and African origins, one woman of size and a wheelchair-bound colleague. Seated on plastic chairs against bare walls, the diversity group watched us in action. We were three Afghans and one Iranian; two women and two older, middle-aged men. The exercise's purpose was to exam our teamwork abilities. Communication, after all, was key to the job we had applied for. The idea, to sum up, was to show that we could work together efficiently.

As the exercise began, the Afghan man in our group launched into a vicious attack against everybody else, gleefully pointing out our faults and mistakes, sometimes telling us plainly that we were ignorant. Given the excitement on his face, he enjoyed this mini-jihad against his fellow competitors. I recalled a poem by Pazhwak, a famous Afghan poet and diplomat. It was about Alexander the Great's bewilderment with the Afghans under his rule. In the poem, which is a letter to his mother, Alexander says something to the effect of, "if you put four Afghans in room together with a non-Afghan in presence, they soon start fighting each other." He then adds, "They are very patriotic but as soon as they smell the soil of their country in each other, they start a war." This was exactly what was happening in the small HR room of BBC Monitoring.

Ten minutes into the performance, the diversity team collectively let its hair down, bursting into laugher and taking pleasure in our tragicomic performance. Looking back, I am not surprised they let themselves relax. I later learned that the HR-team had nothing to lose because they were already facing the sack due to BBC cost-cutting. Besides, no-one could accuse them of discrimination or racism; they had all minorities in their group, big people, disabled people, dark-skinned people. If we had raised objection, it would have been us to face the accusation of discrimination. Be that as it may, the team had a field day of free comedy with us. They left the room without a word, shaking their heads in disbelief. The four of us shared a taxi, acting as if the attack that was obviously for the benefit of the non-Afghan observers, had not taken place and we were all good friends. We even invited each other to tea and future meetings and in a strange and unfathomable way, we really meant it when we said, "Yes, let's stay in touch." As the taxi reached the train station, referring to the HR team building game, the Afghan man exclaimed, "Ah, the British. Strange people! They don't cut your throat with a sharp knife. They do it subtly, with a piece of cotton."

In team-building workshops on the ground in Afghanistan, Afghans tearing each other apart is a regular occurrence. One trainer in Kabul confided in me her own experience of such an exercise. "I asked my class to write anonymous feedback notes about the strengths and weaknesses of their fellow workshop mates. When I opened the notes, I couldn't believe my eyes. They all, men and women alike, were ripping each other into pieces. It was unbelievable. I had to clarify that this was not what feedback was about." The non-Afghan trainers are often appalled at this inter-Afghan hostility but they keep mum for fear of being accused of racism. But the truth is that underneath the surface of the Afghans' polite conformism there lurks a strong spirit of ruthless rivalry. The country is poor and economically unproductive with trade the only financially worthwhile activity. Everybody is basically a business man or woman and the resources being limited, life becomes all about the survival of the ruthless and the beautiful. An Afghan saying sums up the competitiveness, "No-one wants to be a fifty-cent in Afghanistan, everyone wants to be nothing less than a dollar note!"

I got the job and joined my new Afghan team. Recounting the embarrassing episode of my fellow Afghan's aggressive competition in a game that was about cooperation, my colleague, a disillusioned but highly informed man, told me the following story.

In the 1980s Afghan and Polish exiles occasionally held joint, anti-Soviet protests in London. But while the Polish protestors stood out for their organization, having people allocated to distinct roles (banner holders, refreshment providers, and people who simply stood in the crowd in solidarity) the Afghan protesters found themselves in chaotic disarray. The crux of the problem was that no-one in the Afghan protest group wanted to be a mere banner-holder, a nothing of a standing protestor. Everybody wanted to be the keynote speaker. "You see, that is why the mujahedin divided into so many splinter groups. When you split from your group, you have the chance to become a leader yourself, running your own group. Everybody in Afghanistan wants to be nothing less than a leader." With this simple logic, my colleague solved the mystery of the endless internal splits that had ultimately brought down both the communists and the mujahedin. Understanding Afghan politics can be sometimes as simple as this. Sometimes there is no need for complex theories, or to use an American phrase, there is no need for over-think it.

Welcome to Globalized Afghanistan

Some twenty years after my family fled Afghanistan, I returned to Kabul, and felt slightly seedy for it. A bit like a murderess who is compelled to revisit the scene of her crime.

By contrast to my escape flight, the return one was ridiculously international: the pilot was British; the airline Afghan; the passengers global. The cultural influence of the Gulf Arab world on Afghans was already present on this flight. One look at the air hostesses and it became clear that they were the copycat versions of the Emirate counterparts I had met earlier on my London to Dubai flight. They wore the same skirt suits, the same voile hats, and the same hairstyle as the Emirate staff; the only difference was that the originals were taller, wore cream rather than blue uniforms and included natural blondes. The Emirate girls' style itself was a globalized mishmash—a combination of Islamic aesthetics (the voile and the striking eye make-up) and the western taste for smart skirts and bare calves. If the Emirate hostesses were designer goods, their Afghan airline counterparts were high-street imitations. Watching them walk the aisle, it occurred to me that we Afghans were fearful of being original, different, *ourselves*. In piety and politics, in style and conversation, in song and literature, we ended up looking and sounding like the cut-price version of others. This "others" could refer to anyone: American feminists, Iranian secularists or Arab Islamists. We were imitation nation and this, too, was a symptom of our confused identity.

The only Afghan staff of the flight was the head steward, a flirtatious hipster with an expensive hair-cut. Minutes before the plane took off for Kabul, he recited a surah from the Quran. He had a sweet Afghan accent in his Arabic but his intonation was off and his pronunciation jarring. Religion has always been omnipresent and superstitious in Afghanistan. The public surah recitation on the plane was part of a familiar ritual but there was also something new about it—a new pride in one's Muslim identity. A symbolic gesture of defiance, perhaps. An attempt to show that despite the British pilot, the Eurasian air hostesses and the international passengers, this flight was a still an Afghan flight and as such a Muslim flight. (The two always overlapped).

When the plane took off, it triggered a mini buzz of apprehension mixed with excitement that is typical of heading for a conflict zone. Twenty minutes into the flight over clear skies, there he was again, our British pilot with his Estuary English accent typical of Londoners. He said that for our own safety, we had to return to Dubai. The plane had a technical fault and engineers had been called in to look at the problem. The surah had failed to work its magic, maybe because the pronunciation was off. Religion was so superstitious in Afghanistan that even though mispronunciations of the Arabic words of the Quran were commonplace, knowing that one had actually pronounced god's words wrongly could strike terror into the heart of the believers. My uncle, for example, famously shouted during prayers, making sure that every syllable of his prayer was loud and clear for god to hear. Technology or divine intervention, the fact was that we returned to Dubai twenty minutes after taking off. It was a

PART ONE

bit humiliating but the Afghans on board took it with humor while the non-Afghans felt frustrated. If the airline embodied the magic of the new, thriving Afghan economy, then we had reason to worry. The airline was somewhat of a mirage. Its surface was reassuring, complete with a foreign pilot, smiling stewardesses and a head steward with a hipster haircut. But the vital element of the whole venture, the plane itself, was old, cranky and unwell—a little bit like Afghanistan itself.

As the plane returned to Dubai, the mercenaries on our flight (such soldiers of fortune were regulars on most Kabul-bound flights) become restless. Looking like toy troops, with square heads and shoulders, they gesticulated at the staff that they were thirsty, the way London office workers order beer after work on Fridays when the pubs are jam-packed. The only "I-need-hydration" gesture they knew was the one people use to order booze. Given the surah recitation half an hour earlier, the gesture seemed incongruous on this pious flight heading for the Islamic Republic of Afghanistan. The soldiers of fortune were seated in front of me, occupying row after row, after row. They had embarked the plane robotic and silent. But when the thirst kicked in on our return to Dubai, they became irate, awake and talkative. Being a trained linguist, I indulged in my favorite hobby in times of boredom in international surroundings; I tuned in to detect the mercenaries' nationality through their language. I knew that these tough guys tended to be truly international, coming from faraway places such as Germany and Ireland, Australia and South Africa. But the words I heard were Russian. I had a hard time trying not to burst into a fit of loud, crazy laughter, the kind of desperate hilarity that is associated with the corridors of mental institutions. The mercenaries were Russian! Twenty years earlier, I had fled a Kabul occupied by the Russian military. I was now returning home on a flight with a bunch of Russian legionnaires. Same shit another decade? Not exactly but nearly so. If there was any need for evidence for just

19

how pathetic our jihad had been, this was it. The Russians were back, this time as paid security guards.

But they, too, had changed. I remembered an episode from my school days in Kabul. I was called in to the principal's office and upon entering, my eyes fell on the photograph of Lenin on the principal's desk. She had placed the communist leader's black and white picture underneath a glass cover, protecting it from dust as if it were a religious icon. I noticed that Lenin's eyes were projecting unwavering political authority. As if by magic, Lenin's photograph had added power to the principal's authority by linking this ordinary Afghan woman to the seats of power in Moscow. I remember feeling humiliated that through Lenin, my school principal had gained a kind of internationally-supported power over me. At least the Russians I had fled from fought for pathos, myths and ideology in Afghanistan. The ones on the plane were just fighting for money.

What would Lenin have made of this surreal twist in the history of Russo-Afghan partnership? His face is too mummified to show a reaction but had he been buried like other mortal Russians, he would have turned in his grave and spat in disgust. I felt sorry for myself and my fellow Afghans on the plane. The Russians at least had suffered for something of international impact, a socialist empire whose effect was felt throughout the globe. We, on the other hand, did not even have the satisfaction of having suffered for something great. We had suffered for what became a civil war, followed by a stone-age, militant theocracy, followed by an international rescue mission that was about to finish prematurely. The plane was full of international aid workers.

A New, Sort of Lost, Society

Some twenty years had passed since my escape, a stretch of time in which both Afghanistan and I had changed. It would be fair to say that the change in me had been more dramatic. When I returned, I was no longer a typical Afghan girl who kept her gaze fixed to the ground, holding her mouth shut. After all, only the richest and the poorest societies of the world could afford to keep half of their population unproductive, tucking them away in domestic leisure activities or its opposite, plain domestic slavery. Germany, where I was raised after Kabul, was an economically productive society, requiring both men and women to work hard to keep the country going. My female Afghan quality of submissive shyness was not only useless in Europe but guaranteed a life spent in poverty. It took me a long time and much battle with the Afghan community to change and become an individual. My survival instinct sent me to a Maoist-style cultural re-education camp made all by myself. I learned to look men and women directly in the eyes, keep my head high and argue my point just so to be able to function normally in my new society. It was hard work and involved plenty of selfishness and guilt for betraying my roots. Needless to say, when I returned to my ancestral homeland, I was angry and vocal; educated and self-confident. Such qualities were valued in developed, post-industrial societies. In Afghanistan, they were regarded as exclusively male qualities and women who displayed them were regarded sometimes with admiration, but most of the time with contempt and suspicion.

Most men of my country were unimpressed with my new self, even the educated ones. For most of them, my having become an individual represented a negation of Afghan values. They had a name for people like me: "the foreign Afghans." This was their polite term. The more common name was "the pet groomers," referring to the fact that most Afghans who had lived abroad worked as manual laborers, sometimes walking dogs and picking dog poo for cash. Dogs are considered impure beasts among Afghans so the insult was doubly harsh. Ours was a judgmental society. The only people who were given true respect were those who had died for Afghanistan, even if their martyrdom was accidental, in a suicide attack targeting the foreign troops, for example.

My male critics and I had numerous silent fights in the shape of angry staring contests. One such contest took place inside a bookshop that used to be my favorite store as child. Back then, the store was filled with fine Russian literature and run by a friendly young woman with short hair and spectacles. The Moojs regularly bombed the bookshop but the female manager always re-opened it after it was repaired, cleaning its windows until they were shiny. In the dusty chaos of Kabul then, the bookshop was a haven of order and erudition. When I returned to this same bookshop a year ago, it was dirty, disorganized, and was run by a grumpy guy in his forties. The shelves were filled with Afghan-only, government-press books including theological treatises and revisionist histories complete with ethno-centrist historiographies, some of which had turned historically-notorious misogynist rebel leaders into champions of democracy. We were as sloppy with history as we were with everything else. And then there was the "iron man," my angry staring-contest partner. This man was dressed in white traditional loose top and trousers. He was old and had a protruding belly, which made him look pregnant. His belly was evidence that he had enough money to eat plenty and even feed others. In sum, he represented the ideal of the Afghan patriarch, the kind of man that must be respected. (Slim, smartly dressed young men are usually dismissed as "immature nobodies" in Afghan society, though youth television is slowly changing the worship of the old and the contempt for the young).

Browsing the books inspired by Iranian-style political Shi'ism, I noticed that the patriarch was shooting me hateful stares. I was in a bookshop and in his view, given that I was a woman, I was supposed be in the kitchen, my natural place. I was supposed to be doing what Afghan women were made to do: cooking food for eight kids, a grumpy husband and a pair of petulant in-laws. In the process, I was also supposed to grateful, counting my lucky stars for having been born a Muslim woman. This, after all, was what traditional wisdom dictated: that Afghan women belonged indoors and as such, were the luckiest women on the planet. The man was angry because instead of hiding in the seclusion of home, I was in a public place, perusing books in a bookstore. To be fair, I was the only woman in the bookshop but one could also argue that whatever I was doing was none of this man's business. But Afghans have little respect for individual privacy. If one is a woman who is out and about, one is automatically classified as public property and this is the price one pays for being out. This rule is unspoken, which makes it even more powerful. If a woman breaches the traditional code of conduct, she pays the price for it, says the folk wisdom gathered over centuries of isolation and ignorance. The price, in sum, was that everybody out there felt entitled to cross one's personal boundaries by staring, cat-calling, and groping.

If the patriarch in the bookstore was offended by my crossing the frontiers of gender roles, I, in turn, felt appalled by his disregard for bookshop etiquette. Bookshops were quiet places for deep souls who appreciated poetry, for example. This man, however, not only looked like an ignoramus, he acted like one, hissing and staring, while holding a flat iron in his hand. I soon realized that he was in the bookshop not to buy books but to test his flat iron. He must have known the manager of the bookshop, he could feasibly have been a family member. Such stray hangers-on were to be found in all public offices, including the presidential palace. They were unemployed and that's how they killed time, by hanging out in public offices. The lines between the public/official self and the private self were blurred in Afghanistan and that, too, was seen as normal.

The patriarch moved from socket to socket, plugging and testing the iron. During the testing, he still somehow managed to keep his angry stare fixed at me. He would spot a socket, plug in his iron and press the palm of his hand against the sole plate, his gaze fixed on me. The iron was obviously dead but the man just wouldn't give up. This, too, is a common Afghan quality. We are loath to give up and this persistence is called *shalagi*, a derogatory term associated with the stubbornness of toddlers. A family's persistence often pays off, eventually persuading a gay guy unwilling to marry either to flee or cave in and get engaged. An incompetent bureaucrat finally gets the promotion he wants but doesn't deserve. It is a battle between those with principles and the ones who apparently lack self-respect. The latter always wins. If I, the prodigal daughter, had returned home too confident for Afghan men's taste, they, in turn, had become too crude for my liking. I left the bookshop, armed with loads of books, leaving the iron man behind.

It was obvious that in the twenty years of my exile, the homeland I had left behind had changed. Ancestor worship and traditional wisdom still dictated all spheres of life. But there was one striking exception. The society I had left as a youngster used to be Afghan and Muslim in a natural, unselfconscious way. Upon arriving in Afghanistan from Iran, the British explorer, Robert Byron, summed up this quality in his 1930s travel book, *The Road to Oxiana*. He famously said, "Here at last is Asia without an inferiority complex." The society I returned to after exile was no longer matter-of-factly Muslim and Asian. Thirty years of experimentation with supra-national models of twentieth-century identities (from socialism to different types of political Islamism and ethnicized nationalism) had left its mark on the collective psyche. Afghan society had lost coherence and was in the midst of a full-blown identity crisis. Then there was the added factor of exile. Kabul is famously full of returnees, its original inhabitants having settled permanently in Europe and North America. The people I met in Kabul mostly had no idea who or what they were. They had lived as laborers and illegals, students and professionals in all corners of the world and had returned home with new hybrid identities. Exactly what it meant to be Afghan was no longer clear but what was evident was that people had absorbed cultural influences from every spot of the world. On the dusty streets of Kabul, I watched aspirational middle-class girls take hurried steps in their black *niqabs*, following the hijab style of the Arab Gulf women. In 2011, the burqa was no longer the Afghan symbol par-excellence of traditional modesty. Appearing on front pages of newspapers published in London and New York, the negativity campaigns abroad had mirrored back to the Hindukush, rendering the burqa a mere symbol of female poverty. In the words of a young professional, "Nowadays, only women beggars squatting on the roads wear the burqa." Afghans were beginning to look at themselves through the lens of the outside world and in the process they were becoming self-conscious and insecure about themselves. Their former innocence was lost for good. If the girls emulated the sartorial style of rich Arab women of the Gulf desert cities or the more daring girls of Tehran's streets, their male counterparts opted for the spiky, asymmetrical hair-cuts of London's hipsters from the rainier side of the planet.

This new society was carrying a huge burden on its shoulders by trying to be everything at once, democratic and authoritarian, progressive and traditional, Afghan and global. Its politics was equally a chaotic collage of ideologies contesting for primacy in a fledgling democracy. Afghanistan was an Islamic Republic and a democracy during the daytime, and in some parts, it became a Taliban-run Emirate with the sunset. Bits of it were fiefdoms run by local strongmen, with the local policy depending on the warlords' personal taste. The fiefdoms of the south imitated Mughal provincial courts. The ones in the north were turning to Turkey and Iran for inspiration, adopting modernist Islam sometimes complete with a feminist interpretation. What was missing amidst all this diversity was the gel that glued the people together. The new Afghanistan was more than ever a country without a nation.

The Islamic Republic Rises from the Ashes

One evening I found myself stuck in the weekend traffic jam, entering Kabul from the north. It was night and the mud-brick houses on the mountains were lit up, creating a celebratory atmosphere. "When I was a child, we used to have curfews and no-one would be out on the street at this time of the night," I told the driver. He was listening and not listening. He pointed at a car that had suddenly started to drive on the wrong side of the road to bypass the jam and said, "Look at this mule! There are so many idiots like him in this city." Afghans are risk-takers—even the Christian cemetery in Kabul has its fair share of tourists who died in car accidents. There is a theory that the reduced instinct for self-preservation is a side effect of post-traumatic stress disorder. I carried on anyway, doing *shalagi*. "The streets would be empty at this time of the night and unless you had a pregnant wife in your car, you would be sent back home at gun point. I am not used to this kind of normalcy in Kabul. We used to have rocket attacks all night." I was missing the sound of shooting and rockets because they were the noises of my childhood. The driver listened but said nothing.

The truth was that he had been getting on my nerves all day long. He was not exactly sharp but he was trustworthy and that is why we chose him to drive us to the north, to Panjshir. Along the way, we stopped at small towns and villages for horse-riding, shrine visits and people watching. The quiet peacefulness of the atmosphere was eerie and the prosperity obvious. The shops were packed with products including shampoo, groceries, energy drinks, mobile phone top-up cards and even gasoline. Even in small towns, building work was underway, with laborers erecting opium palaces in pink and purple. In between towns, narrow

PART ONE

bridges were widened and old shops replaced by new ones, reflecting the taste of the rural rich. The roads we drove on could have easily competed with the highways of Spain. They were doubtless in a better shape than the potholed streets of New York and Los Angeles. (In the words of one source, if the Taliban return, they are bound to just love driving their land-cruisers on foreign-funded freshly paved roads of Afghanistan). In and outside of Kabul, people owned mobile phones, sometimes two or three of them (for young guys, each phone served a different purpose, calls from work, family, and girlfriends were kept separate). They drove cars and had television sets. They listened to political satire on the radio, having picnics under the shade of ancient trees. They laughed their heads off at political jokes, especially about the president and his ministers. In the past, a joke about the political leadership amounted to suicide as one was bound to get arrested, imprisoned, even killed. Freedom and prosperity was all around us but our driver kept whining. "The situation is bad, seriously bad!" he said. When we reached Panjshir, he shouted at his family on his mobile phone: "Hello, it's me. I am driving in Panjshir. It's so overrated here. Nothing but water and rocks. I don't understand why anyone would bother to come here." When we returned to Kabul, my friend lost her patience, and asked him straight out, "You keep saying the situation is very bad. But tell us why? Exactly how is it bad?" If he had an answer, he did not share it.

On the road back to Kabul it seemed like the whole city was returning from weekend trips to the north. Kabul's air is famously filled with tiny shit particles floating about, courtesy of the inadequate sewage system. Everyone who can leave the city for a while leaves it—sometimes just to remember that there is something called fresh air in this world. Everybody was out but stuck in traffic. The scene around me was a snapshot of the new Afghan society. It was a directionless, diverse and dynamic society. If I looked ahead of me, I'd see the back of a pick-up truck carrying uniformed gunmen. The car was part of a security entourage, protecting a VIP. In Afghanistan, a VIP is basically a man with many enemies. This in turn explained the standard gunmen entourage. The person could be a minister, a warlord or a drug kingpin. It would be fair to say that VIP in Afghanistan stands for a very illegal person; or a very infernal person; or a very insane person.

To my right was a brand new black luxury SUV and seeing the occupants, I felt like grabbing a sledge hammer and smashing the car's windows. Let me explain. In the front seat sat a bearded man with a black turban which basically shouted out, "Hello, I am a Talib!" (So much for post-Taliban society). His beard was so long, thick, and curly that it would have made Noah of the Ark look like a dishevelled hobo rather than a prophet of global fame. In the back of the car (where else, please?) were seated the T-Boy's "honors," a bunch of women dressed in black *niqab*. I felt like getting out of the car, opening the door of the T-Boy's SUV and shouting at him, "Listen 'Mr Don't-I-Look-Just-Like-Prophet-Muhammad?' How come you can afford this expensive car and the five ritzy women who, I suspect, are wearing designer shoes underneath those modesty tents? Are you a plastic surgeon? If not, then what's the secret?" The question was rhetorical because I already I knew the secret. The source of any T-Boy's wealth is opium, gifts from rich Muslims who hate Christians and the 25 per cent extortion tax that the T-Boys take for blowing up roads, bridges and schools—but *only after they are built* (NGOs in charge of such infrastructure projects need evidence of work done to prove that European and American tax payers' money is spent for good use in Afghanistan. They pay extortion tax to the T-Boys or else the T-Boy blow up projects *before* they are completed). And then there was the more recent source of money—vast sums offered by Washington to buy peace from the Taliban. The Americans, too, had understood the truth of the Afghan saying that there was no winning against the insane. Buying peace, it appeared, was cheaper than winning the war. The pompous piety mobile on the right revealed just how pathetic we were as a people. We paid thugs extortion money to stop them from doing the only thing that they had skill for: destroying our country. They took the money, destroyed our country anyway and with the sum pocketed, they went to Mecca to pay god their respect. Piety had become such an ugly thing in Afghanistan. People showed off their devotion with menacing beards and by wearing letter-box tent hijabs. Theirs was a bullying, gangster-style piety. This was no longer Asia without an inferiority complex.

If I looked to my left to check out the other car, I would see a small battered vehicle full to the brim with male hipsters in tight t-shirts. Loud music was playing inside the car and the boys seemed happy and excited. I looked at their colorful t-shirts, their expensive haircuts, their hopeful faces and felt sorry for them. They were the professional class of Afghans, people who earned rather than extorted money. But when it came to wealth distribution, what chance did these economically productive youngsters have against the gangster T-Boy in the piety mobile? The T-Boy was a multiple-wife man, which meant that within three years, he could become father to eight mini T-Boys. Girls with their hymen intact were high-price commodities and weddings ridiculously expensive in Afghanistan. The professionals in the small car to our left would acquire serious debts as soon as they got married and they certainly could not afford a second wife. To picture the future one needed a simple calculation to figure out that per eight T-Boy babies we would get two to three professional babies. The thugs easily outnumbered the civilians. At this rate, the future was theirs.

The situation, however, was not entirely hopeless. I knew many open-minded, professional young men and women who were sons and daughters of formerly zealous Mooj commanders. The old men had mellowed over time and their offspring no longer shared the old Moojs' worldview. Their daughters sometimes popped up on Facebook, though few boys dared to friend them because they feared the wrath of their famous dads. The old Moojs had mellowed but there were limits to their tolerance. Still, there was hope in Afghanistan and the young men in the battered car embodied this hope.

As the traffic jam finally eased off, we headed home, passing by homeless street kids and elderly beggars. I recalled an Afghan saying that summed up the mood in this new, multi-directional society of lost souls: "There are three types of people in Afghanistan. Al-Qaida (the insurgents); Al-Faida (the enriched) and Al-Gayeda (the fucked)."

We Change to Remain the Same

On my way out of Kabul, I discovered that in a nod to the current American intervention and the newly fashionable in-your-face Muslim piety, twenty-dollar notes had replaced the old vodka bribes. At the new, sober Kabul airport I refused to pay the expected dollar bribe that was offered in return for "you won't get searched at all." The important search, the one for drugs and weapons, had already been done by a German sniffer dog fluent in Persian. The dog was one of the few employees of the Afghan government that was not lazy and corrupt. He did his job in a timely and competent fashion, looking content in the process. When he finished the two standard rounds of search, the dog had his tongue out in excitement, looking up at his soldier master, waiting to be petted on the head. I was so thrilled by this rare display of government efficiency that I asked for my bags to be sniffed again. I wanted to watch the dog in action, his competence was so reassuring that it was exciting. The solider understood my enthusiasm, smiled and let the dog do an extra sniff. The three of us, the canine and the humans, enjoyed the performance—the humans with broad grins and the canine with sparkling eyes.

Having refused the twenty-dollar *bakhshish*, I discovered that the sniffer dog was only the first stage in the rigorous searching of my luggage, and my bags were searched punctiliously, again, as if to punish me for being law-abiding. I noticed that of all the items in my bags, my books were the ones that received most suspicion. I stood back, watching the besuited middle-aged official flip through the pages, reading poetry verses and philosophical entries. His eyebrows were raised, his eyes doubtful, looking slightly bemused as if thinking, "Why the hell would anybody bother to read this rubbish?"

I'd bought the large collection of new Dari-Persian poetry, fiction and history books in Kabul. I had detected a thriving book market in Kabul, with numerous bookshops making solid business by selling school and university textbooks, Afghan literature, poetry and alternative, sometimes conspiratorial, history accounts. Education was clearly seen as something worth investing in even though, like the unimpressed airport security guard, the three drunken teenaged school boys that stumbled in and out of the book bazar told a different story. "They are drunk at two in the afternoon?" I shrieked. "Yes, they are bad boys!" said the shopkeeper, who happened to be a poet himself. Poetry and war are hard to escape in Afghanistan—we are the land of poet warriors. "The alcohol is home-made and sold for a couple of dollars over there," the shop-owner pointed at a distant location at the end of the dusty road. "Even in London, school kids don't get drunk at two in the afternoon," I lied.

Alongside destroyed infrastructure and human casualties, the war had also been a serious blow to Afghan literature. With education interrupted, literacy and linguistic skills had suffered. Our Iranian neighbors made little secret of their mockery of our linguistic failures as the lesser-known custodians of the Persian language. Their famous saying that Persian had been born in Tajikistan, flourished in Iran and died in Afghanistan summed up their criticism. I left Kabul, having done my final round of angry stares' contest with all the men in the departure lounge. Like all wars in Afghanistan, this mini staring war had no clear winners.

PART TWO

New Gods, Fallen Deities, Forgotten Demons

In April 2012, Afghan users of Facebook started a trend, sharing and re-sharing the photograph of a horrifically burned man. The man's eyes were filled with terror as he was being put into an ambulance. The photo's caption said in Persian, "Fear the wrath of Allah! Look at what happened to this Danish man when he made fun of Prophet Muhammad." In reality, the man was neither Danish nor a joker. He was a miner, and his burns were caused in a methane explosion that took place in 2001 in Donetsk, a city to the east of Ukraine. His story had nothing to do with Allah, Denmark or jokes. This was the factual side of the story but the god-fearing Afghans who shared his picture didn't care about facts. Like robots without a will or brain of their own, they shared and re-shared the picture together with the threat, "Allah is going to burn you to death if you laugh at his prophet." The numerous comments left underneath the picture (among those who commented were graduates of Yale and Harvard) reeked with terror: "May god forgive us, *tubah, tubah*!"

Watching Afghan superstition in action on Facebook, I raised an imaginary glass to Emile Durkheim. Here it was, evidence for his view that religion was "society worshiping itself." The deity that these Afghans worshipped had little to do with Allah the Compassionate and the Merciful—the words that they utter every time they say Bismellah (which they do frequently). There was no mercy and little compassion in this deity of terror. If anything, it seemed to have some kind of personality disorder, a narcissist, perhaps, who also had borderline sociopathic tendencies. The followers of this deity were so terrified of his radical punishment methods that they felt they had to walk on eggshells even on Facebook. It was clear that the Afghans who believed in this deity had confused Allah the Merciful and Compassionate with one of their many warlords. Many Afghans pretend that our warlords have grown on trees and have nothing to do with our culture. But the truth is that in every family, there is a mini-warlord competing with his rival, lesser warlords. We call them fathers, brothers, husbands and uncles. The heavenly threats from above are a reflection of the darkness below—proving the point of the saying that there are three types of people in the world: Muslims, non-Muslims and Afghans.

Judging by archaeological finds of the last six decades, Afghans have always been excessive believers. Underneath the monochrome soil of Kabul and Herat, Ghazni and Kandahar, lie buried Buddhist stupas, status of Hindu and Greco-Bactrian deities and the gravestones of medieval Afghan Jews. The memories of the defeated gods of the past, of Buddhism, Hinduism and Zoroastrianism, are kept alive in the names of urban landmarks and landscape spots. Tomb shrines dedicated to local saints are scattered throughout Afghanistan, offering peaceful rest on long trips. It is inside such shrines that one finds quiet spirituality—even as a woman. The saints themselves are often wanderers and transients and in more recent times, victims of warlord murders.

If the roadside shrines tell stories of seekers with the power to heal liver break and heart ache, then, their narratives are in stark contrast to the story of Kabul's Muslim conquest. This story drips with blood, and its ending feels like the site of a suicide attack, complete with puddles of gore, scattered body parts and missing heads. The leader of the conquest, the King of Dual

Blades, fought with two swords, one in each hand. His aides were equally remarkable. They were men of Herculean size and companions of Prophet Muhammad—socially speaking they were of impeccable pedigree. It is fair to say that since Kabul fell to Muslim rulers, religion never ceased to demand blood for its survival, protection and sustenance. In Friday sermons of the kind that would make a less desensitized people shudder in horror, Afghan imams tend to wallow in talk of carnage: "The wombs of this land nurture martyrs; the soil of this land is soaked in the blood of martyrs." If the Coen brothers were to make a film about religious Afghanistan, it would be called "There's Never Enough Blood."

The further north one travels, the more Central Asian the shrines become. Decorated with animal horns, the metal bars around the tombs have colorful cloths tied to them. The sacred sites are leftover traces of the fallen gods of Shamanism.

High-up to the east of Afghanistan is the land of the forcibly converted people of Nuristan (Land of Light). The religion of these *jadid al-Islams* (newcomers to Islam) converts of the late nineteenth century was a mystery to the Muslims of the time. In a story featured in the first Afghan newspaper, *Shams-al Nahar*, in 1873, we read about a fugitive man from Nuristan who had broken a Nuristani religious taboo by entering a cave that was forbidden to men. The rascal of our story says he was driven by curiosity. He describes entering the cave inside a formidable mountain at the foot of the Himalayas. As his eyes get used to the darkness of the cave, he slowly discerns the contours of what turns out to be numerous statues of horses—hundreds of them (which should be taken with a pinch of salt, of course, given that Afghans like to exaggerate numbers for dramatic effect). Their appearance—the heads, the eyes and the elegant tails—are of such natural beauty that our taboo breaker believes he is in the presence of horses of flesh and blood. Still in awe but also horrified, he tells the newspaper's correspondent (the paper used the

English word correspondent) about the highlight of the cave—a waterfall behind which is the statue of a deity made of gold and bronze. This idol is crowned and bears a sword. "Shiny scarlet stones were placed inside the statue's eye sockets. The deity was blinking as if alive." The sacred cave was forbidden to all men, and from among women, only those who were about to get married were allowed in. It was inside this cave that the brides to be underwent a ritual of purification. The nubile would leave the cave, sworn to an oath of secrecy. They would never talk about the cave. What happened inside the cave remained in the cave—until the rascal of our story entered the scene and broke the law. He was now a fugitive, and to bypass the wrath of the Nuristani deity, he had quickly converted to Islam. It was under these unusual circumstances that he spoke to the newspaper.

These days, the Land of Light is quickly turning into the land of beards. It has been infiltrated by Wahhabis and turned into a center of the Wahhabis' soulless, legalistic interpretation of Islam. The kind that is all about measuring the length of one's beard and pubic hair.

Part Two is about the state of religion in Afghanistan ten years after the Taliban lost their monopoly over people's faith. It tells the stories of crypto-converts, dejected Sikhs and Muslim and Christian proselytizers' competition over the souls of Afghans.

Nostradamus in Kabul

In 2009, Baba Vanga, a Bulgarian clairvoyant and blind prophet of doom, inadvertently closed down *Payman*—Afghanistan's most respected newspaper—from beyond the grave.

The shutdown came after *Payman* mistakenly published a "blasphemous" article called "Prediction of the Third World War"—the story of Bulgarian visionary Baba Vanga, her dramatic life and her dystopian vision of a nuclear war. The cause of the fuss was a paragraph introducing the article. It said world religions have no evidence to prove their vision of the afterlife, leaving the question of humanity's origins and the hereafter an unsolved mystery. In other words, it suggested that the prophets were liars.

The offending article was apparently published by mistake. It had a title strikingly similar to the one the paper had intended to publish: "Will There Be a Third World War?" An easy mistake in the age of internet journalism. The former had blasphemous content, the latter was harmless, but *Payman* was unlucky and published the wrong one. Its editors were quick to spot the mistake. Immediately after publication, *Payman* itself volunteered the view that the article's content was unacceptable and apologized for it.

"We are in the business of journalism where such mistakes are common," they explained in a public letter of atonement to the country's religious scholars. "A review of the paper's past content shows that the paper has consistently respected Islam and the public's religious sentiments," they said. It was a mistake; we're aware of it and we apologize, they repeated. But to no avail. The paper's headquarters was raided and the Supreme Court ordered the collective arrest of *Payman*'s journalists. They were released hours later but their colleague, the news editor, remained in custody for ten days.

How did this happen? According to the newspaper, the rumour trail points to the Afghan president as the main driver behind the threats that ultimately led to its closure. According to the paper, a rumour made the rounds, pointing the finger of blame at President Karzai. The president, gossip had it, was tired of *Payman*'s constant criticism of his administration and in the mistaken publication of the article, he saw a convenient opportunity to silence it for good.

Payman was an outspoken critic of Karzai. The paper made no secret of its view that his constant vilification of Pakistan was a ploy to distract attention away from the multiple failures of his administration. When reports announced that the war on terror was to spread to Pakistan in 2008, a policy much favored by Karzai, *Payman* warned Kabul not to meddle with Pakistan because if provoked, Islamabad could retaliate. Karzai dismissed such fears, reassuring the public that the Afghan army was capable of defending Afghan borders. Karzai's reassurance left *Payman* sniggering: "How can a government that can hardly ensure security in the capital defend the country's distant borders?" The paper was proved right when some time later insurgents attacked the justice and education ministries at the heart of Kabul. The war on terror had extended to Pakistan but Kabul was no longer safe. *Payman* was right, and Karzai wrong.

The story of Baba Vanga and her accidental entanglement with *Payman*'s closure was sad and ironic. *Payman* was the exact opposite of Baba Vanga. The blind Bulgarian had visions; the Afghan paper had facts. The clairvoyant foresaw a nuclear war between Muslims and Christians; the Afghan paper discussed Krishnamurti's teaching alongside ethnical philosophy and religious pluralism. Baba Vanga was more in tune with old Afghanistan, where political careers were made on myths like the one about Mullah Omar pulling his own eye out when it was injured. *Payman*, by contrast, was all about contemporary, urban Afghanistan, a place where investigative journalism had led to a degree of demystification of politics, separating facts from fabrication, truth from fancy. *Payman* published articles that carried titles like "How to avoid stupid beliefs."

The likeable Baba, on the other hand, believed that in 2111 mankind would become robots. And yet it was the mistaken publication of Baba Vanga's story that led to the closure of Afghanistan's most intellectually open-minded newspaper. In this incidental clash of Afghan rationalism versus Bulgarian supernaturalism, Afghans were the losers. *Payman* served an important public service in a country where religious sentiment had become politicized to the point that Islam was acting as a source of conflict instead of unity. (Consider the irony of the Taliban waging jihad against the "Islamic Republic of Afghanistan").

Payman provided much-needed religious edification by publishing academic but easy-to-understand articles about religion so that its readers, armed with reason, would not fall victim to militant religious fundamentalism. But in the arsenal of weapons deployed by the Afghan government, there's a new, potent one called blasphemy. Anybody can be accused of it on flimsy ground, allowing the mob and the government to take what Afghans call "serious action." Unfortunately for President Karzai, militant fundamentalism turned out to be a much more serious threat to his administration than the paper he allegedly forced to shut down.

Christianity in the Afghan Spiritual Bazaar

"When we arrived in Kabul, we felt the power of evil very strongly," says Christy Wilson, a Christian missionary, in his book *More to Be Desired Than Gold*. An unwittingly hilarious volume of strange and macabre tales which includes the story of a Californian dog possessed by demons in Kabul and the perils of satanic ouija boards, the book is about a group of Christian missionaries in Afghanistan of the 1960s and 1970s.

Kabul of that period is famously associated with the flower children, their rugs, drugs and sheepskins. But little is known about the equally strange, but drug-free parallel universe inhabited by missionaries who were from the same parts of the world as the hippies.

Yet it was in this period that a small group set up base in Afghanistan, opening a church in Kabul in 1970. The triumph of having founded a church at the heart of an exceedingly religious Muslim community was short-lived. News of conversions soon reached the Afghan government, leading it to demolish the church three years later.

According to Wilson, Afghan officials took the term "underground church" literally, digging in vain for a secret church underneath the building. By then a handful of Afghans had already converted to Christianity, among them a blind teenaged boy who became known among missionaries as Saint Paul of Afghanistan.

Conversion being an extremely dangerous decision amounting to a death wish, the early history of Afghan converts has its fair share of what missionaries called Christian martyrs. The irony of Afghanistan as a birthplace of both Muslim and Christian modern-day martyrs is lost on the sanctimonious in both camps, but it nonetheless shows the powerful appeal of the country over the religious imaginations of people from radically different places, from the dry deserts of Saudi Arabia to the green pastures of New Zealand. The attraction is peculiar, given that Afghans themselves tend to regard their country as a God-forsaken place where Satan, rather than God, came to rest.

Be that as it may, conversion to Christianity hasn't stopped since the early days of missionary activity described in Wilson's book. Judging by the fact that Afghan churches have sprung up in places as far apart as Scandinavia and California, the number of converts must have increased drastically since the days of "early martyrs."

According to a reliable source, missionary activity is particularly evident in northern Afghanistan, where Christian concepts are subtly sneaked into instruction materials. So for example, students in computer classes are encouraged to create folders named after Christian theological concepts such as the Trinity, or Christian saints and prophets.

The fear of losing people to other religions has regularly led to protests in the Afghan parliament. But a more sinister version of such protests occurred when the owner of a private TV station desperate for viewers, secretly filmed—and then broadcast—a Christian sermon delivered in Kabul. Led by a disabled man, the congregation was a sorrowful sight, composed of the poor and the starved. But if the missionaries were cynical in luring hungry Afghans into conversion with cakes and fruit juice, so was their opponent, the TV presenter. For the sake of self-promotion, the Afghan presenter put lives at risk, taking advantage of the sensitivities associated with conversion.

Most Afghans tend to regard such conversions with skepticism, given that becoming a Christian equates to a full stomach and, at times, a fast track to Canada on the grounds of religious persecution. But even though there might be a degree of truth in this suspicion, it is equally true that in contrast to the past, Afghan Christians have become more open and vocal about their existence.

They have their own online TV channel, with presenters possessing a remarkable command of their native language. Equally striking is their use of religious terminology to spread their Christian message which draws upon vocabulary usually associated with Islam. Hence, the community members refers to themselves as "mumenin" (believers) and use the Islamic term "din" to describe their faith.

The bravest among the converts have moved a step further, outing themselves publicly, and offering conversion testimonies in Dari-Persian. Reading them, it becomes clear that it is inconsolable grief caused by war combined with the unappealing experience of Islam in its legalistic guise that has driven some of the more sensitive souls away from Islam and into the fold of Christianity.

This same brand of Islam in recent history proved an impediment to progress, leading the Afghan government to create a new class of Egyptian-educated imams from al-Azhar University in the 1960s. Co-opted by the government, fluent in Arabic and well-versed in scripture, the properly trained imams were crucial in allowing progressive laws to enter the 1964 constitution. They used a reformist Islamic theology to argue for progress against reactionary, traditional mullahs.

Needless to say, the war interrupted the move towards religious reform, leaving Afghans vulnerable to proselytizing Christians and Muslims alike. The bold recent entry to the city of Herat of the global pietist movement, Tablighi Jama'at, which already has massive support in Pakistan, is a recent example. There, confident young Tablighi missionaries marched into shops, pressing their pamphlets into the hands of irritated shopkeepers.

Given this context of international competition over Afghans' souls, Christian converts appear to be part of a wider pattern of religious change. The country has become an international spiritual bazaar where religious identities are offered to Afghans alongside equally popular Viagra pills and Korean soap operas. As elsewhere in the world, globalization in Afghanistan has turned out to be, as it were, a mixed blessing.

Hidden History: Discovering a Pre-Islamic Past

"Thirsty when the water jug is full" is a popular proverb that Afghans use to describe the state of their country. The truth of this saying was confirmed with the discovery of an impressive fifth-century Buddhist monastery to the north of Kabul in the winter of 2010.

Judging by geological surveys and historical accounts, the monastery and the copper mine that lies underneath it were only a small part of the natural and cultural abundance buried beneath the ground. It was almost as if there are two Afghanistans, a monochrome—poor—one above, and a colorful—rich—one below.

Afghans had long suspected that the cultural poverty and material scarcity they suffer from was unnecessary. But although the discovery of monastery and the copper mine below it confirmed their suspicion, in the climate of greed and corruption, the exploits of both treasures were likely to be looted rather than shared.

Aside from the probability of looting, the monastery was facing an additional threat. The Chinese company exploiting the mine was urging archaeologists to speed up the excavation even at the risk of leaving behind an unfinished job.

Afghans were then left with the dilemma of choosing between economic growth and cultural heritage, as having both appeared to be a luxury they could not afford. But economic growth has always come at a price to Afghans. If in 2010 it came at the cost of history, a century earlier it came with the threat of a foreign invasion. That is why Afghan rulers of the late nineteenth and early twentieth centuries decided against building railways in spite of the trains' multiple economic advantages. Trains would have improved trade, connecting Afghanistan to the wider world. But at the same time they could have been used for transporting British or Russian troops, facilitating a military invasion.

Needless to say, the fear of invasion prevailed over the advantages of technological progress, with Afghanistan remaining isolated but independent. A century later, economic consideration was likely to overshadow historical heritage, jeopardizing the survival of the Buddhist site.

The moral high ground appeared to be with those who chose economic growth over cultural heritage. After all, they argued, living people should be given priority over the dead objects of the past, no matter how precious. But archaeological surveys are as important because they can play a crucial role in a nation's destiny. In Afghanistan, for example, the lack of a comprehensive archaeological survey has meant that unlike Iran, Egypt or Lebanon, Afghans were not able to formulate a secular identity based on a pre-Islamic past.

While other Muslim majority societies successfully managed to create alternative, secular nationalist identities, Afghanistan had no choice but to rely solely on Islam for political and cultural self-identification. After all, in the absence of a meaningful, fully-conducted archaeological survey, apart from Islam there was little else that Afghans could draw upon for identity. As a result, Afghan nationalism has always been inseparable from Islam.

In the political climate of 2010, the collapse of patriotism and religious zealotry into one led to the absurd situation where serving one's religion often amounted to destroying one's country. The Taliban were a prime example of this conflicted identity, which resulted in the paradoxical situation whereby "true" Afghan patriotism often resulted in killing one's fellow Afghans and destroying what little infrastructure the country had.

This type of patriotism appears bizarre but in the light of the peculiarity of Afghan nationalism, it makes perfect sense. The complications of this model of identity, in which religious vigor and patriotic fervor collapse into one, has resulted in many conflicts in Afghan history, particularly since the 1980s.

The historical weakness of the state in Afghanistan has also meant that religion has served as a source of legitimacy for two conflicting ends. On the one hand, Islam has served to grant universal, political legitimacy to Afghan leaders and states; on the other it has been used to legitimize local rebellions against those same states or leaders.

The religious wars of recent decades were the culmination of the vicious cycle that is linked to the peculiar formulation of Afghan nationalism. According to this formulation, serving one's country and serving god is one and the same even if the country is being destroyed in the process of serving god.

The lack of archaeological surveys unveiling the Afghans' past is at the heart of the dilemma and absurdity of Afghan nationalism. It is here that the importance of preserving the country's past becomes obvious. The evidence of a distinct cultural past that Afghans can claim as their own offers them a chance to formulate an alternative identity that draws upon more than religious zealotry.

Needless to say, this alternative identity cannot be created without evidence provided by archaeology. After all, it is only through such evidence that Afghans can fully understand who they are in addition to being Muslims.

That is why the preservation of the Buddhist site to the north of Kabul is not a luxury but a necessity. The site's acknowledgement could be the first step towards wisdom and true self-knowledge in Afghanistan. After all, as Lao-Tzu wisely said, knowing others is intelligence but knowing oneself is true wisdom.

Afghan Sikhs: The Forgotten Victims

Few people outside Afghanistan are aware of the Afghan Sikh community: a little-known, inconspicuous religious minority whose mass exodus from Afghanistan began with the coming to power of the mujahedin in 1992. The decision to leave at that particular juncture made sense. After all, the new rulers had an established reputation for religious intolerance.

The collapse of the Soviet-backed Kabul regime in 1992 had left Afghan Sikhs in a vulnerable position. With their black *dastar* turbans and neat but untrimmed beards, they stood out from the Muslim crowd, and became an easily identifiable target for crime and harassment. A community of traders with business contacts stretching from Afghan cities to India, Japan and Korea, the Sikhs were perceived as wealthy and this perception, in turn, made them a key target for kidnapping gangs. Even during the famously rigid rule of the Taliban, members of the Sikh community were kidnapped for ransom, and according to one trusted source, the kidnappers included Taliban. One Sikh family, for example, lost six members during the Taliban rule, having failed to collect the required ransom to secure the release of relatives.

In many ways, the Sikh community's experience of loss and forced migration had much in common with that of their Muslim counterparts. Families were torn apart and ended up stranded in refugee camps before eventually settling in whichever country was ready to let them in. But the Sikhs' distinct religious identity came with additional hardships that affected both, those who had been left behind in Afghanistan and those struggling to survive abroad.

In the 1990s, the mujahedin, and later the Taliban, elevated ordinary Afghans' intolerance of non-Muslims to official state policy—depriving the Sikhs of state protection, the only protection that the community ever had in recent Afghan history. Subsequently, the Sikhs were denied their basic rights, including the right to bury their dead in line with the requirements of their faith.

Religious intolerance, especially towards Sikhism and Hinduism, is a deeply ingrained part of Afghan national identity which was formulated in opposition to the Hindus and Sikhs of India. Often, it takes exile and exposure to racism to make mainstream Muslim Afghans realize just how unfair society has been towards the Sikh community. "It was only when I came to England that I realized that our attitude towards our Sikhs had been wrong," said a young Muslim Afghan I met in London's Southall market. With the exception of a restaurant and a music shop, the market is run almost entirely by Afghan Sikhs.

Like most Afghans, the young Muslim was suspicious of my motives for asking questions and refused to let me interview him. Instead he introduced me to an Afghan Sikh friend who was the owner of a small shop, jam-packed with colorful shiny fabrics, South Asian-style garments and bejeweled sandals.

"Talk to Harpal Singh, our community leader. He knows everything," the shopkeeper advised. Such delegation of authority to a community leader, which often results in block voting during elections, is widespread in South Asia, and the Afghan Sikh community has replicated this pattern in British exile. But even aside from this delegating authority to a leader, the Sikhs' fear of speaking out was striking.

Decades, if not centuries, of oppression have left their mark on this community, and their fear manifests itself in other ways, too. Unlike most Afghans, who tend to be unreserved and gregarious, Afghan Sikhs speak in a quiet voice. Their manner of conversation to non-Sikhs is structured to avoid confrontation and often begins with formulations of reassurance.

"We never had problems with the people in Afghanistan," said Harpal Singh. I knew from my own life story that he was not telling the full truth. In my school in Kabul, Sikh children were regularly mocked for their manner of dress and names; the boys were ridiculed for their distinctive headgear and there was pressure on them to convert to Islam. We had a Sikh classmate, a girl with an impressively long plait who, apart from her name and religion, spoke, talked and behaved just like the rest of us. Unluckily, she soon became the target of Muslim proselytization carried out by a zealous little girl. This girl stalked her Sikh classmate, always two steps behind her, and kept asking her loudly, for all to hear: "Why don't you convert to Islam?" The pestering went on for months until finally, the Sikh girl responded, "Why don't you convert to Sikhism?" I remember the classroom bursting into laughter. We sided with the Sikh girl because it was the 1980s and at the time, Afghans still valued individual audacity more than religious hypocrisy.

In Southall market, Harpal Singh offered me what sounded like a standard community leader speech. The community was peaceful, had no problems with other Afghans or the British people. He then told me about the Sikhs' specific problem of having to authenticate their Afghan identity when arriving in England or other western countries. The authentication process involves speaking Dari-Persian and knowledge of the city they lived in before exile. Given that the community's children often grew up in refugee camps outside Afghanistan, young Afghan Sikhs sometimes no longer speak Dari-Persian, being fluent only in their mother tongue, Punjabi. This, in turn, adds to the complication of corroborating their identity outside Afghanistan.

"But these days, the British no longer believe that we are oppressed, that we are still not allowed to bury our dead in line with our religious regulations," said another Sikh shopkeeper on condition of anonymity. "The British say they are running the country, and know what's happening there."

I asked him whether there was anything he could do about this. He shrugged and said: "I have letters of my family from Kabul but the British say they know what's happening there."

Despite daily harassment in Afghanistan and the additional complications that stem from being Afghan Sikhs abroad, the community still feels a powerful sense of belonging to Afghanistan. Its members are known to have helped Muslim Afghans make a living by setting up businesses in the UK. It is this solid loyalty to Afghanistan and touching solidarity with Muslim Afghans that dismantles the popular myth that only Islam can create unity among Afghans.

Being Afghan is about more than religion, and as possibly the country's oldest inhabitants, the Afghan Sikhs have always known this much.

Holy Violence

Martyrdom has become the quickest way to local stardom in almost all Muslim countries. But in Afghanistan, anyone who dies is automatically considered a martyr. It's one of those social trends that starts suddenly and spreads quickly, without much thought. Or maybe it's an act of respect for the dead person. Either way, in January 2010 the Taliban launched a series of spectacular attacks in Kabul just as cabinet members were taking their oath of office. In a report posted online on the Taliban website, their spokesman Zabiullah Mujahid listed the ministries under attack: the ministry of mining, the ministry of justice, and the ministry of finance. The Taliban's message was clear: even though the ministers were taking charge of Hamid Karzai's cabinet, the power in control of Kabul was not Karzai but the Taliban.

The ministers in Kabul may not be used to the idea of dual government, but outside the capital city, Afghans have long

PART TWO

learned to live under two parallel regimes; a daytime government run by President Karzai and a nighttime one run by the Taliban and other local strongmen. Ministers in Kabul had been spared this unsettling reality until now, hiding as they do in bulletproof cars, on blocked roads and behind the protective walls of Kabul's green zone. But the reality outside the capital is otherwise and ordinary Afghans have learned to negotiate their daily routine around avoiding random violence by the Taliban and other troublemakers. The attacks targeting the three ministries might have given the ministers a taste of what life is like for a majority of Afghans, especially those who live in restive regions.

After the attacks, the Taliban spokesman, Mujahid, posted a report written in broken English on the Taliban's al-Emarah website. The report mentioned the names of Taliban commanders who were in charge of the so-called martyrdom operations. Mujahid said that seven of them "gave their lives for Allah the Almighty, and embraced martyrdom."

Afghanistan is a curious place. Those who kill are called martyrs. Those who they kill are also called martyrs and the violence is apparently done for the sake of God. "God is everywhere in Kabul," said a source who recently returned to the city. "It's like a dictatorship. There is no escaping God here." Those who kill do so for the sake of God. Those who die hope that God will punish those who kill.

Baharat, an Afghan woman who watched the violence from behind her office window, told the BBC Farsi service: "I saw terrified stallholders caught in the middle of the crossfire. They didn't know whether to run for their lives, leaving the stalls unsupervised or to stay behind, and risk their lives." The stallholders had two options: to risk losing their livelihood or to risk losing their lives.

But in his report on the "martyrdom operations," Mujahid made no mention of the terrified Kabulis caught in the crossfire. His report read as if Kabul were an empty space, a frontline inhabited only by government soldiers and their Taliban enemies. There was no mention in the report of children hiding in the cellar of the bank that came under attack. The terrified stallholders or the shoppers stranded in Qari Aman shopping center did not exist in the Taliban report. The Taliban spokesman did mention the shopping center, but only to claim that the blaze that burned down the building was the work of Afghan troops who had panicked, opening indiscriminate fire.

The spokesman then went on to mention that a "brave mujahid" by the name of Haji Massod had driven the explosives-filled ambulance to the Malik Azghar roundabout. Again there was no mention of civilians. The spokesman simply said that high-ranking officials and security personnel were killed in the "martyrdom explosion," as if a busy roundabout in a city of three-and-a-half million people had been empty that morning.

Judging by Mujahed's report, the Taliban were either in denial or regarded Kabul's civilians as fair game. Either way, there's nothing new about the Taliban attacking Kabul. Their predecessors, who ironically also called themselves mujahids, began firing Sakar-20 rockets on Kabul in 1985. The people who fled the city and subsequently ended up in Pakistani refugee camps became known in the local language as Sakarbisti, the Sakar-20s.

Later, in the 1990s, Kabul turned into an open battleground under fire by various mujahedin factions "martyring" each other and the people of the city. But Kabul is not the only city of violence creating new martyrs. Afghanistan's soil is full of martyr graves, triggering questions as to how to avoid unintentionally polluting a grave when doing one's business outdoors. In the villages, parents warn their children to tread carefully and avoid soiling what might be an unmarked grave of one of the country's millions of martyrs.

But if the Taliban are in denial, so are the people of Kabul. Reports of the Taliban violence were soon followed by two sets of rumours. The first rumour insinuated that the attacks were orchestrated by Karzai's administration with the purpose of distracting public attention away from the president's failure to come up with an adequate cabinet. The second rumour also held Karzai responsible by implying that by allowing the Taliban to carry out the attacks in the heart of the city, the president was trying to persuade the public that the Taliban simply had to be given government posts or else they would destroy Kabul.

Such rumours made the rounds even though the Taliban had not only claimed responsibility for the attacks, but also were making a point of describing their operations in detail and mentioning the commanders in charge of the attacks by their name. Needless to say, the commanders were either Mullah such-and-such or Hajji this and-that—titles that indicate religious credentials.

Afghans are so used to violence and the way it is justified that they rarely realize just how absurd their situation is. When an Afghan journalist asked the family of a victim of the Taliban's violence, he was given an obscure answer: "May God punish the enemies of Islam." The language of theology has become intertwined with the discourse of violence and the result is bewildering, with murderers and victims called martyrs alike.

Asif Mohseni: Afghanistan's Turbulent Cleric

After ten years of reporting from Afghanistan, international reporters got to know Afghan politicians in a more intimate manner. That is why to describe these men, they started to use euphemisms such as "colorful character" or "unsavory person"—semi-polite ways of describing dubious individuals. So when a new Shia family law (which made it illegal for a wife to refuse sexual intercourse with her husband) was proposed in 2009 by one such "unsavory character" to the Afghan parliament, it divided Afghanistan. The split revealed a nation struggling to come to terms with a complex problem: how to reconcile traditional religious values with the demands of the twenty-first century, which measured a nation's progress by way of its treatment of women. The result was a cultural war between traditionalist and progressive Afghans. In between was a third group in whose view the controversy over the law was an unnecessary distraction from the country's more urgent problems. Why focus on a law whose sole function was to make legal what was already common practice when the country was facing the more serious problems of foreign occupation, extreme poverty and a corrupt central state perpetually on the verge of collapse? According to this third party, under such circumstances the focus on women's rights was simply misplaced, if not hypocritical. This is because the same western forces who opposed the law for its misogynist content were also the ones that created widows in Afghanistan when their air force bombed the south and the east of the country in the war against terrorism.

This, in sum, was the situation as it appeared on the surface when the law was proposed. But digging a bit deeper, a more complex picture emerged. At the center of this complex picture was Ayatollah Asif Mohseni, a Shia cleric and the architect of the new law. He's the boss of Tamadon ("civilization") TV, a privately-owned television station with a visual outlook and religious content remarkably similar to Iranian state-run television channels. The night before the protest demonstration of 15 April 2009, which ended in violence and made headlines around the world, the TV station repeatedly broadcast a message, advising people to prevent their family members from attending the protest. In other words, the cleric had anticipated the protest and indirectly prepared the ground for the counter-protest, which resulted in broken windows and stones being pelted at demonstrators.

This act of public manipulation should not come as a surprise because Mohseni is far more than a prominent Shia cleric and TV station owner. He's a politician whose career has been far from uncontroversial. Born in 1936 in Kandahar, in the south of

Afghanistan, Mohseni is the founder of the Islamic Movement of Afghanistan. This Shia, anti-Soviet resistance movement combined various smaller groups with numerous bases inside and outside the country. The party was founded in the Iranian holy city of Qum in 1978 and Mohseni received much support from the Iranian state. But some Iranian politicians objected to him because in addition to allying himself to the Shia state of Iran, Mohseni also kept communication lines open with rival Sunni resistance group based in Peshawar. His Iranian critics believed that as a leader of a Shia party, Mohseni's contact with rival Sunni groups amounted to betrayal of the Shia political cause. They suspected that even though Mohseni received Iranian support, he still forged secret deals with rival Sunni groups based in Pakistan. Later on, after the withdrawal of Soviet troops from Afghanistan in February 1988, Mohseni still managed to keep his options open, moving between Kabul, Qum and Islamabad where he multitasked as a teacher, politician and prolific writer of religious books, as well as a founder of Afghanistan's official Shia center. Based in Kabul, the center, *Khatam-al Nabyeen* (the last of all prophets), was also the scene of the protest.

The secret to Mohseni's ability to move between the otherwise divided worlds of Iran and Pakistan, the Shias and the Sunnis, is his complex identity as a Qizilbash born in the Pashtun region of Kandahar, which makes him a Shia with Pashtun cultural roots. This is a remarkable combination and Mohseni has taken full advantage of it. An exploration of the realm of censor-free Afghan citizen blogging reveals him as a leader who's accused of believing in the principle of divide and rule. The division in the Shia community, a direct result of Mohseni's proposed law, can be interpreted in this light. Mohseni's chief opponent, Muslim Fahimi, himself an insider in the Islamic Movement party, went even further after the protests, leveling serious accusations against the cleric on a private TV station. They included claims that he had made a deliberate attempt to fuel violence among the Shia Hazara community during the civil war years of the early 1990s; murdered a man who objected to Mohseni marrying his fourteen-year-old sister who had been entrusted to the cleric for religious education; and ordered the assassination of political rivals. As is typical in the largely unregulated media world of Afghanistan, none of the allegations were substantiated with evidence, even though the accuser claimed to possess documentation.

The controversy surrounding Mohseni revealed that the cleric was a typical Afghan politician. He was an ambitious maverick who had his fingers in many pies, was venerated by his supporters and deeply reviled by his opponents. His complex identity (a Shia leader born in Kandahar who speaks Pashto) gave Mohseni the chance to act as a unifying figure, bringing together the Shias and the Sunnis, the Pashtuns and the Hazaras. This, in turn, may explain why President Hamid Karzai didn't hesitate to sign the law, presumably to secure Mohseni's support in the presidential election of 2009. But what both Mohseni and Karzai neglected to take into account was the growth of a small, yet vocal indigenous women's rights group with both local and Western support. Their protest made headlines across the globe, triggering strong emotions and serious objection to the proposed law.

Karzai was left with the impossible task of appeasing the western donors who finance his government while reconciling the progressive and traditionalist forces of Afghan society. Judging by the president's record so far, in all likelihood he'll manage to achieve a half-baked solution and Afghanistan will carry on as usual, deeply divided and in conflict with itself and the world.

Lost in Holy Translation

In March 2009, the Taliban leader Mullah Omar asked his fighters to stop the violence in Pakistan. According to Pakistani media outlets, the mullah told his soldiers not to kill innocent Muslims because their murder gives jihad a bad name. Was this be the first step towards homespun turbans and a Salt March through the Hindu Kush? Far from it.

The mullah hadn't lost an inch of his belief in war, only he wanted it in Afghanistan not Pakistan. And so he told his troops that if they wanted to do jihad, they should only do it in Afghanistan. This in turn raised eyebrows in Kabul, with commentators asking the obvious question: what about the Afghans? Aren't they innocent Muslims, too? But this was Afghanistan, a country where Muslims have been fighting their fellow Muslims for the three decades. This internal jihad had been running parallel to the official jihad against the Soviet army and since 2001, Nato. The post-9/11 version led by the Taliban not only targets "infidels" but also Afghan Muslims—teachers and tribal leaders, women's rights activists and imams.

The sheer violence and absurdity of this unholy war finally encouraged Afghan intellectuals to try to salvage religion from those who are destroying it. Ghows Zalmay, a celebrated journalist turned self-appointed religious reformist, was one of them. As he understood the issue, if Afghans were able to read the Qur'an in their own language, they would become less prone to manipulation by firebrand mullahs and better Muslims as a result. So it was that in the summer of 2007, Zalmay arranged for the pious people of Kabul to be given free copies of the Qur'an in Dari-Persian translation. "You are now in possession of your own Dari edition. Read it and remember us in your prayers," he wrote in its preface. But if anybody did pray for Zalmay, their prayers went unheard and on 27 February a court in Kabul sentenced him to twenty years' imprisonment on charges of blasphemy.

Accused alongside Zalmay was Qari Mushtaq Ahmad, the imam of the Tamim Ansar mosque in Kabul. The imam had read the translation and confirmed its accuracy. In the preface to the translation, Moshtaq had stated, "I, Qari Mushtaq Ahmad ... the preacher of the Tamim Ansar mosque, confirm that when the Dari edition of this pure and heavenly book—which has been translated in America by Ustad Qudratollah Bakhtiarinezhad— was placed at my disposal, I read it in full and found the translation to be accurate, and God forbid, with no change." In other words, the translation had been checked by a man of authority who, in turn, made his approval public by having his signature printed beneath his declaration.

So why the blasphemy charges? Here lies the crux: the translation had omitted the original Arabic text. According to orthodox precedent, the Qur'an is not the Qur'an unless it appears in the original Arabic. Approved translations are acceptable only as long as they are printed beside the Arabic text. For unknown reason, Zalmay ignored this tradition.

What happened next was predictable. Offended piety led to angry demonstrations in which Zalmay was compared to Salman Rushdie. The rumour merchants then did their bit to add fuel to the fire. The translation turns haram into halal, they said. It omits some verses and willfully mistranslates others. It approves of homosexuality. Zalmay must be killed, they demanded. The magnitude of his predicament finally dawned on Zalmay, and with his brother he got hold of a pair of Afghan army uniforms and, disguised as officers, they set off for the Pakistani border at Torkham. There he was caught and arrested. It turned out the notoriously hard to control border was easy to control after all.

That was in early November 2007. In the year between his arrest and sentencing, Zalmay almost entirely disappeared from the news. When he finally appeared in court in Kabul, he was dressed in traditional attire, wearing a chapan gown and an oversized turban. In remorseful mood, he admitted to having made mistakes. He pleaded for forgiveness, but in vain: he received a twenty-year sentence. It was 365 days more than the term given in 2008 to Abdullah Sarwary, the head of the communist-era secret service agency responsible for the killing and torture of hundreds of mujahedin during the 1980s.

Despite its ending, Zalmay's story is no cautionary tale. On the contrary, it is symptomatic of a broader trend towards religious individualism in Afghanistan. In theory, such democratizing of Islam is positive as it empowers the disadvantaged. But in practice, it has led to theological chaos and social fragmentation. Rival interpretations of Islam are competing for followers and clashing with each other, sometimes violently, as more and more people employ Islam as a means of social and political empowerment.

Ghows Zalmay and Mullah Omar are both Afghan Muslims, yet their understanding of Islam is radically different. Omar's Islam is a transnational religion, appealing to an Arab, Pakistani and Afghan following alike. Zalmay's Islam, by contrast, has a more nationalistic character, seen in his attempt to encourage Afghans to read the Qur'an in their own language. A Pashto translation was also planned, but didn't materialize after the reaction to the Dari-Persian translation. If twenty years in prison seemed a lot for translating a book, then buried in the sentence are the implications of replacing a single transnational Arabic Qur'an with a plurality of national versions of it.

Afghan Jews: A History of Tolerance

I was at primary school in Kabul during the Soviet occupation. One day, seemingly out of the blue, a Muslim girl started a campaign of fear and slander against our only Jewish classmate. She declared that the latter came from a morally loose household and incited us to ostracize the quiet blonde girl. As far as we could see, there was nothing outwardly immoral about this exceptionally smart girl who already kept herself to herself. We asked the inciter to explain her accusation and she responded:

"Her mother lets in a complete stranger, a man, into their house every Sabbath!" The understanding was that no decent Afghan woman would allow a strange man into her home, especially if she was a widow with no grown-up son to protect her honor. This example of ignorance breeding cruelty took place at the honeymoon stage of the Afghan flirtation with jihad—before the mass romance with God's soldiers turned into gang rape.

Looking now at old photographs of family life, religious classrooms and bar mitzvahs, the similarities between Muslim and Jewish Afghans are striking. The rabbis' beards, turbans and gowns made them almost indistinguishable from Muslim scholars, while both were referred to by the title of mullah. The community shared with the rest of society a profound mistrust of state interference in family affairs, rejecting secular education and military service. In the 1920s, Jewish rabbis famously protested against Kabul's attempt to enlist Jewish children to state school.

Much like the rest of society, the family structure was patriarchal. Jewish women married young, were deprived of education and led domestic lives away from the public eye. When leaving home, they covered themselves just like their Muslim counterparts. Such resistance to change meant that the community remained conspicuously traditional and close-knit, marrying only among themselves. In the later decades, when Jewish children started to attend state schools, they had no choice but to turn up to classes on Sabbath. They dealt with this problem by simply sitting down but not doing much else. But this religious tolerance was already disappearing by the time of the Soviet occupation, when I had my own first-hand experience.

But I learned later that my experience of Afghan intolerance of Jews was far from representative. From a historical perspective, the story of the Afghan Jews is a tale of remarkable tolerance. It may seem hard to believe today, but historically it was Afghanistan to which Jews turned to when escaping religious persecution in Iran and central Asia. It was in the dusty, ancient cities of Herat and Kabul, to the west and the east of Afghanistan, that they found freedom to practice their faith without getting murdered in the process. A community of leather and karakul merchants, poor people and money lenders alike, the large Jewish families mostly lived in the border city of Herat, while the families' patriarchs travelled back and forth on trading trips, moving between Iran, Afghanistan, India and central Asia on the ancient silk road.

The Jews did not engage in farming, which restricted their means of earning a living. Like many other Afghans, they survived through trade, taking lengthy and often dangerous trips across the majestic mountains on whose rocks their prayers were carved in Hebrew and sometimes even Aramaic.

Like the rest of the population, the Jews of Afghanistan were simultaneously local and transnational, rooted to the Afghan soil by birth and burial but connected to a global faith through religion. Like Afghan Hindus and Muslims, their sacred sites, too, were located in faraway, hard-to-reach places while their holy language was not the official language of the nation. Isolated and yet connected through the invisible ties of spirituality, Afghan Jews were much like the rest of Afghans, sharing with the Sunni Pashtuns in particular a belief in being descended from the biblical lost tribes. Such similarities were ultimately why a peaceful coexistence was possible between Jewish and Muslim Afghans for most of their shared history, which dates back to the medieval times.

The Afghans' isolation from the rest of the world was a blessing in disguise for the Jewish community because being cut off from global political trends meant that ordinary Afghans were untouched by the raging, European-led anti-Semitism of the early twentieth century. Even at the height of the Nazi influence in Kabul of the 1930s, it was Afghan nationalism rather than anti-Semitism that led the government to introduce economic measures that bankrupted Jewish money-lending families.

The laws affecting the Jewish community were soon removed and in the following decades Afghanistan was the only Muslim country that allowed Jewish families to immigrate without revoking their citizenship first. When Afghan Jews left the country *en masse* in the 1960s, their exile to New York and Tel Aviv was motivated by a search for a better life and not by religious persecution.

Like most Afghans, the Jewish community was also polyglot, reading Hebrew and speaking the local language as well as their own Judeo-Persian dialect. Largely illiterate, the community transmitted knowledge and wisdom through oral folktales, the Kafkaesque surreal characters and narratives of which are much like other Afghan folktales. A brutal truth of the cruelty of life in Afghanistan, for example, is summed up at the end of the Jewish folktale Moses and the Ants: "When the fire rages in the wood, it burns the bad trees and the good."

Now all are burned.

Western Muslims: Adapting Faith

At my father's funeral the imam's voice echoed loudly through the speakers from behind the thick curtain that divided the congregation hall into a male and a female section. I listened hard, trying to understand his words. This ceremony, after all, was supposed to give me solace and help me find closure. I waited for the mercy and compassion that Muslims referred to every time they said "bismillah." But all I could understand from the recitation was the term *shaitan*, the devil.

Soon I gave up on listening altogether. The imam might as well have spoken Korean, a language as unfamiliar to me as the Arabic in which the sermon was conducted. I wondered why I was not allowed to hear the words of God in my own language. Why did I have to study Qur'anic Arabic in order to understand what the imam was telling me at my father's funeral? For the first time in my life, I really needed religion to give me solace, but here I was, listening to an unfamiliar language where the word "devil" kept popping up, alarming rather than comforting me.

When the language finally switched to Persian, I hoped to get something out of the Hadith. But to my dismay, even though the Hadith and the imam's interpretation of them were in my language, I failed to understand how they related to the life and death of my father. We were in Hamburg, in the north of Europe, but the imam told a story that took us to the Arab lands of the eighth century, where a group of believers were hiding inside a cave. It was a tale of violence, an attempted mass murder, from which the believers were saved after God miraculously created a spider's net, covering the cave's front and misleading the prospective killers.

Two thoughts occurred to me. Firstly, exactly how was I supposed to relate to the cave, the spider and the desert in this cold German city with its twenty-first-century high-rise buildings made of glass? Secondly, what had this story to do with my father? I lost track of the Hadith and the next words that reached my ears were, "Not all German TV programs are bad. Some of them are good." Aha!

After the service, a long line of complete strangers stopped in front of me, one by one, before kneeling and whispering words of condolence. When the women kneeled, I noticed their huge, expensive handbags and realized that they were wearing full make-up, complete with foundation, lipstick, and colorful eyeshadows. Cheap Iranian-made Botox was equally conspicuous among women of a certain age, whose eyebrows almost reached the end of their temples, their ballooning cheeks covered in red blusher. I realized that for these Muslim ladies, my father's funeral was a social outing, like some sort of disco, where Eve's daughters felt compelled to compete with each other with botox, handbags and make-up. Had these women been allowed social entertainment outside weddings and funerals, they would not have turned my father's funeral into a curious cat-walk.

In the women's section, I looked for a chador, a full body length fabric. They were kept inside a wardrobe and when I opened its door, I discovered utter chaos. The chadors had been shoved into the wardrobe, piled on top of each. One had to go through many in order to find an appropriate one for a funeral.

The chador chaos for me mirrored the confusion in the minds of so many female Muslims who were the most pious believers and paradoxically also the ones who were excluded from a proper religious education. Their faith was blind, a combination of stories from hundreds of years ago mixed with some memorized Arabic suras and Hadith whose meaning was not entirely clear to them. The older ones muttered words in Arabic, kissed the piety banners with Arabic words embroidered on them, looking terrified. Their terror was understandable. After all, if Muslim men were so unreasonably angry, violent and altogether hateful towards women, then, what could these women expect from the god that created such men?

Muslim clerics have a long way to go in order to make Islam relevant to the needs of the diasporic communities of the west. The religion has travelled hundreds of miles but the imams themselves have a hard time adjusting to the west, let alone being able to offer the community the comfort and guidance it needs in order to live peacefully between two civilizations that seem so hostile to one another. It's the blind leading the blind, I concluded, as I left the mosque, hoping to find solace in solitary contemplation conducted in my own language.

Imams and Fingernails

For Muslim women worldwide, the twenty-first century is the age of progress and setbacks. The progress is made possible by women themselves; the setbacks are largely courtesy of some vocal clerics and self-appointed representatives, such as the terrorist group al-Qaida, both of whom often masquerade as the "saviors of the *ummah*."

PART TWO

Call it masochism if you want, but I have taken an interest in what the self-appointed representatives of this religion, whose first believer was a woman, have to say about us, women. What I discovered was far from reassuring. Some imams and also militant terrorist groups, it appears, have taken an unhealthy interest in all things feminine.

This obsessive interest could be a clumsy, if not downright idiotic, reaction to the global push for women's rights, or it might simply be a reflection of such "representatives'" own bizarre mental universe. Either way, the result is humiliating for Muslim women who, after all, are the most pious and caring part of the community and as such deserve more respect.

The surreal nature of this state of affairs was summed up in an Iranian TV program I watched during the celebration of a female saint's birthday. In a room crowded with women dressed in black chadors, I saw a bearded imam on the stage preaching through the microphone to the female congregation. He was telling the hundred or so female believers what it meant to be a Muslim woman, as if the women themselves were clueless about this particular matter.

Judging by the women's almost palpable concentration, they were deeply engrossed in the question, which was fair enough. But why listen to a man who, by virtue of his anatomical, social and cultural programming, was unable to know what it felt like to be a woman, let alone a Muslim woman—the innocent victims par excellence of this century's relentless clash of civilizations. The irony of the situation was missed by both the female congregation and, naturally, the imam himself. The bearded man finished the sermon with the words: "And that's what being a Muslim woman feels like." Seriously?

I, for one, would never dare to tell Muslim men what it feels like to be a man. The beards and the hairy chests are a mystery to me, as are the practice of circumcision and those notorious male hormones. Equally, I never understood the pull of global

jihad that drove so many young men to my tragic Afghan homeland where they practiced shooting in an already destroyed
country. I don't know what's going on in their hot heads and
they, in turn, don't know what it's like to be harassed despite
wearing the hijab on a hot summer's day in Kabul.

But the imams' assumption that they know women's nature
better than the women themselves does not stop with such surreal sermons. I watched an Afghan TV program that in all seri-
ousness broadcast the deliberations of an imam about nail
varnish. Once again, I found myself startled at this interest in
female beauty products. I am a woman and do not remember a
single conversation with my female friends, let alone male
friends, that revolved around nail polish for more than two minutes. But this imam could talk about nail varnish with such ease
that it could only imply either a great deal of prior contemplation, some self-experimentation or, alternatively, a thorough survey of women's feet. Needless to say, all three possibilities were
equally alarming because they spoke of a mind preoccupied by
frivolous and mundane matters that should have nothing to do
with men of God.

This trivialization of religion is not a joke. It's an insult to the
dignity of Muslim women. There is more to Islam than vaginal
vigilantism and the clerics and self-appointed terrorist "savior
groups" should be the first to know this much. After all, it is
stated clearly in the Qur'an that women's mandate is necessary
for the choice of political leadership. If the prophet himself
respected women and saw them as equals, then why can't
today's leaders, both the self-appointed and the legitimate ones,
do the same?

Secular Education

Sohrab Samanian works for an NGO in Kabul where he is
tasked with educating Afghan women about their rights. In a

blog post he describes walking past a stall where a bearded man was selling various tape recordings, including cassettes with Islamic religious content.

To create interest for his goods, the stall owner was playing a cassette through loudspeakers and Samanian noticed that a crowd of men had gathered around to listen. This is what they were listening to:

"Ask the people you know, the ones who send their girls and women to schools, exactly what have you achieved with this? Is it not the case that these schools that they have built for us so that we Muslims send our girls to them have had a negative impact on morality and honor? By building so-called educational institutions, the foreigners are encouraging our girls to become whores."

The tape's misogynist content dressed up as religious preaching angered Samanian but there was nothing he could do. In his blog, he wonders whether allowing this type of incendiary preaching is a necessary part of democracy, given that its content undermines the same women's rights that the government and many NGOs are trying to institutionalize in Afghanistan. But when Samanian raised his concern with the relevant offices, he encountered a dismissive attitude summed up in the following response: "This kind of blathering won't achieve anything."

While Samanian is right about the potential dangers of such incendiary preaching, the truth is that religious scholars' objection to secular educational institutions dates back to the 1910s—a whole century before the international community started building schools or encouraging women's education in Afghanistan.

A newspaper report published in 1915 about the launch of the first state-controlled elementary schools in Kabul illustrates the reason for this objection. It says:

"A group of mullahs had the following request. They said, 'Before this school, children used to come to us to be taught. But now that they have entered this school, we, who have no other qualification but to teach, are left without work and income. The rest is up to his majesty to decide.'"

This example shows that the mullahs' objection to new schools was not religiously motivated but had practical reasons. The king had introduced reform but without taking into account its side-effect of making people unemployed in a professional group that had the power to manipulate Afghans against reform by using its religious authority.

The Afghan authorities of the time came up with a compromise. The mullahs were allowed to continue teaching as long as they stuck to the syllabus authorized by the state. But they were also warned that if they strayed from the syllabus, the state would demolish their mosques. A mixture of concession and violence helped the state to stay in control.

But religious scholars' resistance to modern education must have gone beyond the mullahs' mild request to carry on working. Essays written by the first graduates of the new schools in the 1920s reveal a profound concern with legitimizing modern education. A student writing an essay in Pashto devotes entire paragraphs to justifying that learning to read and write in one's own native language is not in conflict with Islam.

Another student translates a text about Islam from English to show that learning a European language does not make him an infidel.

Reading these essays written nearly a century ago, it is obvious that students felt that they had to justify their education to religious scholars. It is also clear that the clerics saw modern schools as a threat and fought them with the only weapon they knew: religious authority.

The clerics fought against modern education way before cassette recorders, female students or non-Muslim foreign advisers existed in Afghanistan. The anti-education polemic mentioned in Samanian's blog is just an old story told in a new guise.

66

Given this historical background, it becomes clear that the problem that Samanian identifies in his blog has neither to do with democracy nor with religiosity. It has to do with the way Afghan authorities introduce reform without taking into account its possible repercussions, such as depriving people of their jobs without offering them an alternative.

But while the state responded a century ago by threatening to demolish wayward mosques, today's government is too concerned with its own survival to even notice the perils of inflammatory misogynist sermons.

Caught between a state obsessed with itself and ruthless clerics who call them "educated whores," skilled Afghan females are left defenseless in an ugly war of words fought to ensure the clergy's survival in its competition with modern education.

Taliban Attacks and Theological Chaos

A Guardian article in 2010 about an alleged poison gas attack at the Totia girls' school in Kabul, where Muslim believers are said to have come under attack by fellow believers during the holy month of Ramadan, reminded me of a similar incident during the Soviet occupation. I was at primary school and remember watching girls being carried over to an adjacent hospital.

The rumour that later spread at school explained the incident as follows: one of the pupils, from a family of mujahedin sympathizers, had poisoned the school well in protest against the communist-inspired syllabus. The story sounded plausible at the time, given the absence of free media, reliable investigation or international witnesses offering a different, perhaps more objective, take on it.

The parents' reaction was pragmatic. The following day, pupils returned to school, carrying plastic flasks filled with water from home. But this response did not mean parents supported the government. It was true that the syllabus was inspired by communist ideology. But there was a way around that. Children simply learned to differentiate between useful scientific knowledge and political propaganda. To receive an education, Afghans—then as now—had no choice but take the risk of exposing children to state propaganda and its spin-off, insurgent violence.

The two incidents—with the water and the "poison gas"—are separated by decades but their similarity makes it tempting to repeat the old cliché that nothing changes in Afghanistan. But in some ways they are strikingly different, revealing profound changes in three decades of conflict and the way it is perceived.

The key difference is that in the old story the conflict was neat, involving two clearly opposite sides: a communist regime of perceived non-believers versus an Islamist resistance of believers. In the new story, all parties involved in the incident are believers, including the Islamic Republic that is responsible for the school, the pupils who attend it and the perpetrators who allegedly carried out the attack.

Another striking difference between the two stories relates to gender issues. The old story had a female protagonist who was a school insider. In the current story, by contrast, girls appear only as victims and the perpetrator is perceived to be an outsider. We can assume that the girls of my school were still able to sympathize with the mujahedin, since they had never lived under their rule. But the current generation of schoolgirls knows better and there has been no suspicion of an insider act carried out by a girl. These differences are subtle but reveal shifts in the emotional landscape of the people, and the way they relate to the present conflict.

Judging by the parents' reaction to the current story, ordinary Afghans expect the Taliban to break all sorts of traditional religious taboos, including the ban on violence during the month of Ramadan. The parents' reasoning is plausible. After all, a serious taboo such as suicide has been reinterpreted and reintroduced as an act of piety without apparently raising a single eyebrow in

Kabul or beyond. Judging by such precedents, Ramadan, too, could have been reinterpreted without notice and declared a month in which jihad by violent means could continue. What we see is theological chaos and various conflicting interpretations of Islam vying for power and influence in Afghanistan. The result is an Islamic Republic in charge of a Muslim people, which is under attack by an Islamist insurgency.

Little wonder, then, that parents of Totia school girls have been left wondering who is representing Islam, and who defaming it. But this type of chaos is an expected outcome when Muslim states lose control over religion. Faced with the Taliban, the old mujahedin who are in power now are getting a taste of their own medicine. After all, they too had once used Islam to legitimize violence against civilians, schoolchildren included.

Another striking difference between the two stories is content-related. In the old story, the poison incident was explained as an act of protest against the school's syllabus but not girls' education per se. Could it be that the old mujahedin leaders were less rigid by comparison to their contemporary reincarnation, the Taliban? Unfortunately, we cannot verify this assumption because the old jihad was highly dispersed, lacking in a coherent, clearly defined political vision that could provide answers to the question of gender and public education. Be that as it may, the Totia school incident is yet another example of Afghanistan's theological chaos. Rather oddly, the chaos has been ignored, despite the trouble it is obviously causing.

But maybe ignoring the problem is deliberate. After all, the relationship between Islam and nationhood is particularly complex in Afghanistan. Religion has always been a key component of nationalism, so fighting for religion tends to be automatically interpreted as a legitimate act of patriotism. This formula worked well as long as the conflict involved Muslim believers versus non-believers. But since the 1990s, the conflict is no longer about Muslims versus non-believers but various interpretations

AFGHAN RUMOUR BAZAAR

of Islam vying for power and influence. As a result, religion no
longer works as a binding force but has become a trigger of conflict in Afghanistan.

However, since acknowledging this truth amounts to disman-
tling the most sacred of the country's recent myths, Islam is
likely to continue being regarded as the solution rather than the
source of conflict.

Old Habits and New Life-Styles

In the 1930s, Swiss lovers and avant-garde writers Annemarie
Schwarzenbach and Ella Maillart felt they had reached the end
of the world when they arrived in Afghanistan. After all, no
newspaper could arrive at this abandoned frontier spot of
bygone empires in time. The two women soon lost their sense of
time—oblivion, after all, was what they were seeking in Afghanistan, leaving behind the Europe of World War II with its cruel
rationality, crude racism and the cold metallic cars, trains, and
planes. They sought peace in the protective aloofness of Afghanistan from all things mechanical. To such disenchanted creative
minds, the chunk of earth demarcated on maps as Afghanistan
was the embodiment of the idea of anti-civilization. Afghanistan
was the opposite of urbanization, militarization and industriali-
zation. The visitors must have felt like they had entered a time-
machine to land in the past.

Three decades later, Italian artist Alighiero Boetti, another
child of his time, arrived in Afghanistan of the 1970s. He was a
spiritual seeker and a traveler, driven by the same desire for
escape that had tempted Maillart and Schwarzenbach. In Boetti's view, consumerism had rendered art meaningless in Europe.
He said that in Europe, art had become mere dead objects that
people hang on theirs walls. In Afghanistan, he discovered a
minimalist people. The men and women of this land wore the
same clothes day and night. They lived in empty homes, without

furniture or décor. The untouched unproductiveness of this country included the landscape which looked virginal, as if created only yesterday. Boettie admired Afghans: "The resistance with which Afghans oppose our civilization has always amazed me," he said.

When I translated the Persian scripts of Boetti's *Mappa Mundi* embroidery, crafted by Afghan refugee women, I discovered forlorn lines of love poetry and celestial worship scattered across the embroidered maps of the world. There were lines in awe of the sharp edges of a gorge somewhere deep in the mountains of Afghanistan, the footprints of carrier horses, the sighs of merchant travelers of a bygone age. The embroidered writing often looked childish and clumsy, the kind of writing that is made by those who can't read but are skilled at copying shapes. These scattered lines were the splinters of fragmented souls. We were a displaced people and chunks of our imagination were hanging on the walls of a museum in California, for all to see but few to understand.

Everything changed in 2001, when the international community came to Afghanistan complete with soldiers, missionaries, mercenaries, seasoned advisors, fresh-faced aid workers and eager reporters (not to forget the unsung heroes that were the occasional tourists and adventurers). After ten years of journalists' poking, probing and reporting, Afghanistan lost its mystique and the world discovered a nation that was wounded, hurt and traumatized at the same time as it was corrupt, criminal and unreliable. The endless tales of suffering ultimately became dreary and the timing of it could not have been more convenient for Washington. After ten years of war, Washington decided its problems at home were more urgent than that distant war in Afghanistan. If winning against the Taliban was not an option, purchasing their loyalty still offered a solution. While Kabul and Washington arranged to buy the T-Boys' loyalty, the trade-off came at the worst time possible for young Afghans. They were just coming of age, beginning to find their voice; a majority of Afghanistan's population were now teenaged or in their twenties. Afghanistan was becoming young again just when the world was becoming tired of it. Here are some of their stories.

Gay Afghans

The first time he slept with a man, Hamid Nilofar was a young Afghan with little experience of life outside the city of Kabul. His lover, an older Pakistani man, happened to be just the right type—educated, mature and well-mannered. The young gay Afghan met the older man by accident. Hamid, like most Afghans, had family in Pakistan and while visiting his sister there, one day he went for a stroll in a nearby public park. The other man just happened to be there, walking towards Hamid from the opposite direction. In his brutally honest memoirs, *Passing Through a Nightmare*, Hamid writes about other, equally restless lone men, purposelessly wandering about the park. He suspected that they, too, were looking for that forbidden love with another man.

The older man held the young Afghan's gaze as he walked towards him, getting closer and closer. He stopped when he reached Hamid and struck up a conversation. Soon after, intuition kicked in and the two men sought privacy on a bench hidden away from public view. The older man complimented Hamid on his beautiful eyes and asked for permission to touch and kiss them. He cautiously stroked Hamid's face, and carefully watched the young man's reaction. Far from being appalled, Hamid was flattered and already melting. He soon found himself holding hands with and being kissed and caressed by the older man. One thing led to another and for Hamid, this first experience of gay love felt just right. It was, after all, the realization of what he had dreamed about since puberty. "I feel sorry for all those men who die without ever having realized their dream of love with another man," Hamid writes in his memoirs. Such men do exist in Afghanistan. More than often they are married and have children, leading a perfectly "respectable" life on the surface. But secretly, they yearn for this other love—the one that dare not speak its name.

Officially, Afghanistan is a strictly heterosexual, family-based society where sex outside the legal bounds of marriage is a crime punishable by imprisonment. But behind the clean-cut surface of respectability, there's a foggy underworld of chaotic sexuality with no clear rules and boundaries to protect the vulnerable, including gay men. "We fall in love easily and give our heart and soul but only to be betrayed and ridiculed," writes one gay blogger from Kabul. He gives an example of the kind of fear and loathing existence that is part and parcel of being gay and Afghan. The blogger's ex-boyfriend, who turned out to be an intelligence officer, finished their relationship with an action that reeked of self-hatred bordering on sadism. Upon ending the affair, the intelligence officer gave his ex's name and telephone number to all his male acquaintances, encouraging these random men to approach the former boyfriend for sex. Needless to say, the emotional damage of such cruelty can be irreparable and yet it is a piece of cake by comparison with the danger to one's life that can accompany such forced public outing of a gay man. After all, if an Afghan man is outed as a homosexual (sometimes it's enough to just be labeled gay), he is considered a disgrace to his family and runs the risk of becoming a victim of "honor killing." Family is king in Afghanistan—a mini mafia structure that rules over life and death, providing protection for those who comply with its rules and punishing those who dare to stray. To be gay and Afghan means to live life in perpetual fear of discovery and betrayal, a paranoid existence spent in continuous terror of forced outing.

In addition to such soul-crushing anxieties, there's the tyranny of a conformist society with a stubborn image of the ideal manhood to which every male is expected to aspire. This ideal is represented by the figure of the strong and powerful patriarch. To get married and have children is not enough to live up to this ideal. A man has to be tough and masculine, rich and powerful. More importantly, he has to father many sons and raise them as obedient foot-soldiers under his command. That's the kind of man who is envied in Afghan society. (The warlords, with their big bellies and long beards are all but a contemporary reincarnation of this traditional model of brutish, militant masculinity). Needless to say, far from aspiring to this ideal, gay Afghan men dread the prospect of wedding, dodging the barrage of questions and postponing marriage as long as possible. For Hamid Nilofar, the first openly gay Afghan man, leading the fake, pretend life of a married heterosexual man was simply out of question. He fled Afghanistan, and endured years of horrific hardship in Iran and Turkey in order to escape the tyranny of Afghan conformism. It's a conformism where married life is forced upon everyone, young boys and girls, homosexual men and lesbian women as well as those who simply have no interest in sexuality or in leading a typical Afghan family life. Many Afghans don't flee because of politics, they flee their society and escape their culture, Hamid writes in his memoirs after meeting teenage runaway boys who fled Afghanistan to avoid marriage.

Hamid finally settled in Canada where he wrote his pioneering memoirs. It was there in Canada that he met online the man he would have become had he not fled Afghanistan. This other man, also gay, had succumbed to society, marrying and fathering four children. "What bitter life it is to have just one longing and to never, not even for a day, have this longing fulfilled," wrote the other man from an office in Kabul. For Hamid, these words were enough to clarify which one of the two had made the right decision.

Afghanistan's Accidental Gay Pride

If you are gay and proud, Afghanistan is quite likely the last place on earth to show it publicly. How, then, are we supposed to make sense of the conspicuous appearance of the rainbow-cultured gay pride symbols all over the streets of Kabul and other urban centers?

The pioneer Afghan Pajhwok news agency took it upon itself to investigate this unusual sociocultural phenomenon, sending a reporter to interview drivers who had decorated their cars with gay pride stickers and rear banners. After all, these Chinese-made car accessories had suddenly become popular, available in any garage supplying vehicle parts.

Even more remarkably, Afghan drivers seemed to have little concern about using their cars to openly advertise being gay and proud of it. In a country where social conservatism sometimes results in gay men sharing their life with their partner of choice and an arranged wife so as to keep up appearances, there was certainly something very unusual about this apparently new openness.

Needless to say, Pajhwok's reporter soon discovered that Afghans who had decorated their cars with the rainbow symbol had no idea what it stood for. For them it was just the newest car fashion accessory but, on learning of its meaning in the west, drivers immediately started removing it.

The rainbow stickers had first arrived on secondhand cars imported from Canada. Afghans had simply assumed that the color combination was the latest fashion fad in the West, and duly adopted it. Had it not been for the news agency's interest, the gay pride symbol would have continued to flourish in Afghanistan. Uprooted from its original cultural environment and landing in the country by sheer accident, it would have led an existence devoid of any meaning aside from showing that, like everywhere else in the world, Afghan men loved their cars.

But since Afghanistan is no longer an isolated country, imported symbols are bound to be recognized and decoded not only by globetrotting members of the middle class but also the many expatriate internationals and returnee Afghans. Once informed about the symbol's meaning, the stickers were removed en mass. One commentator even expressed the hope that the embarrassing incident would serve as cautionary tale, warning Afghans against their tendency to blindly follow fashions imported from elsewhere.

The confusion that had allowed for the gay-pride car accessories to become coveted goods in Afghan garages is not restricted to the symbol itself. Judging by the way homosexuality is debated in the public sphere, the term itself is understood incorrectly. It is usually used as a synonym for what would be described in Europe and North America as pedophilia. Hence, on the rare occasions when Afghan writers dare to publicly tackle problems related to sexuality, we encounter the local terms *hamjins baazi* (homosexuality) and *bacha baazi* (pedophilia) used interchangeably, as if they both deal with the same phenomenon. There seems to be little awareness of the fact that in liberal democracies of the west the term strictly refers to relationships between consenting adults.

Given that Afghanistan is an exceedingly conservative society, it is astonishing that articles openly discussing homosexuality actually exist. The content of such articles is often surprising. Hence, in what—by Afghan standards—is a frank and almost judgment-free article, one writer establishes that it is the country's social conditions that contribute to unorthodox practices. Blaming strict gender segregation, the author points out that since desire is natural to humankind, its suppression is bound to make it resurface in a different guise: "For example, monks and those who renounce worldly pleasures quite often tend to be fat, with big bellies. Their desire has resurfaced as greed for food."

Following this rather strange line of argument, the reader is then confronted with a curious assessment: if necessary, relations with underage persons should be conducted with girls rather than boys because even if they are physically immature, the female anatomy still renders girls more natural partners.

A recurrent theme in all such debates is a juxtaposition of European countries' treatment of the hijab with their attitude towards homosexuality. Authors are genuinely puzzled that France has banned the hijab, which in their view is a religious obligation, but protects the rights of homosexuals—which they say is banned by all religions. Such articles as a rule make generous use of question and exclamation marks. These loud orthographic markers, in turn, echo the profound divide that separates the Afghans' traditional society from the liberal markets from whence secondhand cars make their journey across continents, sometimes complete with dangerously loaded but misunderstood ornamental accessories.

The Trials of Transvestitism

"Take off your chador," the police officer orders an Afghan cross-dresser in a video that has been shared endlessly on social networking websites.

"Take off your wig!" Beneath the shiny black locks, the head is revealed as male with receding, closely cropped hair.

He's also wearing a scarlet short-sleeved shalwar kamiz—sexy but traditional female attire. The feminine look is accentuated by large sparkling bangles and see-through embroidery.

The victim's ordeal goes on for what seems like eternity as he endures humiliating comments and laughter from the police officers.

"Please have mercy, don't make fun of me," he whispers.

"Boy! Face the camera," they shout, forcing him to remove the fake breasts from inside his top. The breasts turn out to be a pair of socks filled with dough.

"Dough to make the breasts feel softy-soft," an officer shouts amid laughter. Male cross-dressing is familiar enough in Afghanistan for the locals to have coined a special term. The word is *ezak*—a vague but deeply derogatory noun referring to anything from a eunuch or a hermaphrodite to a transvestite or a male homosexual.

Following the discovery of the dough, a barrage of questions ensues in the video. "Why are you dressed like this? Where did you put the makeup on? What is all this about? What have you two been up to?"

This final question is addressed to a shy young man leaning away but standing next to the transvestite. The two were arrested together. "I was shopping for clothes," the cross-dresser whispers, taking off the bangles. He is trying to tell the officers that his dressing up is just a silly, harmless game.

"Put the bangles back on," a police officer orders. The victim reluctantly obeys, his eyes filled with tears.

"Please, officer, we haven't committed a crime," the victim's companion pleads, turning away from the camera.

Like most of the sensationalist Afghan news that is spread online, the video gives no information about the date, the source, or the victim's fate following the arrest. The clip made the rounds, creating lively debate before people tired of it.

My immediate reaction was to regard it as a clear example of ignorance breeding cruelty. From the officers' tone it was evident that they felt proud of the arrest, believing they had protected ordinary families from a couple of "dangerous perverts." But the officers' pride was also mixed with utter bewilderment. This confusion was neatly summed up in the video's title: "A man dressed as a woman—but why?" The title cried out for explanation and the numerous comments left by viewers revealed a wide range of interpretations, including political paranoia, with some viewers suspecting that the cross-dresser was in reality a suicide bomber trained by the Pakistani ISI to infiltrate Kabul disguised as a woman.

There was also a more sober reaction, with commentators criticizing the police for wasting their time on mundane incidents while the threat of terrorism was all too real. A few comments interpreted the cross-dressing as a sign of cultural anarchy, a symbol of Afghans straying from the path of Islam. A couple of people demanded the cross-dresser should be executed, while others said that even though the cross-dresser was misguided they still felt sorry for him.

Amid such voices of confusion, and at times outright cruelty, it was heartening to read comments expressing anger at the police's humiliation of the victim: "The man has committed no crime. Cross-dressing is a psychological condition. What he needs is treatment rather than public humiliation."

Others recalled their own encounters with transvestites:

"During the Taliban, we had an *ezak* in our neighborhood. His brothers used to hit him for acting like a female and finally killed him."

"I am worried about this man's future. His family is bound to kill him because of the shame he has brought on them. To protect this unfortunate person, people should stop sharing this video."

It was the presence of these voices of sanity among Afghans themselves that encouraged me to write this article. It showed that people are beginning to realize the importance of psychology in making a society more humane. This is vitally needed but much neglected in Afghanistan. Students are often discouraged by their own families from pursuing their interest in psychology. "Do you really want to end up a doctor to the crazies?" is the usual reaction. The prejudice is widespread, even inside the medical community.

The result is a nation deeply in need of psychological treatment but left with little choice but to turn to "traditional treatments," which include chaining patients to the walls of saintly shrines or depriving them of food and drink for long periods. Amid such dark despair, the sane voices of compassion that appeared alongside the aggressive comments offered a glimmer of hope because they showed that Afghans are beginning to understand that transvestites are not criminals.

It is true that different cultures create distinctive personality traits, but as the case of the unlucky Afghan transvestite revealed, such non-standard but deeply felt psychological needs are universal, with transvestites from the dusty roads of Kabul to the sparkling clubs of New York feeling the same urge to dress up as women with or without society's approval.

Hollywood Burqas

Images of Afghan women have become part and parcel of the ideological battles of our century. Compare the big-toothed confidence of Hillary Clinton with the missing nose of Bibi Aisha (her husband hacked off her nose after she tried to flee his abuse) on *Time* magazine covers and you get the picture. But how do such stereotypical representations of Afghan women come about? I didn't know the answer until recently, when I was asked to be a cultural adviser on the set of a film in Los Angeles. The film's story was the familiar tale of an Afghan girl who is forced to marry against her will.

The movie was my chance to add much-needed nuance and complexity to the fashionable genre of international films on the plight of Afghan women. I was filled with anticipation when I began to read the screenplay. But my heart began to sink with every page I turned. The storyline was an unimaginative take on an outdated Orientalist fantasy at best, and crude political propaganda at worst.

Its hero is an idealistic American UN worker who meets a beautiful Afghan girl at a border checkpoint. She is about to be wedded against her will but a brief misunderstanding between her and the American leads to a flirtatious argument. The American idealist is intrigued and captivated by the girl, as is the Afghan girl by the blue-eyed American. The ensuing platonic romance between East and West culminates in the girl lifting her veil to look the idealist deep in the eyes. The problem is, she is caught in the act and ends up being flogged in public by her angry Afghan father. The film ends with the UN hero shouting: "Stop it, Stop it"—but his cries are useless. His job is to observe and document, but not to interfere.

There were numerous problems with the plot but when I registered my concern, the director set me straight: "Honey, this is a movie!" It is true that films are fantasy and make-believe, but then again what was I, the cultural adviser, doing on the set?

A friend explained the situation. "This is how it works: You rubber-stamp them and they rubber-stamp you." I had a sinking feeling but withdrawing at this point was bound to be deemed unprofessional so I stayed on.

There were visual inaccuracies. The signs were in Arabic, the Afghan father was dressed as an Egyptian while the women sported Moroccan jilabas. This was a serious mix-up but the key decisions about Afghan culture had been made in my absence and judging by the team's happy energy, I was alone in my dismay.

I clung to the hope that the Afghan-American lead actress might share my concerns. After all, it was disheartening to watch everything that was meaningful to our culture turn into a farce. I tried to test her reaction and asked: "Did you see the dad?" She replied: "Yes! Doesn't he look great?" I was flabbergasted and protested: "But this is NOT how Afghan men dress!" She watched me in silence and resumed piling makeup on her face.

Later, I watched the actresses improvise the scene after the girl is caught flirting. The mother was distraught and a melodrama unfolded. The mother shouted with a thick Iranian accent in Persian: "Why did you do this to me?" But by then I had already given up on correcting her accent to sound Afghan.

"Language is not important," I had been told sharply. The Afghan girl started to defend herself. She was skinny in a trendy, self-imposed way, unlike the involuntary starvation of real people in Afghanistan. Her screeches were heartrending and implausibly loud, given that they came from underneath protruding ribs.

"That's a lie. I didn't show my face," she shrieked. This was a plausible scenario. An Afghan girl who had the guts to flirt with an American guy would be one capable of defending herself with kicks and shouts. But the film's Chinese director had her own take on female Asians' psychology. She interfered, directing the actress to project "shame."

"You are not supposed to be angry. You are supposed to be ashamed," she told the actress. And so Chinese morality was added to the film's Arab dress code and Iranian accent, leaving little that was recognizably Afghan.

I decided to tell the producer not to credit me in the film. There was no way I was going to dignify this farce with cultural authenticity. These thoughts were on my mind when I heard a crew member address me: "Would you mind being an extra and wearing this burqa for the next scene?"

I looked up and saw a crimson burqa floating in front of me. The whole crew had assembled, watching me with anticipation. As a professional woman it was expected of me to be a team player and don the burqa. "But I have never worn a burqa in my life," I heard myself protest. "We realize that it must be hard for you and we appreciate it," said the man, still holding the burqa. The irony of the situation was lost on the crew.

Minutes later, I found myself wearing a burqa for the first time in my life. "This is incredible," fumed a self-righteous extra from under her blue burqa. I found myself wanting to defend the burqa and was startled at my own reaction. I was surrounded by bossy international liberals born into wealth. They shaped the entertainment industry and ran its moralizing side-project of glamorous charity events about the plights of other people.

A realization dawned on me: so this is how it happens, the misrepresentation of Afghan women. Then I heard the word "Action!" and the camera began to roll, filming a crowd of self-righteous female western extras dressed in fake Afghan burqas.

PART TWO

Osama bin Laden Was Not Our Hero

What will they think of my hat in Poland in a hundred years?"
wondered Pablo Neruda in *The Book of Questions*. A curious
question, but not as queer as the one I have been asked: how will
historians remember Osama bin Laden? The answer depends on
whose history, what sources, and which language we're talking
about. We can easily imagine future American commemoration
of Bin Laden. So instead of tales of heroic firefighters and their
bearded nemesis, this essay draws on stories from little-known
places of even lesser-known people. In 100 years, were she to sift
through Afghan materials, an imaginative historian might come
across these stories and write a history of what Bin Laden meant
to those other partners in the tale, the Afghans.

Let's start with Zazi, the district in eastern Afghanistan where
Bin Laden first found fame fighting Soviet troops in 1987. (Type
in Zazi to YouTube and you get a thirty-seven-second amateur
shot of the district). Future historians may note that Bin Laden's
formative jihad years were spent under a pale open sky, in a valley ringed by snow-capped mountains and hills of fern trees.
Here he set up his first regiment, with the name al-Masada: "the
Lion's Den."

Since then, his Arab fighters have moved further north, to
Korengal in Konar province, where they married local women.
They are fighting US troops stationed nearby, flinging to the fog
of war the chance that memories of their old commander will
reach future historians. US troops have placed a bounty of
$350,000 for the fighters' current commander, Qari Ziya al-
Rahman. He doesn't mind being photographed, showing off his
taste for cream pakul flat caps. In 100 years our historian might
link his photo to those of American soldiers, posing for souvenirs in the same local headgear.

We are moving among the obscure places and people whose
lives have been touched by Bin Laden. One of them, Sher Akbar

from the village of Bagh-e Metal, had his life ruined by another photograph when a Peshawar magazine noticed his striking resemblance to Bin Laden. The result was massive manhunts, twice resulting in Akbar's arrest. He still crosses the border to Pakistan for business and fears the Hellfire missiles used against vehicles believed to transport al-Qaida leaders.

Future historians may also come across Jan Ali Zaki's account of his trip to Indonesia, published in Kabul in October 2008. The Afghan journalist wrote: "The majority of the Indonesians I met believe Bin Laden is a hero, which is why some of them print his picture on T-shirts. When I tell them Osama's jihad is causing suffering to Afghans, that his actions have killed more Muslim children than infidels, they're surprised and say: 'But he is Islam's hero. How can he do such things?'" Like many other Afghans, Zaki despairs that Bin Laden has become to Afghanistan what Che Guevara was to Cuba: a revolutionary internationalist coupled with a country not his own. "They ask me where I am from. I say: 'Afghanistan.' They say: 'Oh, Bin Laden's country!' I tell myself, what a strange country! Our whole history has been lost to a foreign Arab!" Bin Laden was killed in 2011 but his accidental association with Afghanistan is to survive even after his death.

Kabul Street Style

A new generation of young people is quietly reviving the Afghan capital's urban fashion culture.

"Is this supposed to be culture?" demanded an onlooker dressed in the loose trousers and shirt of the traditional *pirhan tumban*. This conservative clothing stood in contrast to the Afghan hipsters posing for our photographs. Like everything else in Afghanistan, fashion, too, is a question of politics and identity.

We took fashion pictures in Kabul's Macroyan neighborhood. This former Soviet quarter is now famous for young men who unashamedly follow the fashions of New York and London, parading their skinny jeans and spiky haircuts on Kabul's dusty streets.

In the 1980s, Macroyan was partly home to the communist elite. Their teenagers started going on evening strolls, dressed in the latest western styles. Today's youth are too young to recall Macroyan's socialist past, only the Taliban. "Even kids had to wear black turbans," recalled Yusof, our nineteen-year-old guide. "My turban was stylish, I used to wrap it in a unique style and became famous for it at school."

Yusof was ten when the Taliban regime fell. He joined a crowd that chased the last Talib official from the neighborhood. "What happened to him?" I asked. "We cornered him and stoned him," Yusof said, blushing with embarrassment. These young professionals, who work in private banks, the media and the telecoms industry, were also shy and needed persuading to pose for us. "Do you really think me stylish?" some asked.

Their carefully chosen accessories combine functionality with fashion. Pulled over one's head or mouth, the colorful scarves combat Kabul's dust and air pollution, safeguarding lungs as much as expensive haircuts. The necklaces and armbands are contemporary renditions of traditional Islamic talismans which protect the wearers against the evil eye and suicide attacks. Survival is often a matter of luck in this contested fringe of departed empires, but some young Afghans are determined to look good, war or no war.

Fighting Women

Perhaps it is misogyny, or sheer desperation that is breeding this kind of women, but among the females of Afghanistan, there are some who stand out for their exceptional courage, doing dangerous jobs that most ordinary men would be loath to do. One such woman was Malalai Kakar. Needless to say, she ended up being killed in September 2008.

"Killing Malalai Kakar was an unmanly thing to do," said a UN official in Kandahar, Malalai's home city, after Afghanistan's most famous policewoman was murdered.

Ordinarily in Afghanistan, the shooting of a woman by two armed men on motorbikes would be considered naamardi— cowardly or, literally, unmanly. But Kakar was no ordinary woman: she was a senior police officer who had shot dead three men about to launch a suicide attack. When the press approached her at the time, she said that kind of thing happened every day in her line of work.

The Taliban claimed responsibility for Kakar's death, saying she had been a long-term target. In a perverse nod to gender equality, in killing her, they acknowledged that an Afghan woman can be as deadly an enemy as any man.

Unusual as she clearly was, Malalai Kakar was also part of a long-standing tradition of Afghan women who "outman" their men in bravery. These are women who take sides in wars, taking up arms for or against the government. In the past, such women used to be mainly the stuff of legends. They were admired and held up as role models but not feared, since they weren't real.

Early Afghan historical works are full of such women. Reminiscent of the epic German poem the Nibelungenlied, these tales of warriors, horses and fortresses feature young women such as Shah Bori, described as a girl with a taste for male clothing and horse riding. She is said to have liked living the life of a warrior, refusing for a long time to get married. She is also said to have died fighting the troops of King Babur, in the sixteenth century.

Then there's Nazauna, who, legend has it, single-handedly protected the Zabol fortress with her sword; that was in the eighteenth century. And in the nineteenth century, there was the original Malalai, after whom Malalai Kakar was named: Malalai of Maiwand, who turned her headscarf into a banner and led a successful rebellion against the British.

But for a long time, Afghan girls could only read about these women and fantasize about being one of them. In real life, their biggest adventure was walking alone between home and school. That was in the times of peace; then the communist coup of 1978 and the subsequent wars changed things, and real Afghan women proved themselves every bit as courageous as their legendary role models.

In recent decades, the first girl to make a name for herself by living up to the heroines of the past was a sixteen-year-old schoolgirl by the name of Nahid. In February 1980, Nahid led a demonstration of schoolgirls and female university students on the streets of Kabul. It was one of the very first public protests testing the loyalty of the communist regime's army and police force. Would the government shoot at unarmed schoolgirls and students? The answer, it turned out, was a firm yes. Soviet helicopters were heard hovering over the protesters, and shooting soon followed. Nahid fell immediately, and so did many of her companions.

The people of Kabul were stunned: this was naamardi of serious proportions. Nahid was immediately declared a heroine, a contemporary Malalai of Maiwand. Her death was tragic but also reassuring: Afghanistan was still capable of producing courageous, patriotic women who had no fear of death—just like those in the country's founding myths.

In 1982, a few years after Nahid's demonstration, Malalai Kakar joined the Afghan police force. At the time, she would have been considered brave and patriotic by some sections of Afghan society; others would have seen her as a traitor, for collaborating with the Soviet-backed government. The same split opinion is probably true after her death.

The Taliban killed Kakar because she worked for an Afghan government with the backing of international armed forces. But many other Afghans see Kakar as a patriot who risked her life to ensure the security of her fellow Afghans. This is also what President Karzai said when he "sharply condemned" Kakar's assassination, calling her a woman who toiled for the safety of all Afghans.

Around the time when Kakar first joined the police force, another Afghan woman, called Bibi Ayesha, made the opposite decision. Her son was a mujahid who had been killed by the Soviet-backed army. Bibi Ayesha set off to avenge her son, and rumour has it that she killed her son's murderer with her own bare hands. That was the start of her career as the militia commander who later became known as Commander Kaftar. Her career has since stretched over almost three decades, and she fought against almost everyone: the Soviets, the Taliban and, more recently, the Karzai administration. In June 2008, she was captured and told a press conference: "I had to sell my cows to buy weapons."

The people in her native province, Baghlan, still fear her and want her kept in captivity. In July this year, an anonymous local told the Institute for War and Peace Reporting: "Kaftar has joined hands with the Taliban commander Mullah Khodaidad, who recently fled the Bagram prison." Together with another commander, the source said, the three of them were controlling the local drug routes.

In custody Kaftar denied all charges against her. There was, however, one charge she proudly admitted to: that when she fought the Taliban, she had 2,000 men under her command.

Neither Kakar nor Kaftar are feminists in the conventional, or even the unconventional, sense: what they represent is an alternative model of Afghan womanhood that is much older than the Taliban, the mujahedin or the communists. In that sense, we can rest assured that even though Malalai Kakar is dead, the female spirit she represented will live on.

Love Kills

Dear Rabia,

I am writing to you across centuries—from the land of the living to the realm of the dead. The year is 2012 and you were murdered

exactly a thousand and sixty-nine years ago. You have the dubious privilege of being our first recorded case of honor killing.
Let me tell you, Rabia, that I don't care for your poetry. I
know that you are the first female Afghan poet. I know that you
are famous, a saint and a celebrity. I know that men and women
worship at your grave and that you were there when our language, Persian, was born. But everybody is a poet in this land of
love, lies and blood. Everyone writes poems, even the warlords.
Our girls write poetry, too—sometimes in their prison cells,
other times behind the mud-brick walls of their village homes.
There is even a radio station for women's poetry and our girls
sneak out of the kitchen to call the station on their cellphone
and read their poems. They use poetry to tell the truth and to
veil it at the same time. I believe that our language was shaped
in response to dread. It is full of ambiguity, perfect for a people
who dare not speak the truth. Everybody escapes into poetry,
saying everything and nothing. It is a questionable kind of bravery. Let me tell you, Rabia, among Afghans, poetry is the language of cowards.

I am not interested in your poetic legacy, the seven ghazal
poems and the scattered verses you left behind—not even the
ones that you wrote with your own blood. I am Afghan, a
woman from the land of self-immolation where the soil is
soaked with the blood of accidental martyrs. I am interested in
your brother Haris, the king who was your murderer. He
planned your death carefully, and he loved you. You were, after
all, his only sister. Let me tell you that the year is 2012 and
Afghan brothers still kill their sisters. We have remained loving
and passionate, cruel and murderous at the same time. We love,
honor and cherish our girls and we stab them with knife
wounds, burn and drown them. Let me tell you, Rabia, that we
haven't changed. The love-hate carnage still goes on.

I am interested in Baktash, your lover. Legend has it that it
was you who saved his life. There was a war (there still is a war)

and you came to his rescue. You were a rider in an armor suit, your face covered. The story is, Rabia, that your cries frightened the men, and the battle came to a standstill. As you grabbed Baktash and took him away from the battleground, the soldiers took you for an angel. I smile at the way Afghans write about you. She was a high-flying dove; a maiden with ruby lips and pearly teeth. Worse of all—she was a girl whose bird of a heart was imprisoned in the cage of love. Let me tell you, Rabia, that we are still full of platitudes.

And Baktash, was he worth it? I know how you "met" him. There was a party in the court and being a girl, you were not allowed to take part. You came to the rooftop, lured by music, laughter, and perhaps, by the deep voices of men. You saw Baktash, watching him from the rooftop as he poured wine, played music and sang. He was tall and handsome and you fell in love—what a cliché! You got yourself a problem there, Rabia. Baktash was your brother's slave and a court entertainer. A princess in love with a slave? Only over your brother's dead body. Or yours.

Let me tell you, Rabia, that we are still like that. I saw a photograph of a boy and a girl shared and re-shared endlessly on Facebook. The caption said, "This boy and girl were friends." Their bodies hang listlessly from trees, like ripe, forgotten fruits. One of the comments left underneath the picture said, "This is how it should be!" Many other men agreed with this ruling and the girls remained silent. If you were alive today or a century later, chances are, Rabia, that you would still be killed. Afghanistan is still no country for lovers.

Legend has it that when you saw Baktash, love hit you like a "hurricane," making you sick and turning you into a fine poet in the process. You were a girl with a secret and the secret was killing you. The story is, Rabia, that poetry poured out of you as if a dam had been broken open. You didn't eat; you didn't sleep; you didn't drink. You nearly died, silly girl. It was your nanny who saved you. She coaxed you into revealing your secret. She let you get it off your chest; she saved you but she also killed you. Your secret was out. Let me tell you Rabia, that life is still like that for us. We are doomed if we don't tell and killed if we do.

You listened to your nanny and wrote a love letter to Baktash. I smile when I think about the way you drew an image of yourself in the letter. Legend has it that you were beautiful—eyes bewitching, teeth like pearls, mouth like ruby, blah, blah, blah. I don't care for your beauty, Rabia, and maybe you were not even pretty. Maybe our poets beautified you because who, after all, likes a story about an ugly girl in love, or a princess who is plain?

Our men of pen, even those who lived closer to your time, twisted your love and turned you into a spiritual seeker, a Sufi. They declare that in truth, the love you felt was for God, not for a handsome creature made of flesh and blood. There is even a story that when Baktash recognized you in a crowd, he came to you eagerly but you were cold. The story is that you confused him, you told him that your feelings were not of lust but of love; how dare he get close to you. You told him that he should be content with being your source of inspiration, the passive recipient of your bombardment of love letters. You see, Rabia, since your death, a campaign has been underway to protect your reputation even from beyond your grave. You had talent, and as the first recorded Afghan poetess, you're a figure of historical importance. But how can such gravitas be reconciled with a young, infatuated girl whose own brother killed her to save his reputation? And so your story was edited to "purify" you, turning you into a "respectable" saintly woman. Let me tell you, Rabia, that we still don't respect the dead. On the contrary, it is only when the people are dead that we start properly telling lies about them.

The story goes that one day you bumped into Rudaki, the court poet par-excellence of the time. The two of you conversed in poetry, with ex-tempore verses to show off your command of rhyme and syllabus, metaphor and innuendo. He was impressed with you, so much so that he memorized your poems. Or perhaps he had a fine ear and memory because he was blind. Did you get carried away in the heat of the moment, Rabia, and reveal too much? If love was on your face, he could not possibly have seen it. But he was sharp. He had memorized the entire Quran by the time he was eight and he learned his craft with... blah, blah, blah.

I don't care for Rudaki's poems, even though others worship him. I am interested in his part in your death. Legend has it that it was during the post-battle party (the same battle during which you saved Baktash) that Rudaki outed your secret. Was he too drunk to curb his tongue or was he jealous of your gift for words? Perhaps both. Either way, his tongue was loose that night and he launched into reciting your poems. The crowd of poets and warriors was intoxicated and asked Rudaki to come clean. "Tell us, whose are these fine verses?" It was then that your fate was decided, in your absence, without your knowledge. That's what they do to us, Rabia, they still plot our murder while we are asleep.

The story is, Rabia, that Rudaki blurted out (or maybe he carefully chose his words), "These fine verses belong to Rabia, King Ka'ab's daughter. And let me tell you, they are fine poems only because the girl is in love. With Baktash, the slave, of all people!" This is how it happened, Rabia, at night, during a drunken party in the town of Bukhara, far away from your hometown. Rudaki not only betrayed you, he also belittled your talent and put your life in danger. He was a co-culprit in your murder. Let me tell you, Rabia, that we still can't be trusted with secrets.

Your brother was there when Rudaki made you famous and infamous. He left the party, keeping a straight face. Inside, he was enraged; you had "dishonored" him. Rabia, if only you knew how your story is told today—in textbooks, web-blogs, and old

92

women's tales. The tone is matter-of-fact. There is no outrage, no sense of wrongdoing, only the usual submission to the self-generated carnage that is sold to us as destiny, as the tragedy of life.

This is how the end of your story is told. Your brother ordered that you should be taken to a bathroom and that both your wrists should be cut. He ruled that you should be left alone in the bathroom, and that the bathroom door should be blocked from the outside with heavy stones. Blood streamed through the cuts of your wrists, and they heard your cries, Rabia, but no-one came to your rescue. Your body was picked up the following day. You were drenched in blood and so were the walls of the bathroom where you had written poetry, dipping your fingers in pools of your own blood.

Let me tell you, Rabia, that in death you became harmless. They call you "the mother of Persian poetry" now, even though you died a young, infatuated maiden. We are still liars, Rabia, and the love-hate carnage and the poetry goes on.

Rest in peace, Rabia. I just wanted to tell you that love still kills in Afghanistan.

The Lingua Franca Controversy

Afghans have a rich body of expressions based on *zabaan*, a word that can mean language, tongue, or manner of speaking. The triple meaning of *zabaan* opens the door to all sorts of puns and figures of speech. "The tongue interprets what the heart says" is one example; "the tongue is flexible so you can twist it this or that way" is another. Then there's a subset of expressions that carry a warning. For example, "your red tongue can cost your green head." In other words, watch your tongue or you'll be dead. Surely a fear of the past now that freedom of speech has been enshrined in Afghanistan's new constitution? Well, it's complicated.

Judging by reports in the Afghan media, the problem in the noughties is not so much the words you say in public, but in which language you say them. If you opt for Iranian Persian, for example, chances are you'll be in trouble. But why would an Afghan want to speak Farsi, the Iranian form of Persian, rather than Dari, the Afghan form? The answer is simple. Some Afghans argue that Afghan Persian and Iranian Persian are one and the same language. Hence, they take the liberty of uttering words such as *daneshgah*, an Iranian word for university, to refer to, for example, Kabul University. Hang on, their opponents cry out, *daneshgah* is not just a harmless Iranian Persian word that you can throw into the conversation. It carries political baggage because it's official terminology for an Iranian institution. You're prejudiced, say the pro-*daneshgah* camp, pointing out that when they say *daneshgah*, they're not being pro-Iranian; they're just making use of their right to speak in their mother tongue. And so the argument goes back and forth, sometimes ending in violence. That's what happened when a group of Afghan students in Balkh and Kabul universities played a prank, placing a *daneshgah* sign right next to the official Pashto entrance sign of their respective universities. Needless to say, the prank led to clashes between Persian and Pashto-speaking students. Later, the police were called in, and of course they added their bit of violence. As a result, over 200 students ended up injured, two of them seriously. A similar story unfolded at Kabul University, but fortunately there were fewer injuries.

So what's happening? Having spent the last three decades fighting its ideological and religious wars, is Afghanistan now on the brink of a cultural war between Persian and Pashto speakers? Again, it's complicated.

The key figure in this simmering linguistic conflict is Abdul Karim Khorram, the culture and information minister. With his finely tuned ear, the minister is quick in detecting culturally delinquent words like *daneshgah* and handing out punishment to their users. Since 2006, Khorram's obsessive control of public language has often raised eyebrows. The minister presents himself as a patriot whose sole concern is the protection of Afghan cultural identity from foreign influence.

But a close look at Khorram's decisions reveals a more complex picture. His critics have noted that his definition of foreign contains a double standard. For example, he doesn't mind hearing or seeing English words in public spaces. On the contrary, he actively encourages the use of English words—and here's the rub—as long as they serve to replace Persian and not Pashto words. According to Khorram, what is foreign and threatening to Afghan culture is not so much western linguistic influence but the influence of Iranian Persian. So when he recently ordered a new entrance sign for his ministry, the word for culture that appeared on it was the English word "culture" written in Pashto script. One critic was so infuriated by this snub that he published an article meticulously listing all the uses of *farhang*, the local word for culture, in canonical Persian and Pashto literary works. If the seventeenth-century poet Khoshhal Khan Khattack, the Pashto point of literary reference bar none, had no problem with *farhang*, what exactly was Khorram's problem? Khorram, of course, didn't give a clear answer, which added to his critics' incomprehension.

My suspicion is the minister is fighting a very Afghan paradox. That is, even though the Pashtuns have always been political leaders, their language never managed to assume a corresponding level of cultural dominance. In 1924, when Norwegian linguist Georg Morgenstierne made a research trip to the country, he reported that the Afghan king, Amanullah Khan, was trying to introduce Pashto as an official language but the efforts met with little enthusiasm. The lack of enthusiasm was not ideological but had to do with practicalities of everyday life. According to Morgenstierne's Report on a Linguistic Mission to Afghanistan, "The fact is that, while most Pashais, Kafirs, Turks, and probably very many Afghans, know a little Persian, comparatively few Parsivans know Pashto. If they speak it at all, it is often of an execrable kind." In a rather clumsy way, Khorram is following King Amanullah's path in trying to turn Pashto into an Afghan lingua franca, as well as a language of education and officialdom.

So much for the minister; what about the students? I sifted through local reports but most of them stuck to the facts and refrained from comment. A few quoted politicians as voicing concern that "foreign countries" and "political parties" were using linguistic divisions as a political tool to destabilize Afghanistan. Otherwise, the media were understandably silent. After all, in the absence of a strong government, Afghans have always had to reach out to each other beyond ethno-linguistic divisions in order to survive.

As a British anthropologist pointed out to me, such is the complexity of personal and professional ties in Afghanistan that most people have "a friend among the enemy," even if the enemy in question is the Taliban. The complexity of daily life makes it impossible for most people to take sides in the debate on the proper national language. Nonetheless, the debate is real enough—at least among students, journalists and politicians. In the bazaars, Afghans still mix their words like before: the tongue, as they say, is flexible.

Girls Will Be Boys

It may seem strange, if not downright unbelievable, that in a society obsessed with maintaining strict gender roles, one form of transvestism has become widespread and even acceptable. We are talking here about little girls sporting closely cropped hair, dressed in boys' clothing and carrying male names—the phenomenon known in Afghanistan as *bacha posh* ("dressed like a boy"). Discussing it with my Afghan friends, I discovered that many knew at least one *bacha posh*, if not several.

"Remember that famous theatre actress?" one friend recalled. "She lived on our street. During the Taliban rule, she dressed four of her daughters as boys."

PART TWO

"I knew a girl in Herat," another told me. "She used to do occasional labor work and sometimes beg on the streets."

There is also a celebrity *bacha posh*: Bibi Hakmina, a politician who was previously with the mujahideen. Proud of having spent all her life as a man, she never leaves home without a Kalashnikov. She never felt like a woman either, she told the BBC in a documentary film, explaining what it felt like to live one's life as a man in a society where gender roles are so strict that being a man or a woman often feels like coming from different planets.

Bacha posh is one way of adapting to a rigid social environment where having a son is a must for any family desiring prestige and security. Families that can't produce a son sometimes resort to this deception, dressing up one of their girls as a boy and presenting her as a male offspring to society. In this bizarre form of keeping up with the Joneses, everybody, from the *bacha posh*'s extended family to her schoolmates and teachers, become part of the deception game. They all pretend that the girl is a boy, even after discovering the child's real gender.

The pretense stops at puberty, when the *bacha posh* is overnight forced to become a girl again. The world of boundless male freedoms is thus replaced with the invisible chains that mark an Afghan woman's life. The hardest part of this sudden boy-to-girl transformation is the behavioral change it requires. Having learned to face the world with an Afghan boy's direct gaze, she is suddenly required to be coy, averting her eyes in a show of feminine modesty. On television, it's easy to spot a former *bacha posh* from her erect posture, her direct eye contact, and the way she speaks up with the confidence of a man.

Women who were once *bacha posh* talk about the psychological impact of their imposed gender change with mixed feelings. They feel anger over lost freedoms, bitterness over never having had a carefree childhood but they also appreciate that they are possessors of a unique experience: they have seen the world through both male and female eyes.

To have known and lost freedom still remains a most bitter pill to swallow, but such is the uncompromising nature of Afghan society. There is little room for individual suffering because what matters is what people think of a family, and if a *bacha posh* can help her family gain respect by pretending to be a boy, then so be it.

A generous take on this would be to look at the *bacha posh* as gender bridge-builders with unique insight into the normally separate worlds of male and female. Some of them have gone on to shine in political careers where negotiation skills are crucial. The head of the Balkh Women's Affairs Department, Fariba Majid, the previously mentioned MP, Bibi Hakmina, and Azita Rafat, one of the first female Afghan MPs, belong to this category.

But while Bibi Hakmina broke the rules by never becoming a woman again, Rafat not only returned to her original gender but also became a wife and mother to four girls. Living the life of an MP, she found herself subjected to malicious jibes for not having a son. In reaction, she then repeated her own life-story, turning one of her daughters into a *bacha posh*, complete with a boy's name, short hair, and looking like a perfect mini-man in a shirt and suit.

If prestige is one reason for this radical but common deception, poverty and safety also make families opt to join the *bacha posh* game. Many poor families without sons find themselves caught between the devil and the deep blue sea. On the one hand, allowing their girls to work as street vendors amounts to losing their moral integrity. On the other hand, the family needs money, and has no choice but to let its daughters work. Unsurprisingly, the child street vendors one encounters in Afghan cities are often such girls pretending to be boys.

More recently, Afghan human and women rights groups have begun to criticize the *bacha posh* practice as not only a manifestation of misogyny but also a violation of the girls' rights to be themselves. But to deal with this problem is far from easy. Like much else in Afghanistan, even though *bacha posh* exist in everyday reality, they do not exist officially. Ghost-like but real, the unfortunate fake boys are another symbol of a creative and resilient society that is often in denial of its own role in creating its own social ills.

Ethnic Conspiracy

They parted ways but not without a smile, and a friendly squeeze of the arm. The atmosphere was relaxed. "Give me a Kalashnikov," said the Talib. And without complaining, the policeman took the gun from his shoulder and handed it to the Talib.

The rest of the video broadcast on YouTube in 2009 showed a larger group of policemen and Taliban chatting and milling around together amid what seems to have been a larger handing over of weapons. This surreally sociable encounter between supposed enemy parties took place in Baghlan province in northern Afghanistan. A Taliban fighter filmed it and sent it to the BBC. His message: even the police force has sided with the Taliban.

The Afghan interior ministry was quick to dismiss the video as Taliban propaganda, implying the film was a forgery. An article in Sorush-e Mellat was worded along similar lines, speculating that the Taliban had staged the meeting to make the public lose trust in the Afghan government. If this is true, the Taliban are fighting a pointless battle because the public has already lost trust in Kabul. The fraud-ridden 2009 presidential election did the Taliban's job for them in undermining the credibility of the central government.

Be that as it may, the video's reception on the part of the government, the public and the media was revealing. What is particularly interesting is that what might seem to a non-Afghan audience the most obvious interpretation of the event—as a run-of-the-mill act of police corruption—is the one that has been least accepted by Afghan commentators.

Instead, in line with the Afghan penchant for seeing political motivations and machinations everywhere, most commentators saw the encounter as suggesting a political strategy rather than financial transaction. Thus, for some, the meeting represented an example of Pashtun ethnic solidarity overriding loyalty to the nation as a whole. This is because the conversation between the police and Taliban in the video was conducted in Pashto, in a relaxed and friendly manner.

Critics have often accused President Karzai of deliberately allowing emotional attachment to ethnic affiliation to compromise the country's security and institution-building. Karzai's refusal to pursue a consistent aggressive policy with regard to the Taliban has been interpreted in this light. Critics argue that the chain of ethnic loyalty begins at ministries in Kabul, infiltrating the police force and reaching the Taliban, as evidenced in the film.

The theory is neat, but there's a serious flaw. Pashtun civilians have died in their thousands in Nato airstrikes, and Kabul has done little to protect them. Karzai may offer peace to the Taliban but the people in the south and east are dying nonetheless. Ethnic solidarity is not protecting them.

Amid accusations and counter-accusations between the government and its critics, it remains unclear exactly what motivated the policemen in the video to simply hand over their weapons to the Taliban without putting up a fight or even showing anger. But there could be many reasons, some of which may have more to do with local rather than national politics.

There is the possibility that the pockets of Pashtun settlement in the north are feeling under threat after the presidential elections brought to the fore Abdullah Abdullah, a Tajik leader in close competition with Karzai. The possibility of a non-Pashtun power takeover could be a terrifying prospect for the Pashtun populations there.

After all, there are allegations that forces loyal to the Afghan-Uzbek leader General Rashid Dostum killed 2,000 Taliban prisoners of war in 2001. The Obama administration ordered a review of that incident, which allegedly took place soon after the collapse of the Taliban regime. But Dostum's followers raised objections, correctly saying that singling out Dostum while offering negotiations to the Taliban leader, Mullah Omar, smacks of injustice and hypocrisy. The ordering of the review did little for inter-ethnic trust in Afghanistan. It is, after all, Dostum's troops who are fighting the Taliban in the north.

Anecdotal evidence is also widespread that families are hedging their bets between Kabul and the Taliban by sending one cousin to fight for the Taliban and another to serve the police force. This kith-and-kin interpretation of the meeting seen in the video may have an element of truth to it. After all, keeping one's options open with both—the power in charge and the power that might be—is a known survival strategy dating back to the war in the 1980s. Those who deployed the strategy in the 1980s turned out to be wise. Solid ideological loyalty is a luxury that few can afford in Afghanistan, especially since the international community started offering negotiations with the Taliban.

Ultimately, the commentary that surrounded the video was more revealing than the footage itself. It was always clear that the Taliban were getting their weapons from somewhere, and in an economy so reliant on notionally corrupt transactions as that of Afghanistan, it would be surprising if some policemen were not selling their weapons to Taliban "enemies" with whom they may well have grown up. What the video and the discussions around it revealed was the paranoia of ethnic conspiracy that embroils Afghanistan. And no amount of cracking down on police corruption is likely to put a stop to that.

The Machinery of Corruption

When the Taliban arrived in a village in Farah in May 2009, the village elders approached them and asked them to leave. They told the Taliban that if the fighters stayed, NATO planes would bomb their village. The Taliban said: "We are fighting and dying for Islam and so should you. Why should you be spared death? Is your blood redder than ours?"

The planes came, dropped bombs and, according to the villagers, killed more than 100 civilians. "What could we do?" said a local man to the BBC's Afghan service. "The Talibs were young men with guns and grenades. We had no weapons to protect ourselves and no young men to help us."

But the western intervention in Afghanistan has long ceased to be about improving the lives of civilians. It has become a separate entity with its own economy, creating lucrative jobs for those who know how to exploit the situation. Not all Afghans have come out of this war poor and destitute; not all foreigners are dying there. Formerly unemployed expatriate Afghans from the west have returned to the country, setting up NGOs and flying around their relatives—who have become their employees—in helicopters with foreign aid money. After all, 80 per cent of foreign aid is channeled through NGOs. Reckless Afghans with expertise for violence have been recruited to provide security for foreign special forces.

A cabal of discredited Afghan warlords accused of war crimes and ousted by the Taliban allied themselves with the foreign troops against the Taliban, and were co-opted into the system, becoming ministers, MPs and governors. To Afghans they remained just that—warlords—albeit warlords with new "democratic" titles and western friends. The 2001 intervention was a knee-jerk reaction to 9/11 done on the cheap. As local wisdom has it, there are three types of people in Afghanistan today: *al-Qaida* (the fighters), *al-faida* (the enriched) and *al-gaida* (the fucked). Most Afghans belong to the third category.

From the perspective of Afghans on the ground, the West is part of this machinery of corruption which thrives on the continuation of the current situation. If the Afghan leadership is corrupt and incompetent, so is the western leadership involved in Afghanistan. If Afghan warlords ignore international standards of warfare and engage in torture, so does the US in Bagram and Guantánamo. If the Taliban endanger civilian lives by suicide attacks, so do the foreign troops by carrying out reckless air strikes. The lines between the bad and the good, the problem and the problem-solvers, have become blurred. Moreover, the problem-solvers have themselves become part of the problem; they are costly but ineffective. Every little project, from digging a well to conducting research, involves hiring an entourage of armed security guards.

Far from disarming the many Afghan militia gangs, the current intervention has created a new set of armed men who are highly trained and well-equipped. Their daytime job is to protect foreign problem-solvers. But in their spare time, they run their own criminal businesses, robbing and intimidating locals.

The local population is capable of doing many of the projects for a fraction of the cost (and without a single bodyguard) but they are not being employed. The civilian and military problem-solvers are cut off from the population they are supposed to help. They talk to each other but not to Afghans, unless the Afghans in question are part of the English-speaking elite. In the words of an MEP I met recently, "We have good ideas; the only thing missing is the Afghans themselves."

From a local perspective, Afghanistan has become a laboratory where a disparate set of international military and civilian problem-solvers and their Afghan colleagues are trying out and dropping various ideas and making a comfortable living out of it. Not everyone is starving in Afghanistan. The *al-faida* are doing well.

It took Afghans many years to openly criticize western involvement in the country. The fear that criticism might dishearten the international well-wishers was a powerful incentive to remain silent, and those who spoke out, like presidential candidate Ramazan Bashardost, were punished for daring to antagonize westerners. So the conspiracy to whitewash problems carried on until the truth came home in coffins. The Afghan population shares the British people's anger and bewilderment at the situation. With every dead foreign soldier, the chances increase of the west abandoning Afghanistan. Afghans are aware of this but what can they do? After all, beggars can't be choosers.

"Corruption" Confusion: A Sin or a System?

In December 2009, the international community gave President Karzai six months to rid his administration of corruption or face the consequences. Washington was also pressing for the appointment of a "high representative" to keep watch over his government.

The news created excitement among Afghans waiting for the first heads to roll. There'd been much speculation about the identity of the potential victims and the possibilities were endless. After all, corruption is a murky term in Afghanistan.

The vernacular translation of the English term is *fesaad*, a word which refers to moral corruption, conjuring up images of strip clubs and gambling halls rather than the Ministry of Islamic Endowment, one of the first government offices accused of corruption. The ministry's director responded to the accusation with indignation, and threatened to unleash 162 angry imams against Tolo TV for broadcasting the allegation of corruption against the ministry.

The privately owned station had broadcast the news, quoting an article published in the *Guardian*. This episode is illustrative of a much broader problem which has to do with imported terminology and its failure to make sense in the context of Afghan reality. Like gender equality, democracy and agency, no one knows exactly what is the meaning of the word corruption.

There's a form of corruption, *reshvat* or bribery, with which all Afghans are familiar. It involves petty officials who compensate for their meager wages by requesting extra cash in return for perfectly legitimate services. The amount of cash is in proportion to the services required and nowadays involves hard currency such as dollars. Depending on the nature of the service, the bribe can be offered as a "present," with intermediaries receiving a commission for establishing contact and ensuring a smooth transfer. But the international community is not concerned with this type of petty bribery.

One can safely assume that when Hillary Clinton was discussing corruption with President Karzai, she was using the term as understood in developed countries. In this usage corruption is a deviation from the existing legal standards, and hence a crime. But using this term in the context of Afghanistan is at best confusing, at worst meaningless. After all, what is the meaning of legality in the context of a country where entire districts are not under government control and where the president himself has been accused of conducting a fraudulent election?

The term corruption is also often used to decry personal enrichment as a result of contractual business deals. International and Afghan critics of capitalism tend to point at the class of newly rich business families who all have a family member in the government. The bitterness felt towards such families is understandable, given the sheer poverty of the majority of Afghans, but the automatic equation of wealth accumulation with corruption doesn't bear scrutiny.

Besides, accusations of corruption could easily be thrown back at the international community itself. After all, it has awarded no-bid, open-ended contracts to global corporations whose reconstruction projects have often turned out to be both defective and unnecessarily expensive. And so the blame game goes on endlessly, resulting in rumours, speculation, and even more corruption. This is because evidence of corruption has now become a commodity, tempting prosecutors to provide evidence in return for money.

Because Afghan bureaucracy has not yet been fully computer-ized, documents are often handwritten and forgeries can easily be produced and sold as evidence. Those willing to pay for "evidence" are not only local actors but international media organizations. And so the international hunt for Afghan corruption is threatening to increase "corruption," instead of paving the way for more transparency.

The reason for this apparent chaos is simple. The term "corruption," as understood in developed countries, does not make sense when applied to Afghanistan, a country where hyper-corruption is simply an economic system with everybody, from the simple office guard to Taliban insurgents or senior officials, trying to have a share of the hard currency available. Hence, the more money is poured into the country, the more corruption is to be expected. This is not to say that it is justifiable—after all, such parasitical economic systems are ultimately self-destructive. But the fact remains that this is simply a way of making a living in Afghanistan. Everybody and nobody is corrupt in Afghanistan.

Judging again this complex reality, the current international obsession with Afghan corruption is nothing but a political game. A focus on corruption has served to set the Obama administration apart from the Bush government, which is now being denounced for leniency towards Karzai and his family. For Afghan and international critics of capitalism, corruption is equaled with the multimillion reconstruction contracts that have resulted in defective roads and clinics. But ultimately such examples are not about corruption per se, but are a means of under-lining one's case against the free market economy. For political players on the ground, corruption has become a welcome means of undermining one's rivals, only this time with the chance of shaming them internationally through global media.

Meanwhile, those with access to evidence of corruption would probably be tempted to offer it for sale and so undermine its validity of the evidence. As for the rest of the country, it's much ado about nothing.

PART TWO

Progress and Pessimism

"What have the Romans ever done for us?" shouts an indignant Reg in the Monty Python film *Life of Brian*. Reg's comrades then come up with an impressive list of development projects— all of which fall flat on Reg. "All right, but apart from the sanitation, the medicine, education, wine, public order, irrigation, roads, a freshwater system, and public health, what have the Romans ever done for us?"

Thirty years after the film's release, this conversation neatly sums up the mood in Afghanistan. There is much development and progress, freedom and prosperity but the Regs of this world, from Malalai Joya to a whole host of diasporic armchair patriots, refuse to admit that since 2001 Afghanistan has indeed improved a great deal.

During my visit in summer 2011 we had an indignant Reg as our driver. We were driving from Kabul to Panjshir along a fine highway that apart from bits near Bagram was perfectly smooth and most of the time empty.

It was then, in that peaceful moment, that our driver suddenly blurted out: "The situation is bad, very bad!"

He was being paid in dollars and had us—a bunch of friendly and respectful passengers—in his solid Land Cruiser. When my family lived in Kabul in the 1980s, a driver would have given his right arm to be paid in dollars. But today, Afghan drivers take hard currency for granted.

During the drive, Reg's mobile phone kept ringing. His boss, and many friends and family members, wanted to chat with him. In the 1980s, only a handful of families owned a landline and mobile phones were only seen in Bollywood movies. The people I met this summer in Kabul and elsewhere all owned mobile phones, sometimes two or three.

I had no idea exactly why our driver thought the situation was very bad. The villages and small towns where we stopped for breaks were doing fine. The shops and stalls were bursting with goods, from foodstuffs to drinks to mobile top-up cards to soaps, shampoo bottles and DVDs.

The sheer number of cars owned by villagers and small-town people along the way meant that we struggled to find parking space. In every village there was at least one brand new multi-storey home, either already built or in the process of being built. The economic boom was clearly not limited to Kabul and had trickled through to rural outskirts all the way to Panjshir.

When we stopped in the village of Istalif, famous for its divine yoghurt and unique pottery, families were having picnics under lush green trees. The sound of a comedy show was bursting through loudspeakers as I watched Istalifis double up with laughter every time the comedian cracked a joke about the president. Only a decade earlier, making fun of the Afghan leader would have cost the comedian and his audience their heads.

But Afghans seemed to take their political freedom for granted. If in Iran opposition to the regime leads to jail, in Afghanistan men and women are free to grab a microphone and shout with full force to all and sundry that they want their president to resign. But they still insist that "the situation is bad," even though only fifteen years earlier they wouldn't have been able to walk in Kabul without the risk of being hit by a stray rocket.

Aside from resurfaced roads and highways, refurbished schools and new health clinics, to name just a few, one of the most overlooked aspects of progress in Afghanistan is the wide reach of social mobility. Among the new business class there are numerous examples of individuals who had fled the country on the back of mules, surviving with their families in Pakistani exile' on US$20 a month.

Today, many of these former refugees are proud owners of successful businesses, looking back at careers that began with simple jobs paid for with hard currency, working as translators for NGOs, being fixers for foreign reporters or simply serving as security guards for the international community's offices.

PART TWO

In the last decades, it has been possible for Afghans to become middle class in one generation. The new middle class stands out for its ethnic and religious diversity and includes women. For a country where for most of its history one had to be born wealthy to be well off, this represents tangible progress.

On the way back from Panjshir we found ourselves stranded in traffic jams because there were too many cars on the road. Inside the cars around us were families and sometimes groups of young men dressed in tight T-shirts and sporting stylish haircuts. Only a decade earlier, the T-shirts and haircuts would have led to public punishment and there would have been no women in the Land Cruiser behind us. Entering Kabul would have amounted to visiting a ghost town covered in darkness.

"So why do think the situation is very bad?" we asked the indignant Reg. After all, the terrorist attacks and violent crimes did not cancel out the real progress that was visible all around us. He paused and thought, but had nothing to say.

Afghan Manners and Fatalistic Security

It was the first group of security guards at the Intercontinental hotel in Kabul who gave us tips about how to sneak in. "Don't tell them that you just want to hang out in the hotel. Tell them you are here for a meeting." My friend and I thanked them happily. We had fond childhood memories of the hotel—the scene of a suicide attack earlier this week—and just wanted to enjoy seeing our old haunts.

The little wooden cabin where female visitors underwent body searches was even more relaxed. A TV was running in the corner and the women dressed in traditional clothing took only a cursory look into our bags. There was no proper search. The women who do body searches in "secure" places in Kabul are often too polite or too embarrassed to conduct a proper search. Looking into my bag, one of them said: "Don't worry sister, I

AFGHAN RUMOUR BAZAAR

know you only have women's stuff in your bag." Frequently, I found myself asking female security staff to search me properly, to look carefully into my bag, but often they refused out of embarrassment.

Whether young or old, male or female, rich or poor, Afghans can be exceedingly polite people and it is this culture of politeness that makes conducting a proper search a rather awkward endeavor. A friendly visitor who speaks the language and greets security guards in a friendly and respectful manner unwittingly culturally disarms the guards, rendering them incapable of conducting their search duty vigorously.

This is one reason why security is lax in Kabul and why attacks such as the one in June 2011 at Hotel Intercontinental can easily take place despite security guards and barricades. That is why the attack did not come as a surprise to many of the hotel's visitors.

A friend told me about her experience of visiting the Intercontinental days before the attack. "My driver told me that the security guard had simply asked him whether he had weapons on him and he told the guard that he had none. He was then allowed to drive up and park the car in the upper section of the parking lot."

From the upper parking lot, the driver had an excellent view of the pool area and the ground level. Had he been a terrorist, he would have had a field day.

Afghans are perhaps just too polite to be good security guards. Social interaction is informal and people can be easily persuaded to compromise and not fulfill their security duty as vigorously as they should. Taxi drivers in Kabul are fully aware of the lax security because it makes their job dangerous. According to Mohammad, a driver, "When police stop your taxi, they only look into the glove compartment. They don't look anywhere else and they only look in the glove compartment because they hope to find and confiscate dope there." Mohammad calls Kabul

"Shahr-e Kharbouza" (melon market), a derogatory phrase that sums up not only the security chaos but also the city's nerve-racking traffic.

Kabul's drivers often have little idea of the name or meaning of the city's historical landmarks. The map of the city stored in their brains is full of terrorist attack locations. "This is where the co-ordinated attacks against Serena and Golbahar Centre took place. Here is where I had to turn back because there was a suicide attack. This place is when I called my company to tell them not to send anyone to this address because there was an attack." The drivers tell their tales of terror in a low and monotonous voice; they have resigned themselves to living in a city that can turn dangerous at any time.

The continuation of security threats has two more equally significant sources. First, there's the widespread belief that terrorism has nothing to do with Afghans but is something that outsiders do to Afghans. Regarding another attack on a hospital that resulted in the killing of numerous patients, a young, trendy Afghan told me: "There's no way the Taliban carried out the attack. Our Taliban would never do such a thing. It was al-Qaida with the help of the US."

The denial that terrorism in Afghanistan is also a local problem that needs a local solution is widespread among all classes of people and might be a reflection of a desperate psychological need to believe in Afghanistan as a good and safe homeland which owes all its problems to foreign interference.

Certainly, to accept that one's compatriots can be a people of such brutal cruelty as to not even spare hospitals is tough and this, in turn, makes denial as a psychological coping mechanism understandable. But the downside of denial is that attacks keep happening again and again.

The third factor that allows terrorism to go on is fatalism. When discussing ways to reduce the threat of terrorism, one often encounters a shrug followed by: "Well, if it's your destiny to die, you end up dying. It's not up to you." To people who are not culturally part of Afghanistan, this fatalistic mindset is disconcerting. But Afghans believe in destiny and that's why they interpret death in suicide attacks as something that is predetermined for the victims rather than a political act of intimidation. Such belief means that guesthouse and hotel managers neglect to double-check escape routes or make adequate security preparations. "We have an escape door," a guesthouse manager told me, but when I tried to open the door, it was impossible to unlock it, let alone open it. In a less fatalistic society, the door would have been checked every day.

When I tried to explain to a friend that believing in fate was not a solution to security threats because those who planned attacks were not God but human beings who plotted them carefully and deliberately, he laughed, and said: "You know what's the only solution for this place? We should all be put into a spaceship and sent into space so that the international community can finally sort this place out in our absence." This jokingly delivered "solution" was a rare example of Afghan self-criticism. But even though it was delivered laughingly, the bitterness lurking behind the hilarity was hard to miss.

Who's to Blame? The Burden of Unresolved Grief

The small, passport-size picture showed a strikingly handsome young man. "He was killed by the Taliban the night before the first day of his new job at an NGO office," said the bereaved Afghan father who turned to me for comfort. The father had been helping me with my research in Kabul, quietly going through documents and putting them on the desk for me to read. His young son had led an active life, studying, working, socializing and going to the gym every day. "We hardly saw him, that's how busy he was. He would come home happy and hungry," his father said.

"How was he killed?" I asked the father.

"He was stabbed on our street at night," he replied. "I know his killers. They lived on our street and had connections with the Taliban. They fled to Paktia [a province on the eastern border of Afghanistan] the same night. They told the Taliban that he spoke English and was spying for foreigners. We went to courts in search of justice but it was to no avail. His killers had already fled to Pakistan and then India."

My only way to comfort this grieving father was to tell him about the recent death of my own father. "I know what you are going through," I told him as he put the picture of his son back into his wallet, staring out of the window into a solemn afternoon in Kabul.

There was a question about this brutal and untimely death of a young civilian Afghan that kept me preoccupied but I didn't dare to put it to the father. The question was: given that the Taliban focus on killing high-profile individuals for maximum publicity, what were the chances of their killing a young graduate from an ordinary, apolitical family that was neither rich nor powerful? Since the young man had not even started his first job, the only power that he could possibly have had would have been his strikingly handsome looks—he had a strong body and the face of a film star. My suspicion grew that the cause of his death was something personal: a love story in all probability involving the family whose sons ended up stabbing him. But I kept this suspicion to myself.

When I left the office, the father was watching the news on television. There had been yet another suicide bombing, killing dozens of people. "The Taliban are so brutal." He shook his head, probably thinking of his son. I suspected that it comforted him to think that his son's murder had something to do with Afghan politics rather than the Afghan honor system which allows for punishing love affairs deemed illicit with murder. I began to wonder just how many murders disguised as political assassination were in fact pure personal crimes caused by jealousy, business rivalry and sometimes just perceived slights to someone's honor. After all, blaming criminal murder on the Taliban served all parties involved.

The Taliban readily claimed any murder because the publicity increased fear of their power and brutality among the population. The perpetrators, in turn, distracted attention away from themselves by placing the blame on the Taliban. The families of the victims were also spared the uncomfortable realization that the victim might have crossed the perceived boundaries of decency or had personal enemies among his friends, colleagues and even family members. The denial allowed them to grieve for the lost son, brother and friend as a political martyr rather than the victim of a crime, especially since criminal cases hardly ever get solved in Afghanistan's corrupt and chaotic justice system.

Afghans are world masters in covering up the true causes of death, tending to fabricate stories to make dealing with bereavement easier for the victims' families. In reality, what the stories do is to create confusion and avoidance of the grieving process.

The consequence of this is unresolved grief, which can lead to depression, anger and rage and in turn trigger new acts of violence against others or self-harm. The suffering often lasts for generations, with children growing up confused as they hear conflicting stories about a family member's death without ever learning the true cause, or perhaps more importantly, finding justice.

In June 2011, yet another mass grave was discovered by Rustaq villagers in the northern Takhar province of Afghanistan. By the time the news reached the international press, speculation was already high as to the grave's date, the number of the bodies found and the possible perpetrators of the mass murder. Given the unimpressive record of the Afghan people and state in dealing with such violent deaths, the chances of ever finding out the truth about this new mass grave are exceedingly small and the villagers' unresolved grief is bound to carry on for yet another generation.

It is true that Afghans find comfort in the theological notion that we are all guests in this world and that our real, eternal life only begins after death. But the thousands of cases of drug addiction, female self-immolation, violent crime and mental illness speak of a very different reality that is grounded in the brutality of life here and now.

Schoolbooks: An Insult to Afghan Literature

The Afghan education ministry announced the issuing of forty million new school textbooks in November 2010. A ministry spokesman told the BBC that the new material—financed through international aid and costing about US$20m—responds to the needs of contemporary Afghan society.

The emphasis of the texts is on peace, he said, adding that the material represents harmony between modern and traditional knowledge. Such lofty pronouncements cry out for verification—which is why I did just that, perusing the Dari literature (the variation of Persian spoken in Afghanistan is called Dari) textbooks intended for secondary school students. What I found was a reflection of the literary tastes of a parochial village mullah, but not an accurate representation of Dari literature. Year Nine students, for example, are made to read a badly written text of polemical content, not only sanctioning intolerance towards non-Muslims but elevating it to patriotic duty. Exactly why such a poor text had been considered worthy of inclusion in a book of Afghan literature remains a mystery. A semiliterate militia commander fighting in the mountains might be forgiven for confusing this graceless, incendiary piece of propaganda with literature. But the board responsible for the books' content should have known better. Or so we hope.

Judging by the books' content, hagiographies of early Islamic figures are a key part of the board's definition of Dari-Persian literature. Let's assume that the board believes literature is a tool of moral improvement and hagiographies help students become better Muslims. Even so, how is a student supposed to respond to the following passage about Uthman, the third caliph? "It is clear that both through his mother and father he is closely related to the Prophet (Peace Be Upon Him)." It seems that being part of the prophet's family adds kudos, but how are students supposed to reconcile this hierarchical vision of Islam with an earlier statement that says Islam is an egalitarian religion? Even if we are generous and assume that students are taught to understand such contradictions elsewhere in the curriculum, what they learn is, strictly speaking, not hagiography as a style of literature. The biographies of early caliphs are there for pietistic reasons and, as such, they are not literature. There is no need for them to be included in Dari literature because religion is already extensively covered in three other school subjects exclusively dealing with Islam.

The board's perception of non-religious literature is also peculiar. There is an obsession with poems about spring. As students grow older, the poems grow longer but the content remains the same: spring and, occasionally, birds and flowers. If this is supposed be a literature of escapism, the repetitive nature of the themes makes escape into a fantasy world as difficult as an actual escape from Afghanistan.

Unsurprisingly, the textbooks have no clear structure, but some content stands out for its oddity. For instance, lost amid randomly put-together illustrations of classical poetry and hagiography we find a couple of texts about human rights and freedom of speech. This is where the board offers a little nod in recognition of those who have financed the whole project. But what are we to make of a text entitled: "Watt and the Invention of the Steam Engine"? How does this text fit with the righteous caliphs, poems about spring, and tales of wisdom involving Socrates? Needless to say, we don't know. But does the board know?

The only other type of prose offered to students is hekayat, traditional moral tales, the purpose of which is to illustrate proper conduct. It is here that we finally find mention of a female figure who is not a relative of Prophet Muhammad (PBUH). But unfortunately for female students, the woman in the tale represents the category of "how not to behave." The hero of this timeless tale is a sheikh, and we are supposed to admire him for his grace and generosity in ignoring the woman's ill manners. The tale ends with the standard literary platitude, "and so no harm was done and many were moved to tears."

I, too, was moved to tears. Do Afghan girls risk acid attacks and poisoning for this? Afghan literature is rich with female contributions. Why not include Golbadan Begum, born in Kabul in 1523 and author of one of the earliest court biographies? Why not publish Nadia Anjuman, whose fine poems are the voice a generation? And Homira Qaderi, whose short stories represent artfully crafted modern prose, and a frank reflection of the inner lives of women during the Taliban period?

To be fair to the board, their choice of representative literature does not only discriminate against girls. It also disregards boys. It represents men. Not any men, but grownup men of social standing. So there's consistency, a reassuring thought that disappears when the reader bumps into Schiller, Lamartine, and La Fontaine. Rather generously, the board has decided to include them in its definition of "authentic" Dari literature.

Representing a lofty world of moral superiority occupied almost entirely by the male establishment, there's absolutely nothing in the books to reflect young Afghans' experiences of war, exile and hardship. In their haughty disregard for reality, taste and lack of structure, the books are an accurate reflection of the ministry's intellectual poverty and cultural parochialism. But they are certainly not a fair representation of the diversity, wit and eloquence of Afghan literature.

The Self-Immolation of Afghan Women

When Vietnamese monk Thich Quang Duc set fire to himself at a busy intersection in Saigon in 1963, few of the Afghan women who later followed his example were even born. Most of them had probably never heard of the burning Buddhist monk, of the way pictures of his spectacular protest made the then US president, John F Kennedy, famously shriek "Jesus Christ!" or of the way, as some say, his self-immolation speeded up the downfall of the regime against which the monk was protesting.

His death triggered many questions and interpretations. In the words of one commentator at the time: "To set oneself on fire is to prove that what one is saying is of the utmost importance." Thinking of the Afghan women who set light to themselves, just what is this thing of utmost importance that they are trying to say? Since March 2008, there have been a hundred cases of self-immolation in southwestern Afghanistan alone; 100 women who got hold of fuel, soaked themselves in the liquid and lit the match to stage a small-scale domestic revolution of a spectacular nature. If they wanted to say something, they wanted to say it with vehemence. If they wanted to leave this world, they didn't want to leave quietly. But what is their motivation? And who or what is the subject of their protest?

Unlike the burning monk, who wrote down all his hopes, wishes and complaints prior to his death, little is known about what motivates the Afghan women. Few of them survive to tell the tale and those who do survive are unwilling to talk. Afghan documentary film maker Olga Sadat spent months at a hospital which specializes in treating burns. She waited patiently but persistently to win the trust of the women she interviewed for her film Yak, Do, Seh (One, Two, Three). The film is a documentary cautionary tale, the aim of which is to discourage self-immolation. In an interview with Germany's Deutsche Welle international radio, Sadat said, "Unfortunately, in the eight months that I was working on the film, only one of the many women who had set themselves on fire and were brought to the hospital managed to survive. But even that woman is in a bad state." The woman had set fire to herself in protest against maltreatment on the part of her husband. Sadat told Deutsche Welle that she believes that the women who set themselves on fire are confident that someone will come to their rescue while they are in the process of catching fire. Those she did manage to interview for her film said that when they lit the match, their aim was not suicide. They just wanted the people who maltreated them to take notice of the suffering they had caused.

Forced marriages and maltreatment by husbands and fathers is often cited as the cause of the despair that leads women to use household fuel to set fire to themselves. But a closer look reveals a more complex picture. Sometimes the protest is directed against other women, such as an unkind mother-in-law. Other times girls have set fire to themselves for the love of a man they could not marry. And then there's protest against institutions, like in the case of the woman in Laghman, northern Afghanistan, who came to the court hiding petrol under her burqa. She had petitioned for divorce and was awaiting the verdict when she set fire to herself.

Female drug addiction is an equally powerful trigger that has led to self-immolation in places like Ghore, in western Afghanistan. But the fact remains that the women themselves are usually silent on the meaning of their own suicide attempts. The meaning of their acts remains essentially ambiguous because they don't leave notes, maybe because many of them can't write.

In a statement, the Afghan women's affairs minister said, "As long as all individuals, but especially the families, fail to ensure women's social and human rights, it's impossible for the government or the related offices to have any notable success in reducing violence against women."

Other officials, like Sima Shir Mohammadi, the head of the women's affairs department in Herat, blame the war. They say violence stops government offices and aid agencies from reaching remote areas. That's why cases of self-immolation have fallen in the cities but increased in rural areas.

Earlier, in an interview with an Iranian feminist website, Shir Mohammadi said her department had worked hard to tackle the problem: "We had meetings with religious scholars and asked them to make use of religious texts, Qur'anic verses and the prophet's sayings in their Friday sermons and in radio and television speeches to tell the people in rural areas that suicide is not the solution." The clerics also tell worshippers that maltreatment of girls and women is not allowed in Islam. Both Shir Mohammadi and the women's affairs minister believe that the cooperation of religious scholars is essential in solving this problem. Afghan society is traditional and the people respect the clerics and follow their advice.

Time will tell whether the preachers' message will prove effective and discourage women from resorting to fuel and matches to get their message across. What's certain is that the traditional path of "patience and forbearance" has lost its appeal to Afghan women.

Child Rape: Speaking Out

"The moment I saw the blood-stained sandal, I knew that my child was dead," said Abdul Khalid. Khalid, from Takhar province in northern Afghanistan, was talking about the day in the autumn of 2008 when he discovered his eight-year-old daughter's body. The girl had been kidnapped, raped and then killed. It turned out later that she was only one of the many child rape victims in the northern provinces of Afghanistan. There were others, children like the twelve-year-old daughter of a man called Nurollah. Nurollah was from Sar-e Pul, also in the north. He said he knew the rapist, the son of an MP, and he wanted justice for his child. He went all the way to Kabul in search of justice but they told him at the police station: "No one is going to listen to your story. Go home."

In the past, this would have been the end of the story. Nurollah would have gone home and his story would have remained a private tale of injustice, a family secret disconnected from the wider Afghan society. Bad luck, basically. But we're talking about Afghanistan in 2008. A country with plenty of problems but a media that is both brave and vigilant. The media listens where the government is deaf. The media speaks out where officials say shush. So when Nurollah approached a private TV station, they listened to him. His story was aired, as were the stories of other victims and their families. Like the twelve-year-old gang rape victim whose family faced ridicule when they sought justice. The families—mothers, fathers and uncles—spoke out, showing their faces and allowing their names to appear on TV: "My name is Nurollah and I'm the father of a girl who has been raped."

I watched the clips again and again and was stunned. Here were Afghans who spoke about rape in their families. They spoke clearly, publicly and openly. I felt a deep admiration for them. It takes guts to go public about rape in any society, but to do so in Afghanistan requires courage of a special sort, of the sort that entitles people to bravery medals and cheering crowds.

The bravery of Afghans is limitless, but when it comes to honor or *naamoos*, the lions of the Hindukush turn into the trembling rabbits of South Asia. Few have the heart to stand up for the victims and their rights. In the words of one editorial: "In our society, it is not the perpetrator of the act of violation who carries the shame of dishonor. It is the victim, who's condemned to an eternally cursed life." The victims know this much. A young boy was raped by a commander but couldn't face going home with his honor "stained." Instead he stayed with the commander, becoming his "mistress." A girl's family killed her as soon as they discovered that she had lost her *naamos*. Fearing a similar fate, another rape victim fled to the local police station for protection from her own family.

As the week went by, more and more reports of this nature came to the surface. A group of people had been arrested in Kabul for filming children while they were being abused. It's unclear whether the film was for the market or private use. A family accused an Afghan human rights official of spreading "lies" that the family's toddler had been raped. The toddler's mother said: "The human rights woman keeps coming to our house and taking pictures of my daughter. My daughter has not been raped. She just injured herself when she was out playing." The mother said the official was using her daughter to get funding for her office. The official rejected the accusation, saying the woman had first reported rape and later changed her mind. The human rights group said they believed the mother had been pressured into changing her original complaint.

The media campaign to ensure justice for child rape victims has finally paid off. President Karzai was forced to take action. There were dismissals, arrests and religious scholars told the public that sexual abuse of children is a "grave sin." The president later met the family of a twelve-year-old girl who had been gang raped. He embraced her and told her that she was like his very own daughter. To me this is social progress and a sign that Afghans are beginning to use the peaceful pressure tools of civil society. They are learning to create change through civil courage and media pressure, a method that is much more desirable than coups, wars and revolutions.

While I was researching this article, I kept thinking of the nation's self-appointed moral guardians in the government and parliament. Usually they're quick to spot "un-Islamic" behavior and protest against it: Indian soap operas, blue jeans and lipstick. How is it that they miss this gravest of all sins?

We'll Grind This Axe For Donkey's Years

"What kind of people are we? We spot a bunch of quiet birds and right away plot, 'let's make them fight and see who wins.'

It's sick!" This was my friend's reaction to Kabul's bird fighting shows that take place every Friday. My friend is Afghan and he is a peacenik. They do exist, Afghan peaceniks, as do die-hard vegetarians who lose the culinary purity battle soon after returning to notoriously carnivorous Afghanistan (such is our predilection for meat that we use "grilled kebab" as a metaphor for suffering in empathy).

Needless to say, peaceful Afghans have a hard time in this country founded by dynastic clans of martial aristocracy. The martial values of the ruling clans (who, to be fair to them, did use to have empires in the past) trickled down to the masses, blurring the lines that separate a soldier from a civilian. As a result, audacity, fearlessness, and toughness make top of the list of acknowledged Afghan values. All Afghans, except for the very young and the very old, are expected to have combatant qualities—as if life itself is a type of war. This blurring of boundaries between civilian and combatant value systems has made differentiating between friend and enemy impossible in Afghanistan. It would be fair to say that, as a rule of the thumb, everybody is a frenemy and that every man and (and sometimes woman) is simultaneously a civilian and an irregular fighter.

Ironically for a desperately poor, aid-reliant country, national independence is equally high on top of the list of identity markers. To be Afghan means to fight for god and our motherland. God, needless to say, comes first and hence, if the motherland is destroyed in the process of fighting for God, so be it.

The result of the indoctrination into this particular model of Afghanness is ultimately that peace and forgiveness are as elusive to us as is a trip to the moon for a woman from Kandahar. We are stuck in an endless cycle of revenge and counter-revenge, like a machine programmed to self-destruct. We are masters of the art of cutting off our nose to spite our face. We don't need outside enemies because we are our own worst enemy.

This section is about war and since wars are fought because of myths, it is also about the myths of Afghanistan; about national narratives, emotional buttons and the money trail of the war.

Pashtuns Caught in Another Proxy War

The anniversary of Afghan victory over the Red Army in May 2009 should have been a day for Afghans to step back and commemorate the death of the war's two million victims; a time to take pride in the victory of a small country of mud-brick huts and outdoor toilets over a global nuclear power with an ambitious space program and an impressive record of military conquest. But Kabul decided to ditch pomp and ceremony for a low-key commemoration event at the presidential palace with key government and jihadi figures. The budget originally allocated to the ceremony was instead given to relief projects for earthquake victims in eastern Nangarhar province and flood victims in northern Badakhshan province. A fine gesture of unity and charity by a president intent on remaining in power despite his administration's numerous failures.

But according to some Afghan commentators, the gesture was simply a clever ploy to disguise Hamid Karzai's fear of a repeat of 2008 embarrassing incident, in which the Taliban infiltrated the victory celebration, firing shots and killing two people and wounding more. In other words, by staging a low-key event and spending the budget on relief projects, Kabul managed to kill two birds with one stone: avoiding the risk of a Taliban attack while appearing caring and charitable towards the destitute from the north to the east of the country. Be this as it may, the ditching of the celebration of such a significant anniversary showed that something had gone wrong in Afghanistan. One could go a step further and argue that the victory had never been completed, and that the war has continued, albeit in a different shape, with a new set of contenders. Afghanistan in 2009 was once again a scene of proxy wars, this time the strategic conflict between India and Pakistan and the ideological war of the US and its Shia and Sunni Islamist opponents, Tehran and al-Qaida. Caught in the middle were once again Afghan civilians, especially the people of the south and the east who happened to be Pashtuns, just like the Taliban.

Pashtun civilians are under attack from various directions. Internally, the leaders of indigenous minorities, who have been empowered in the years of war, feel resentful towards the Pashtuns because they belong to the sole ethnicity that has been running the country since the beginning of Afghanistan. These leaders feel cheated out of a chance to run the country even after helping Nato fight the Taliban in 2001, and accuse the Pashtuns of deliberately fuelling the violence, growing opium and depriving the country of a chance for peace. Needless to say, not all Pashtuns are Talibs and a distinction has to be made between civilians and fighters. Even those who do join the Taliban do so for reasons that are often directly linked to the present invasion's failures.

Some new recruits are driven by the desire to avenge family members killed in Nato air strikes. The air strikes regularly result in civilian casualties, but since Helmand, unlike New York, is neither well-known through Hollywood films nor well-liked via cultural and linguistic familiarity, their deaths fail to hit international headlines and their stories remain untold.

But empathy is scarce even within the country. Reading between the lines of editorials representing the views of indigenous minority leaders, one cannot help but sense a profound feeling of hatred and betrayal. These sentiments are directed at Pashtuns and Kabul's international allies alike; the latter for dismissing indigenous minorities soon after 2001 and for considering negotiations with the Taliban. Given these circumstances, tears are rarely shed for Pashtun civilians outside their own regions.

Other Taliban recruits are lured by the financial rewards offered by the Taliban which exceed those provided by Kabul.

Once again, the recruitment of new foot soldiers is directly linked to Kabul's failure to pay its army and police force decent wages delivered on time.

In addition to bearing the brunt of air strikes, Pashtun civilians find themselves in the unfortunate position of having to defend their reputation against accusations of fanaticism while helplessly watching the Taliban systematically destroy the foundations of their cultural identity. An example of this is the Taliban's bombing of the tomb of Rahman Baba, a renowned seventeenth-century Sufi and poet buried in Peshawar. This is in addition to the systematic killing of Pashtun tribal leaders, which has been going on for years. One could argue that at least a part of the Taliban is intent on destroying the traditional Pashtun way of life, complete with its tribal system of justice, its poetry, and its cultural memory. Leaders of indigenous minority groups do not tire to point out that key power positions in Afghanistan are occupied by Pashtuns, but having a Pashtun president or culture minister has little impact on the conditions of these forgotten civilians. If anything, their Pashtun president, Karzai and his Pashtun nemesis, Mullah Omar, clearly view civilians as fair game; Karzai by allowing Nato to carry out airstrikes and Mullah Omar by encouraging the Taliban to fight in Afghanistan, instead of Pakistan.

Against this backdrop of proxy wars and profound ethnic divisions, the decision against a pompous victory ceremony seemed appropriate regardless of Kabul's true intentions. This is because the country is still struggling against what is arguably the most damaging consequence of the Soviet war: the ethnicization of Afghan politics. Ethnicized politics breeds lazy politicians who have an interest in the continuation of ethnic hatred. Such politicians have no motivation to perform well or make themselves useful for the nation as a whole. This is because support comes to them automatically because of the ethnic group to which they belong. Hence, 27 April 1992 was not a day of victory. It was simply a new page in Afghanistan's struggle to come to terms with its own difficult history and complex identity. The victory is yet to come, but to get there, Afghanistan first needs to overcome its obsession with ethnicized politics.

Remembering Afghanistan's First President

Afghan flags were in at half-mast when in March 2009 Kabul reinterred the body of the country's first ever president, Sardar Daud Khan. The state funeral was a pompous affair, complete with foreign dignitaries and artillery gunshots. In short, the kind of over-the-top ceremony Daud Khan was known to despise in his lifetime. He was an old-fashioned statesman, compassionate yet reserved and authoritarian.

Had he been alive he would have found Karzai's pomp and Mullah Omar's mendicant airs equally exaggerated. The last of Afghanistan's long line of Pashtun gentlemen rulers of dynastic pedigree, Daud Khan was born into privilege. When he was murdered in a communist coup in 1978, a whole way of traditional Afghan statesmanship died with him.

The public display of respect has long been due but it took thirty years for his body to be discovered and then another eight months passed until a burial place was chosen. Prominent provinces of the country, from Herat in the west to Kandahar to the south, vied for the honor of becoming Daud Khan's final resting place. His appeal was nationwide, a rarity in today's atmosphere of ethnic hatred. The decision finally fell on Kabul, the city where Daud Khan first opened eyes to the world in July 1909.

Writing about Daud Khan's time, the temptation to romanticize life under his leadership is hard to resist. Khalid Hosseini succumbed to this temptation in his bestseller, the *Kite Runner*. In doing so, he irritated some of his Pashtun and Hazara readers who objected to the rosy picture he drew of Kabul in the 1970s. The truth is that, though undoubtedly respected, Daud Khan was also a complex character and a controversial politician.

His own coming to power in 1973 was far from innocent. He launched a coup with the help of Soviet-trained army officers. With their aid, he dethroned his cousin, King Zahir Shah, and established the first Afghan republic. This military venture jointly carried out with Afghan communists earned him the nickname, "the Red Prince." But the reality was less stark, given that "the Red Prince" that ran Afghanistan was a member of the royal family. Daud Khan liked to refer to the coup as a White Revolution. It is true that only one person died in this otherwise bloodless power struggle.

In Daud Khan's view, the communist officers who aided him were a tool that he had used to his own end. But the officers had a different view and saw themselves as the chief operators. They had control over the army, which made them kingmakers (or as it then became, president-makers) of the modern age. Daud Khan responded to this by gradually removing communist officials from ministerial posts. He either demoted them or sent them abroad on insignificant diplomatic missions.

By 1977, the army was the only entity unaffected by Daud Khan's communist purge and around 800 officers known for their loyalty to the Soviet Union remained in charge. Daud Khan didn't dare to purge the army for fear of antagonizing the Soviet Union. He had already pushed his luck with the Soviets by diversifying the country's aid sources and gaining promises of technical and financial support from oil-rich Muslim countries such as Iran and Saudi Arabia.

He had approached the United States, encouraging Washington to play a more active development role, particularly in Helmand province. He was also on the brink of a breakthrough in negotiations with Pakistan over the question of Pashtun self-determination. Step by step, the president was moving his country away from the sphere of Soviet influence. In his own words, his policy amounted to lighting his American cigarette with a Soviet match. It was a gamble that could backfire anytime and Daud Khan was fully aware of the risk.

To be fair to Daud Khan, Kabul had devised this round of Russian roulette decades earlier, when it asked Moscow to help modernize its army in the 1950s. At the time, Afghan leaders believed a modern army was needed in response to the new Pakistani state. Kabul had initially hoped to find in the new Muslim replacement for British India a more willing partner in negotiating the matter of Pashtun self-determination. But Islamabad saw the Afghan leadership's interest in their "kith and kin" inside the Pakistani territory as interference in Pakistani domestic affairs.

In the early years of Daud Khan's republic, tension intensified to such a degree that the two countries found themselves on the brink of a war. Muslim leaders around the world, from Gaddafi to the Shah of Iran, were alarmed and offered to act as mediators. The conflict settled gradually and by the end 1977, both countries launched a series of state visits, displaying an eagerness to solve the conflict. This was presumably because both countries had realized that in this petty inter-Muslim conflict, the only true winner was the Soviet Union.

With the benefit of hindsight, by the end of 1977 there were clear indications in Kabul of a communist coup in preparation. First, the two rival factions of the communist party united. Then, there was the assassination of potential leftist rivals. Finally, there was the BBC commentary broadcast by the World Service's Persian desk in March 1978 that said in no ambiguous terms that a coup was imminent in Afghanistan. In his personal memoirs of the time, Abdul Samad Ghaus, Daud Khan's deputy foreign minister, described approaching the president with a transcript of the commentary. Daud Khan was not alarmed; he simply said that the BBC sometimes spoke off the top of its head.

An old-fashioned nationalist, Daud Khan had the country's interest at heart but at the same time he had an unhealthy obsession with the Pashtuns on the Pakistani side of the border. Fearing a potential war with Islamabad over this conflict, Kabul had asked Moscow to help create a state-of-the-art Afghan air force. Ironically, it was the same air force that turned against Daud Khan, bombarding the presidential palace on 27 April 1978. The communists had mastery over Kabul's skies, resistance proved useless as the army lacked land-to-air missiles. Daud Khan became the victim of his own military modernization. The rebels later found him inside the palace and shot him dead along with sixteen members of his family. The bodies were dropped into an anonymous mass grave. After thirty years, in June 2008, a soldier guided officials to the grave and Daud Khan's family easily identified his body. The clue was a golden Qur'an found in the remains of a skeleton. It was a gift from the Saudi king, the last relic of his quest to find friends beyond Moscow.

The Soviet Invasion

The night the Red Army invaded Afghanistan, Jalil Porshor, a member of the Parcham communist party, was in prison expecting to be shot dead. In his memoirs, posted online from Holland, Porshor says prisoners could hear the sound of warplanes and explosions but had no idea what was going on outside in Kabul. Convinced that they would be killed, the Parchami comrades embraced each other for a final goodbye. They arranged that if there were any survivors, they should meet their comrades' friends and families and give them this message: he remained loyal to the party and its leader, Babrak Karmal, to his last breath.

The farewell done, the prisoners resumed waiting and listening. The sound of explosions could be heard from nearby, as if the prison itself was under attack. Unable to contain his curiosity, Porshor went to the cell window and looked out. There, inside the prison court, he saw soldiers "who didn't look anything like our own troops."

For Porshor, this was good news. It meant that the Red Army had finally come to his rescue and that of his fellow Parchami prisoners. Afghans might have been the only people in the history of the communist movement to have needed a Soviet intervention to stop them from destroying themselves.

In 1978, a curious cabal of idealist poets, would-be intellectuals, officers and KGB spies launched a coup, bringing down President Daud Khan's reign in the course of an afternoon. Victory was easily won but the communists had trouble winning the peace. Their violence was not only directed against the mujahedin, but also against rival leftist groups, the pro-Chinese Maoists, and members of the ethnically Tajik communist party, the Parchamis. The violence culminated in the murder of KGB-agent-turned-leader-of-the-Afghan-communist-party-turned president, Nur Muhammad Taraki, in September 1979.

Taraki had forged a personal relationship with Brezhnev (such intimate couplings include Mullah Omar and Bin Laden, Hamid Karzai and George Bush). According to some Russian historians, Taraki's murder at the hands of his fellow communist party member, Hafizullah Amin, deeply upset Brezhnev and, feeling personally affected, he decided to invade Afghanistan to avenge Taraki's murder. The result was a ten-year war of little benefit to the Russians and much suffering to Afghans.

Since that fateful December night in 1979, Afghanistan has commemorated the Soviet invasion every year. Newspapers publish soul-searching editorials ("it's a time of both pride and pain"); TV stations broadcast anniversary specials ("90-year-old woman tells TV viewers that she used to plant mines to blow up Soviet soldiers") and jihadi leaders grab the microphone to boast about their own role in world history ("it was us who freed Berlin"). But the sad truth is that Afghans paid a heavy price for this victory.

To match the might of the Red Army, resistance groups had little choice but to turn to foreign countries for military and financial support, and in doing so, they gradually lost their independence. In return for this support, the resistance had to open the countries' borders and allow all sorts of foreign armed forces and spies, from Osama bin Laden to the International Security Assistance Force, to enter the country and leave it as they wished. No visa required, no passports shown, no accountability requested. The local population was equally forced to ignore borders, illegally crossing into Iran and Pakistan in search of refuge.

In so doing, they in turn allowed the two neighboring countries to dismiss Afghanistan's territorial integrity. In the words of the Afghan activist and writer Dr Mehdi, "In the last thirty years, Afghanistan has been practically a country without borders and subsequent regimes in Kabul have made a habit of inviting foreign armed forces to help them win the war against this or that group." He explained that the Soviet invasion was the start of this turn of events, the Soviets being the first to illegally cross the northern Afghan border to enter the country. In the process, they created the conditions for all the subsequent border violations, including those we see today.

Christmas 2008 was the twenty-ninth anniversary of the Soviet invasion. But only a few newspapers bothered to publish anniversary editorials. Those who did pointed out that even though the Soviet troops withdrew from Afghanistan many years ago, the country has not seen a single day of happiness since. Others lamented the Afghan leadership's failure to demand compensation from Russia for the total destruction of the country's basic infrastructure. Instead of asking for reparations, the papers said, the Afghan leadership allowed Russia to re-categorize its war spending as aid provision.

Another sad truth is that the communists are back on the political scene in Afghanistan, showing little shame and even less remorse. They appear on TV with their thick moustaches and trademark jargon. They're sent abroad in an official capacity and show off their broken Russian in encounters with native speakers. Puzzled by their easy resurrection (or recycling?), I turned to an Afghan academic who used be involved with the mujahedin during the 1980s. I asked him, "How is it that the communists have been allowed back? I've noticed that they don't even bother to shave their moustaches to hide their past." He said, "They compare themselves with the mujahedin and realize that in comparison they were not that bad after all. They say, look around you, can you find a single former communist who has enriched himself through the war, built himself a palace or owns a shopping center? You won't find a single rich communist but there are plenty of rich mujahedin." In the kingdom of the blind, the one-eyed man is king.

The All-New, Same-Old Taliban?

They were expected to blow themselves up at polling stations in August 2009. Instead the Taliban issued its fighters with a manual of conduct, cautioning them to be careful and courteous in the quest for Afghan hearts and minds. The manual was in Pashto, had over sixty pages and a copy of it was presented to al-Jazeera. The Arab TV station has a large international audience, and the Taliban have been successfully using the station to spread their ideas beyond Afghanistan.

Reports of the manual coincided with news that London and Washington were ready for talks with the Taliban after the Afghan elections of 2009. The Taliban showed indifference to democracy or the upcoming election, but the timing of their manual told a different story. They were undergoing an image makeover just in time for the elections and wanted the world to know about it. The new, more presentable image was interpreted in the local media as a concession to London and Washington, allowing them to feel less embarrassed for wanting to hold talks with the "terrorist" enemy. After all, holding negotiations with the Taliban would mean that the latter had come out of this conflict as the winning side. From the point of view of many Afghans, this would mean that terrorizing the nation had once again paid off, and this time, the UK and the US would become party to the process.

Afghan analysts agreed that the code of conduct signaled the Taliban leadership's intention to change their tactics and focus on winning over skeptics by displaying a more humanitarian attitude towards civilians. For example, in contrast to the Taliban's past unforgiving attitude, the manual offers people who work for the Kabul government protection in return for giving up their jobs. The manual also registers a change of attitude towards suicide attacks, permitting only those that involve important targets. Any other suicide attack is considered a waste of Muslim lives. More importantly, the manual advises Taliban fighters not to discriminate against other, non-Pashtun, ethnic groups. The Buddhas of Bamian might smile at this, were their faces still intact, but Afghan commentators singled out this point as marking a significant shift in policy. Had the manual included equality for women and followers of non-Sunni strands of Islam, the image makeover would have been complete. Afghan commentators noted that the manual resembled a constitution and its focus on fair and lawful conduct, its ban on ethnic discrimination and its condemnation of brutality certainly required the ordinary Taliban fighter to dance more in tune with global norms of political conduct. A new Taliban manifesto, then?

Not everyone was buying into the image makeover. Although the manual's core message was winning over the civilian population, its rules unwittingly revealed the Taliban's own troubles. The manual explicitly banned factionalism and the setting up of new armed groups, underlining the fact that Mullah Omar was the movement's only legitimate leader. Similar rules also showed that Taliban fighters had been taking decisions that were outside the scope of their authority, deciding over life and death, and issuing punishment without consulting religious authorities with the required expertise in Islamic law. If Kabul had trouble controlling its officials, so, it seemed, did the Taliban. Brutality and corruption on both sides had alienated the civilian population whose support was now being courted by both Karzai's administration and the Taliban in time for the elections on 20 August. Be that as it may, the question remained whether the change, like many other phenomena in Afghanistan, had taken place on paper only. The Taliban's initial reaction appeared to be in tune with their new manifesto. A peace accord in Badghis Province between Kabul and the Taliban, for example, allowed for voter registration to run smoothly. Elsewhere in southern and eastern Afghanistan, in a reverse of their previous policy, the Taliban granted people to register for voting cards and according to local reports, even the fighters themselves registered to vote. Skeptics saw this as a ploy, allowing the Taliban to pass themselves off as ordinary civilians with voting cards in case they were stopped and searched. But just when Afghan observers started to describe the Taliban's attitude towards the elections as something between indifference and compliant, the fighters issued a message on their website, asking Afghans not to take part in the elections. The message said that participation in the elections amounted to supporting US policies in Afghanistan and Afghans should join the Taliban's jihad instead of voting for a new president. The message marked a radical departure from the Taliban's early indifference and was followed by a bomb set off in the relatively calm city of Herat and eight rocket attacks, some of which reached the diplomatic neighborhood in the heart of the capital.

In theory, the 2009 election was bound to be irrelevant from a Taliban point of view for three reasons. First, as Afghan analyst Wahid Mojzdah pointed out in an article, the Taliban believe that only practicing and pious Muslims should be given the right to vote. Hence a leader chosen by a majority regardless of their religious credentials is lacking in legitimacy. Second, the Taliban believe that Washington pays only lip service to democracy, failing to accept democratically elected groups such as Hamas or the Iranian government, for ideological reasons. Third, an election campaign held in a country under occupation is by definition meaningless, as the nation is not sovereign.

But still, the Taliban's early indifference was in stark contrast to the high-profile attacks of the election period. What triggered the change? There were a number of possibilities. The attacks might not have been carried out by the Taliban, even though they were attributed to them. The chaos of war was best described with the words of an Afghan jihadi figure, Sediq Chakari, when asked about his responsibility as a commander in war crimes of the 1990s. He said, "Look, this is Afghanistan. Someone fires a rocket; it falls on something, kills some people. Who fired it or why? No one knows." To add to the already existing disorder, the Taliban rarely denied involvement in attacks attributed to them because the attribution serves as free publicity, making them appear more powerful than they are.

But since the attacks immediately followed the Taliban's boycott message, chances were that it was their fighters who fired the rockets and planted the bomb in Herat. In that case, the Taliban might have been reacting to something that had gone wrong in the ongoing negotiations with the Kabul administration. Since the negotiations were kept secret, and were being carried out without consultation with the people, it was impossible to figure out what might have gone wrong. But the fact remained that the Taliban were likely to be economically better off if they continued their self-styled jihad.

After all, the Taliban had exclusive access to three lucrative sources of income—zikat or charity from international sympathizers in Gulf states and the West, drugs money, and income from kidnapping and extortion. If they joined the government side and became co-opted into the Kabul administration, they would lose their international supporters' donations and would have to share zikat from the US with their former enemies in the Kabul administration. The incentive for the Taliban to fight on was powerful and the additional sense of moral superiority that came with it a welcome bonus. With so much at stake, the Taliban were not likely to lay down their weapons.

The Shifting Idea of Jihad

The original mujahedin of the 1980s and today's Taliban may use the same language of holy war, but their understanding of jihad is worlds apart. The key difference between the original mujahedin and the Taliban is that the former waged a traditional type of jihad. In a traditional jihad, if waged locally, a contest over control of resources takes place between rival strongmen who each run their own private armies. In this scenario, the ultimate legitimacy to rule draws upon military strength, but the contest itself is called jihad simply because Islam is the sole language of political legitimacy.

Crucially, in a traditional jihad, the victorious party has an unspoken right to pillage, rape and loot the conquered population. This is because militia fighters are not paid soldiers in a regular army and hence looting is the material reward they receive for fighting. The original mujahedin followed this traditional pattern of jihad upon coming to power in 1992. Since competition over resources rather than ideology is key to traditional jihad, the mujahedin's war focused on Kabul where the nation's wealth and the foreign embassies, another potential source of funding, were to be found.

Judging by a historical account from the 1920s, back then the women and girls of the conquered populations also belonged to the pillage package offered to militia jihadis. Hence, in the diaries of court chronicler Katib Hazara on the siege of Kabul in 1929, we read that the victorious mujahedin of the time had demanded to see the list of girls registered at a Kabul school so as to allocate female students to militia fighters.

Katib's account might be exaggerated, but the story still reveals that there was an unspoken rule that women and girls were part of the conquest package. As such, the mujahedin's struggle over Kabul was a continuation of traditional jihad complete with internal rivalries, pillage and looting. The mujahedin were part of the realm of traditional politics in which a conquered region is a turf that can be exploited by strongmen, who call themselves mujahedin so as to appear respectable.

The Taliban's conquest of Afghanistan in 1996, by contrast, strayed from the path of tradition. In a striking breach of precedence, the Taliban militia did not make use of their unspoken right to pillage and loot. They searched the conquered populations' homes, but only to confiscate weapons and so ensure a monopoly of violence for their state.

In a comical incident that features in Sabour Bradley's documentary series The Extreme Tourist, the Taliban saw a poster of Rambo with a machine-gun in the home of an Afghan bodybuilder fan of the Hollywood star Sylvester Stallone. Ignorant of the world beyond the sharia law, the Taliban assumed that Rambo was a family member and told the bodybuilder: "Tell your cousin that he must hand over his machine gun to us." The bodybuilder's protestation that the poster depicted a fictional Hollywood hero fell flat with the Taliban, who subsequently imprisoned the man.

The Taliban were exceedingly ignorant—which made them cruel—but there's no doubt that they saw jihad as a means to establish a state rather than legitimacy to pillage a conquered territory. Building a state was of utmost importance to the Taliban because without it the sharia law could not be enforced. If the mujahedin struggled over resources, the Taliban were concerned with religiosity.

The Taliban's choice of their capital city, Kandahar, was further evidence of their radically new approach to conquest. As already mentioned, historically Kabul drew its importance from the fact that the nation's wealth and the foreign embassies were concentrated there. The mujahedin's vicious fight over the city, which resulted in thousands of dead, and their disregard for public buildings, which they indiscriminately destroyed in rocket attacks, was rooted in the view that the capital city was there to be pillaged by whichever party that came out victorious. The Taliban, in contrast, disregarded Kabul, moving their capital to the much poorer city of Kandahar. Accounts of Afghans who met Taliban officials all reveal a lack of interest in material goods or symbols of social hierarchy. Meetings would be held seated on the floor in a circle, erasing all signs of hierarchy that traditionally has been part of Afghan court etiquette.

Ironically, such egalitarianism was what the communists had dreamed of in 1978. But in such a deeply religious society, it is not surprising that egalitarianism had to come as part of a religious doctrine. With the Taliban, rural Afghans came to power, ruling over the more sophisticated urban populations. This, too, was a breach of precedence.

Fighting for resources in a traditional fashion complete with looting and pillaging versus fighting for a state that would enforce sharia law even to the point of an obsessive preoccupation with the correct length of young men's pubic hair is what distinguishes the original mujahedin from their Taliban nemesis.

Both parties use the same language of legitimacy—Islam, jihad, and mujahedin—which adds to the confusion, but their similarities are skin-deep.

Taliban Negotiations: The Key to Peace?

"I pray night and day that America will destroy the Taliban," said Fatima Syed, a woman who had lost her husband in a Taliban massacre. That was in 2001 and seven years later it's clear her prayers have not been heard. Nato has failed to pacify Afghanistan and the Taliban are still fighting. To add insult to injury, they may soon even become *salonfähig*—socially acceptable at the tea parties of Kabul. This is because the view that talking to the Taliban is the only way to establish peace has become increasingly popular inside and outside Afghanistan, albeit only among the politicians.

People like Fatima Syed have not been asked for their view but they're likely to agree with Kamran Mirhazar, the editor-in-chief of the Kabulpress website. Mirhazar says co-opting the Taliban would be the natural conclusion of the appeasement process which began with the return to power of the war criminals of the last thirty years. After all, he says, what are the Taliban but the final missing piece in the government's colorful collection of warlords?

Be that as it may, everyone—from Karzai to party leaders like Ahmad Shah Ahmadzai—seems ready to negotiate, what's stopping the talks? According to Mullah Zaif, ex-Taliban ambassador to Pakistan, it's the foreign troops. In a recent interview with Quqnoos news website, Zaif said: "As long as the foreign troops are here, negotiations with the government will be difficult."

Later, during a BBC discussion program, he elaborated, saying the Taliban claim foreigners operate scot-free in Afghanistan and that you can't trust a government that lets this happen. Reading between the lines, this means that the Taliban fear that if they enter into negotiations, there'll be no guarantee that Nato will stop bombing them. This is because Karzai has no control over the troops and they can't be held accountable for their actions in Afghanistan. In the Taliban's view, this is a serious risk and as long as the risk persists, holding talks is going to be a challenge.

Mullah Zaeef held senior posts during the Taliban regime and was envoy to Pakistan when the US attacked Afghanistan in 2001. The Pakistanis later handed Zaif over to the US and he spent four years in Guantánamo. Though he is no longer a Taliban member, many see him as an unofficial mediator between the government and the Taliban. If this is true, then his statement above should be taken seriously because it indicates a shift in Taliban policy. In the past, the Taliban's response to offers of peace talks has always been the same: the "crusaders" must go and so must their "stooge," Karzai. But this statement seems to suggest that the Taliban have changed their stance and that Karzai is no longer a problem. So can we expect to see Nato troops packing up to go home because there'll be peace with the Taliban?

No, not if you listen to Mullah Ibrahim, a Taliban commander in Helmand province. According to him, there's still another impediment to talks: the mujahideen leaders of the Northern Alliance. In an interview, he said: "The government lacks the required mandate to start negotiating with the Taliban. Divisions within the government and the presence of Northern Alliance leaders in the government have prevented the start of negotiations. That's why the Taliban have no choice but to carry on fighting."

In other words, the Taliban fight because they have no alternative. It's a-man-has-to-do-what-a-man-has-to-do scenario and the Pashtun code of honor requires them to fight. The reason is simple. When the US attacked Afghanistan in 2001, it doubly dishonored the Taliban. The first dishonor was that it attacked them without providing evidence of Bin Ladin's involvement in 9/11. The second was that the US helped the return to power of the Taliban's enemies—the mujahedin leaders whose civil war had paved the way for the rise of the Taliban. It's an often forgotten detail that the Taliban movement was a response to mujahedin corruption and that Karzai, like many other disenchanted mujahedin, was an early supporter of the Taliban, and makes no secret of it. To refresh the reader's memory about the Taliban's view of the mujahedin leaders, here is what the BBC said when Kabul fell to the Taliban in September 1996:

'Ousted President Burhanuddin Rabbani, his prime minister and his military chief are being hunted by the radical Islamic group who branded them "national criminals."'

Needless to say, the "national criminals" are back in power and so if you're a sincere Talib you have no choice but to fight on.

If Mullah Ibrahim is right that the Northern Alliance is a serious problem for the Taliban, then the fighting will go on for the foreseeable future. That's why many suspect that if Nato leaves now the fighting will turn into another civil war. But this would not be a simple return to 1992 because now there are additional players in government to consider, including former communists, royalists and former exiles from the West. Iran, Russia and Pakistan have also become bolder in their policy towards Afghanistan than they were in the 1990s. Needless to say, a full-blown civil war is far worse than the current scenario and so some Afghan commentators suggest that Nato must stay for as long as it takes to pacify the country.

To go back to Mullah Ibrahim's view that they are fighting an honorable war, the Taliban's behavior does not always reflect this attitude in a clear or coherent manner. For example, their leader, Mullah Omar, recently asked "the mujahedin" to join the Taliban in the struggle against the government. If the Taliban have a problem with the mujahedin, then why does their leader ask them to join the Taliban? There is an explanation for this contradictory behavior. Mullah Omar's invitation could be an attempt to divide Karzai's administration along ethnic lines in response to Karzai's efforts to split the Taliban into moderates and hardliners. Karzai has repeatedly said that there are two types of Taliban. The first are brain-washed youths and those who fight for money. To use Karzai's phrase, these are "the sons of the Afghan soil" and reconciliation with them is possible. The second are the ideological extremists with links to al-Qaida. Critics, like the young Afghan intellectuals in charge of the Omid-e Vatan website, say negotiating with the latter would hammer the final nail in the coffin of Afghan democracy. Karzai is conveniently vague about exactly who he plans to talk to, though sometimes he explicitly mentions the name of Mullah Omar.

Politicians like Ahmad Shah Ahmadzai believe that whatever Karzai's choice might be regarding his negotiation partners, his

PART TWO

opinion is inconsequential. In a recent interview with Radio France's Dari-Persian service, Ahmadzai said that in his view negotiations depend on two parties alone: the US and the Taliban. When asked if he supported negotiations, he said: "Yes, yes, I do, but it's not up to me." (Hats off to Ahmadzai! Such modesty is rare among Afghan politicians). If he's right, then the future of talks depends on whether America is ready to negotiate with ... urm ... what was that word again? "Terrorists." Some commentators believe that Mullah Omar's name has already been crossed off the US terrorist list in preparation for precisely this.

The Taliban's Strength or the Government's Weakness?

On the first day of Id al-Fitr in 2008, President Hamid Karzai had a treat in store for his people. In a speech he said: "A few days ago I pleaded with the leader of the Taliban, telling him 'My brother, my dear, come back to your homeland. Come back and work for peace, for the good of the Afghan people. Stop this business of brothers killing brothers.'"

My brother? My dear? Yes, and yes again. Karzai is an Afghan version of the metrosexual man. He sometimes even cries publicly, though that's not to everyone's taste. My favorite Karzai moment was a couple of years ago when he told Iranian president Mahmoud Ahmadinejad: "In this country [Afghanistan], women are in charge." He was daydreaming, of course, but I still felt flattered.

The truth is that Karzai has been beseeching Mullah Omar for a long time. So, in a way, nothing new has happened. This, however, is not entirely correct because there is one new element. Ladies and gentlemen, please stand up to welcome the leader of the Muslim world (not my words, Karzai's): King Abdullah of Saudi Arabia. He's been asked to help enable high-level negotiations with the Taliban. Or, as one Afghan website put it: "Karzai stretched out his arms and grabbed the Saudi King's cloak, asking the king to help him negotiate with the Taliban." And the Saudi reaction? Their king welcomed an Afghan delegation led by Abdul Ahad Shinwari, the chief of Afghanistan's state-sponsored mullahs. Then there was an editorial in the Saudi newspaper, Al-Watan, which irritated some Afghan newsmen. The editorial was penned by the paper's editor-in-chief, and suggested Afghanistan is in trouble because of both al-Qaida and the Americans. Remove these two from the scene and you get a peaceful, stable country. To which an Afghan website retorted that during the Taliban regime, the Saudis had offered Mullah Omar military equipment and millions of dollars. The website alleged that such support continues today. Quoting a source close to the Taliban, it said: "The generosity that wealthy Saudi and Gulf Arab sheikhs are displaying now by far exceeds the openhandedness they showed during the time of the jihad against the Soviet Union ..." In other words, al-Watan is not entirely honest. Or suffering from memory loss. Or both.

As for local reaction in Afghanistan, opinions varied. Ahmad Behzad, an MP from Herat province, made clear his opposition. He said: "If the government and the international community entered into negotiations with the terrorists, it would be an utter disgrace. It would mean that the international community has accepted defeat in Afghanistan." He went on: "The international community came here to fight terrorism, not to come to an understanding with it." Ouch!

The Afghan daily *Hasht-e Sobh* was equally unhappy, but for different reasons. In an editorial headlined "A deal-making that's been called peace-making," the paper listed its objections. First, negotiations are kept secret and that makes them objectionable on principle. Second, the Taliban are presently under threat because Islamabad has turned against them. Why should we offer them peace now, of all times? Third, and more importantly, if calm in Afghanistan is reached through negotiation with the

Taliban, this will translate into more violence in Pakistan. After all, this has been the Pakistani experience. They tried "for many years to ensure security in their own country by enflaming violence in Afghanistan." But the violence finally caught up with them, too. Do unto others as you would be done by.

Fahim Dashti, editor-in-chief of *Kabul Weekly*, was similarly doubtful in a recent interview with Radio France International's Dari-Persian service. He said the two sides in this negotiation have absolutely nothing in common. This is because the Taliban is totally against everything that Kabul apparently stands for, "democracy, the rule of law, human rights, women's rights and free speech." Fahim said the offer of talks could in fact be a tactic to create disharmony among the Taliban. This is because the Taliban "are finding themselves under immense pressure because of Pakistani military operations." In other words, they're weak and may succumb to temptation and accept the peace offer. Dashti added that the offer has another, more personal dimension. It could be Karzai's way of trying to ensure the support of the conservatives in the 2009 presidential elections.

And here is yet another version. Since it was the English (yes the English, not the British) and the Saudis who originally created the Taliban, now they have to support them and this is how they are trying to bring the Taliban back to power. (Hang on, I thought Benazir Bhutto was the one who created the Taliban. After all, that's why she was called Taliban Mom).

Be this as it may, the main question is whether the people of Afghanistan support negotiation with Mullah Omar. I put this question to an Afghan journalist whose opinion I regard highly because he travels to the far corners of the country to speak to ordinary people. His answer was a solid, firm "No." The people most certainly don't want Mullah Omar back. What do they want? The same things that westerners want: security, electricity, running water.

In his view, the problem is not that the Taliban is strong but that the government is weak. Here's an example. You've got a district near the Pakistani border where there are 40,000 people. But they've only got forty policemen. So a bunch of Taliban come and take over a village willy-nilly. They're not strong. We're weak. And the Saudis? Karzai's cabinet is too westernized for their taste. It's their way of trying to regain influence in the administration, by bringing back Mullah Omar.

Suicide Bombers

In the summer of 2007, a stranger appeared in the city of Kandahar in southern Afghanistan. He flagged down a taxi and asked to be driven around the town. The taxi passed public squares, mosques and bazaars. All the time, the passenger sat silently in the backseat of the car, watching city scenes unfold in front of him. After an hour, the driver was asked to stop the car. But before getting out, the passenger had this message for the driver: "You are an unlucky man. Today you missed the chance of becoming a martyr." That was when the driver realized that he had been giving a lift to a suicide bomber looking for potential targets. He decided to quit working as a taxi driver and find a less risky occupation.

The story first appeared in Afghanistan in 2007 and soon reached England via the internet. It is quite likely a fabrication, simply because the story is too good to be true. The suicide bomber in the story is efficient, the innocent driver has a lucky escape and there is no bloodshed. This is the opposite of the reality of suicide bombing in Afghanistan—a reality of confused teenage bombers, poorly planned missions, premature detonations and heavy civilian losses.

Like everything else in contemporary Afghanistan, suicide bombings have tragi-comic elements. To illustrate, here is a true story. The protagonist is a wannabe suicide bomber. He fills his car with explosives and sets off towards his target. Halfway through the journey, it suddenly dawns on him: Petrol! He is running out of fuel. A change of plan, then. He drives to a petrol station, the backseat of the car piled with explosives. The station attendant notices and becomes suspicious. He calls the police and the driver is arrested. If Hollywood made a film based on the story, they'd call it *Dude, Where's my Petrol?*

Now picture the failed wannabe bomber lying on a shrink's couch, undergoing therapy. What would the doctor say to him? Most probably this: deep inside, you wanted to be caught. That's why you forgot to fill up the tank. Interviews conducted with arrested wannabe bombers support this view. They show that far from acting out of personal political conviction, Afghan bombers are often either brainwashed, coaxed into action by the offer of money or simply forced to carry out suicide missions. They usually die faceless and nameless and the government denies them their Afghan identity. A regular comment that is made after a suicide mission is this: the bomber's body has been left behind at the scene of the attack. In plain English: nobody is claiming the body because the bomber is a stranger. In the absence of proper forensic tests, assumptions are regularly made about the bombers' identity. In the early days, comments like this were common: judging by the bomber's complexion and the shape of his nose, he is clearly an Arab. A Yemeni, probably. Information collected from arrested bombers helps explain why the body is often not claimed and the identity not established. The bomber's family simply doesn't know. Sometimes they only find out when the Taliban visit the family to hand over post-suicide compensation. According to a UN survey in 2007 only 11 per cent of the population backs suicide bombing. That's probably why the family is left in ignorance. They would interfere otherwise and stop the mission.

The evident lack of political conviction among bombers and of popular support for such missions does not mean that they have stopped or that there are fewer of them. Two suicide attacks were reported as I wrote this article, one in Kandahar and one in Helmand. Two alleged wannabe bombers were also arrested in Kabul but, not surprisingly, the police say they are foreigners.

Chaotic, violent, and lacking in conviction and popular support, Afghan suicide bombing mirrors the current military occupation of the country. It is not surprising, then, that the Taliban call suicide missions "equalizers." Sadly the irony of this label is lost on them.

Armchair Jihadis: The Glamorization of Jihad

If you are an Afghan who lives in the West you always run the risk of bumping into armchair jihadis—people born and brought up in the west but with the mindset of the Taliban leader, Mullah Omar. When they figure out you are Afghan, they engage you in a conversation, telling you how much they admire the Afghans for their jihad against the infidels. The conversation often ends with a statement along the lines of "You people are the only true Muslims in the world."

Well, thank you. We are flattered, but you are quite wrong. There are thousands of young Afghans who would gladly swap places with you. This is because, as an Afghan saying goes, the sound of the drum is always sweeter when heard from a distance. In other words, there is huge gap between the reality of jihad and fantasizing about jihad in the comfort of your bedroom in Bradford or London. Afghans know this because we've been there, done it and are now facing the consequences.

Here are the consequences. The jihadi fighters of Afghanistan were no doubt excellent fighters but they turned out to be incompetent and despotic politicians, incapable of creating a coherent government or bringing peace to their people. Once their common enemy was defeated in 1992, they started fighting each other. In Kabul alone, 60,000 civilians were killed.

The utter disregard shown to the civilian population is documented in a video footage taken during this time. The footage is available on YouTube and illustrates how the warring jihadi factions had turned the Afghan capital into their own private battlefield. The footage shows a group of civilians stuck in the crossfire, with rockets flying over their heads in every direction. Civilians explain in the video that they have been stuck at home for days on end and do not dare to leave for fear of being hit by rockets. The survivors of the battle for the control of Kabul remember this period as a time when you could not bury your dead for fear of being hit by missiles.

Afghanistan's first-hand experience with jihad made it clear that Islam works as a unifying force only as long as you have a common enemy. As soon the common enemy is overcome, Islam as a political ideology fails to overcome the differences or prevent the power-hungry from committing atrocities. The jihadi fighters of Afghanistan and their leaders in many ways behaved just like their communist predecessors. They plotted against each other, fought each other, created a regime of chaos, fear and hatred and left behind mass graves. In doing so, they deprived the nation of a chance to take pride in its success against the Soviet army. This is because what came next was, to put it mildly, a period of shameful disgrace.

The Afghan leaders involved in the civil war of the early 1990s have been approached and asked for explanations. Some of them admit to having made mistakes but refuse to apologize. Most of them view themselves not as warlords or criminals but as national heroes—Afghanistan's equivalents of Gandhi or Jinnah. They say that civilian casualties are the price you have to pay when you are fighting for a higher purpose.

What was that higher purpose? Jihad against your own Muslim nation or other Muslim leaders? We don't know. What we know is that for whatever reason, the fighting didn't stop, but intensified. When the demand for justice and accountability for the war crimes of the last three decades became harder to ignore in Afghanistan, the communists and the jihadis joined hands to pass a bill granting them immunity from prosecution.

The jihadis' failure to bring peace and stability to Afghanistan is the reason why many Afghans today support the presence of foreign troops in their country despite the humiliation of foreign occupation. After all, the people of Afghanistan are famous for their desire for independence. But, ironically, this time we are more afraid of our own leaders than of the foreign occupiers. Maybe we are wrong but we don't trust our leaders. We fear that as soon as the foreign troops leave, they'll start to settle accounts again, plunging the country into yet another civil war. Thirty years of war is quite enough for any nation, let alone a weak and poor nation like Afghanistan.

This, in brief, is the Afghans' first-hand experience of jihad. It's far from heroic, glamorous or even honorable. In all this, the footsoldiers of jihad have turned out to be the biggest losers of all. Their families live in poverty and their protests are ignored. Many of them were disabled during the war and now have no chance of competing for jobs that require health and strength.

The armchair jihadis of the west should better get real and stop idealizing Afghanistan. They should see Afghanistan for what it is—a cautionary tale that speaks against jihadi zeal—and certainly not as a role model.

The Myth of Independence

In an interview with the Guardian, Afghan human rights activist Orzala Asharf-Nemat said it was the responsibility of the Afghan people to create their own national identity. Her point is absolutely valid. But since transnational concepts such as socialism (1980s), Islam (1990s) and democracy (2000s) have all failed to create a stable nation, we need to ask ourselves: what is the single idea that resonates with all Afghans?

Unfortunately for Afghans, the idea that makes them feel that they are part of a distinct nation is the myth of their independence. This myth was the narrative upon which the Afghan state was founded in the late nineteenth century. Since then, it has continued to serve as the key story for political legitimacy and nation-building.

But the myth of independence is a double-edged sword that can be turned against foreign invaders and legitimate local governments alike. When turned against local governments, the myth of the Afghans' natural right to independence turns into license to riot and rebel but without any sense of wrongdoing. The myth of independence is the sole idea that resonates with all Afghans, regardless of their age, gender and ethnicity. The jihadi leaders, their Taliban enemies and vocal dissidents such as Malalai Joya all draw on this myth for legitimacy and popular appeal. In the mood for rebellion, Afghan MPs at times have threatened to "hit the mountain," a euphemism for justified rebellion against an oppressive state.

The strong sense of independence has historically served to legitimize many acts of anarchy and subversion, which is why even the president sometimes threatens to join the Taliban rebels.

A myth that is as old as the country itself is obviously hard to shake off. Most Afghans are emotionally helpless against the call for independence which is why they desert the army, rally around subversive clerics and plant bombs that blow up their own people. The myth's power is such that it makes the legitimate question of what will happen once independence is achieved sound ridiculous.

Afghans should be forgiven for allowing the myth of independence to deprive them of their only chance to rebuild their country with the help of international allies. After all, generation after generation were raised with the idea that what made them unique was their martial qualities, their ability to be independent even to the point of defeating empires. In reality, Afghans did not defeat any empire, as both the British and the Soviet empires were already in decline and in the process of disintegration. But Afghans could not let go of the myth and were instead encouraged to take pride in their country as the graveyard of empires. But Afghanistan remained a graveyard while the capitals of the former empires, Moscow and London, thrived and flourished after their so-called defeat by Afghans. The myth persisted even after the entire country had turned into a giant cemetery.

Afghan jihadi leaders still talk proudly about a nation that gives birth to independence-seeking martyrs. The myth is politically useful as it turns subversive rebels into heroes, thieving highwaymen into politicians. Ironically, international writers and journalists have also adopted the myth, perpetuating it by publishing books and articles about "the graveyard of empires." At times, it feels as if the whole world wants Afghanistan to be just that: a massive graveyard and symbolic two fingers to superpowers. That a country incapable of sustaining itself is further destroyed in the process seems to matter little. Neither does it seem to matter that those who destroy cannot rebuild and hence expect the population to live in ruins and feed themselves with the pride of a myth rather than actual food.

The uncomfortable truth is that Afghanistan has never been a truly independent country and has always relied on outside resources and expertise for survival. Historically, much of the country's limited wealth came through control of trade routes by local tribesmen who also acted as highwaymen, making travelling in Afghanistan a famously dangerous endeavor. Other sources of income included military raids into richer neighboring territories and foreign subsidies in return for implementing superpower policies. The government in Kabul has always received foreign aid and subsidies to implement modernization projects. The border tribes have always been hard to control and repeatedly undermined the central state, refusing to pay tax or supply soldiers to the army, again drawing on the unspoken right to independence.

The myth of independence also legitimized internal rebellions. Hence, in 1919, King Amanullah was declared a ghazi in recognition of his jihad against the British which won Afghans' independence. But in 1929, new rival strongmen had emerged, contesting Amanullah's power. They called the amir an infidel, which amounted to a declaration of war.

That a heroic Muslim leader could willy-nilly be declared an infidel might seem alarming, but in Afghanistan the clergy has always been subversive, often siding with the enemies of the state. After all, the absence of a strong state empowers both clerics and rebels, which is why both groups traditionally join hands, appealing to the myth of independence to mobilize the masses against the state. The riots in the Spring of 2011 in Mazar, Kandahar and Kabul were a continuation of this historical trend.

Independence, the national narrative that binds Afghans together, is simultaneously the force that helps mobilize rebellions, undermine the state and destabilize the country. If there is one lesson Afghans should learn from the past, it is that the inclusion of the myth of independence in their national narrative has to be done with great care, or the endless cycle of internal independence-seeking rebellions will never end.

PART THREE

War in Afghanistan? *Yes but No but Yes but No*

"I am sorry for what we have done to your country," said an American man as I soon as he heard I was Afghan. Masochistic liberals approaching one and apologizing on behalf of their country is a quirky little perk that is the exclusive privilege of Afghans (and Iraqis, I guess). It's such a strange happening that it makes being Afghan, for once, almost worthwhile. There they are, citizens of countries with mighty armies, apologizing to us, the people of a place where unless held at a gunpoint no-one says sorry. This experience is breathtaking for Afghans who are new to Europe and the US because back home, rumour has it that the "infidels" are either morally loose hedonists with little care for the rest of the world or crusading Islamophobes.

The newcomers' bewilderment inevitably makes its way to Facebook, reaching other Afghans via status updates ending in exclamation marks. "My landlord is eighty-five and so ill that he can't walk by himself. But when he heard that I was Afghan, he told his grandson that he *had* to see me. His grandson helped him walk up the stairs and they came into my room and he said, 'I just wanted to tell you how sorry I am for what my country has done to you.' Isn't that amazing!" The comments that pour in are praise mixed with awkwardness, "What a good man!" and, "Wow, how sweet of him!" and the open for interpretation, "Lolz…!" We are not used to being told "sorry." Our own war-

155

lords never said sorry. Among Afghans, to say sorry means you are weak and out of the political game. It means you have admitted defeat. Humility, humanity and generosity is in this way interpreted as subjugation, triggering a victory *atan* dance among the Taliban—for that's how they read "sorry."

Guilt-ridden American and European liberals who offer apologies for "what my country has done to you" are popular among Afghans. They validate the Afghans' views of themselves as victims, encouraging them to indulge in not taking responsibility for their own actions. It's a comfortable position, soothing and simplistic for both parties. The liberals feel morally superior and the Afghans smug. But the reality is more complex. The truth is that it was our own people who started the war with the communist coup of April 1978. Since then, all Afghan groups that came to power at some point allied themselves to international partners in battles waged against their own fellow Afghan rivals. In reality, the conflict in Afghanistan is three decades of civil war in which we have dragged in international partners—from Soviet communists to global Islamists and more recently, the North Atlantic Treaty Organization. In all these conflicts, Afghans have been both victims and perpetrators. They have been manipulated but have also acted as manipulators. It is this complexity that has created much confusion, leading to policies that are marked by hesitation, deviation and repetition.

In 2001, when the BBC's burqa-clad John Simpson single-handedly liberated Kabul, I manically collected front-page articles filled with promises that *this time* the world leaders were not going to abandon us. I have kept the pages as historical souvenirs and when I look at them, I am reminded of a failed love-affair (in fact, in the early days, there were many Afghan with non-Afghan marriages, with foreign girls converting to Islam and making the top evening news in Kabul). Ten years later, the world can't wait to leave Afghans to their own devices. We have lost our mystique as an exotic people tucked away in the Hindu-

PART THREE

kush and our qualities of hospitality, generosity, and kindness
are questioned with every kidnapping, suicide attack and shooting of foreign trainers by their Afghan trainee soldiers. The honeymoon period finished in 2004 and by 2008 the seven-year itch
set in. Currently, we have reached the divorce stage and as
expected, this phase is all about money, custody and division of
responsibilities.

From the beginning of the rescue mission, what was neglected
was the Afghans' own inference of the intervention. With little
to zero understanding of the way democracy works in developed
countries, a majority of Afghans failed to grasp why the meaning and purpose of the mission changed radically over time.
After all, until their recent history, Afghans had only been
exposed to invasions by the Soviet Union and Al-Qaida, an
authoritarian regime and a dictatorial shadow state respectively,
each with coherent policies based on dogmatic ideologies. An
intervention led by a host of democratic societies with pressure
groups, political parties, lobby groups and powerful media vying
to shape public opinion and policy was new and bewildering to
Afghans. Little wonder, then, that the mission came across as a
mess full of contradictions. "On the one hand, they bang on
about women's rights and help for widows. On the other hand,
every time there's an air ride, Afghan women become widows. It
doesn't make sense," my source in Kabul summed up the confusion of many Afghans.

Afghans themselves played a role in furthering the lack of
clarity because with unexpected sudden access to dollars, they
became sidetracked with business opportunities dressed up as
NGOs and soon lost track of what they wanted to achieve as a
nation. In terms of diplomacy, they were in toddler stage, just
beginning to babble incoherently. The key rival country to the
east, Pakistan, already had seasoned diplomats who were graduates of Oxford and Cambridge, Harvard and Yale. They knew
how to influence policy in London and Washington to serve

157

Islamabad's interests, which were usually detrimental to Kabul. Afghans, by contrast, were just beginning to learn English properly and the frequent foreign missions of diplomats often ended in shopping sprees rather than shaping public opinion abroad in the interest of Afghanistan. It is not an exaggeration to claim that the notorious ousted MP, Malalai Joya, who is the most famous Afghan dissident in exile, had more impact on shaping public opinion abroad than all Afghan diplomats put together. The fact that at home, she was becoming the butt of jokes at exactly the same time as she was becoming a heroine abroad sums up the gap of Afghans' own understanding of the situation and the representation of this situation abroad. The same is true of Khaled Hosseini's bestseller, *The Kite Runner*. It took eight years for the book to be translated into Dari-Persian, the local language thus becoming one of the last languages in which the book appeared. If readers abroad read a story of redemption, vocal Hazara ethno-nationalists saw in it an attempt to represent the Hazara as helpless victims even though they had become empowered and emancipated over the last thirty years. The book was banned for a long time in Afghanistan, owing to fears of ethnic violence. But abroad it was celebrated as a feel-good Afghan story. Still, Khaled Hosseini's heroic attempt at giving Afghans their humanity is often annihilated by the Taliban's relentless inhumanity. *The Kite Runner* has done more good to Afghan image building abroad than all international conferences put together but the author himself is not exactly appreciated by his own people.

The aim of Part Three is to show the Afghans' own narratives and readings of the 2001 mission and the policies that followed it. What readers encounter in this chapter is news in retrospect—in other words, a mini history of recent foreign policy in Afghanistan.

Our Brothers to the East Are a Mixed Blessing

From an early age, Afghan girls are imparted a life-saving warning: never trust a guy who says he is like your brother because unless he really is your brother, he is bound to have other plans for you. The plans, needless to say, tend to be dishonorable. The same is true about our fraternal nation to the east, Pakistan. It would be fair to say that key politicians in both Kabul and Islamabad live in la-la land. Both are in charge of impoverished, aid-dependent countries with large populations of illiterate, unemployed young men about to explode in rage and still, they both have designs for each other.

Some ethno-nationalist Afghan politicians dream of a land called Pashtunistan. The land has a name and even a flag, the only downside is that this land has historically never existed. The idea of this imaginary country is to unite the Pashtuns from both sides of the border and in doing so, gain Afghans access to the sea through the Gwadar port. Pakistani politicians live in their own fantasy land, though their fantasy is more like a nightmare. They are paranoid that Delhi is dead set on destroying Pakistan and because of this paranoia, they feel that they need to gain strategic depth in the region, through running Afghanistan by proxy. If you visit Afghanistan, make sure you have no good words for Pakistan because apart from misogyny, anti-Pakistani sentiment is just about the only attitude that almost all Afghans share. They regard the Taliban as a purely Pakistani creation and if Benazir Bhutto is famous as one of the few female Muslim leaders in the West, in Afghanistan she is chiefly known as the woman who gave birth to the Taliban. Against this background of hostility, the shift in the US strategic plans in South Asia in 2008 (changing the focus of the "war on terror" in the direction of the Pakistani border regions) should have been received with high emotions of joy, belated indignation or at least Schadenfreude in Afghanistan.

Afghan newspapers extensively reported the shift in the strategic plan. But when I explored the Afghan press, I found none of the responses I had expected. What I found was a tired sigh of relief and some apprehension. The idea was that finally, the Americans got it. Got what? That "you can't trust the Pakistani government." That "all suicide attacks that happen in Afghanistan are organized in Pakistan." That "you can't win the 'war on terror' without taking this into consideration." The papers said President Karzai had been stressing this over the years but his western allies "didn't trust him," shrugging off the warnings. The papers were not exaggerating. Such was the repetitive nature of Karzai's warnings about Pakistan that one time a colleague of mine fell asleep, translating the news of one of his warnings into English. After being rudely awakened by the sound of our laughter, my colleague said: "Karzai has lost his credibility. To the point that even when he breaks wind, no one bothers to laugh."

In Afghan society, this lack of credibility is equated with sinking seriously low. But what happened when the US seemed to finally follow Karzai's advice? What were the local reactions? One paper, Mosharekat-e Melli, said: "Western politicians trusted the Pakistani government and because of this trust many opportunities were lost. But there is no doubt that if the situation continues unchanged, terrorists and the Taliban will pay back America not only in Kabul but also in Washington and New York."

But not everyone shared this view, and freedom of speech meant that alternative opinions were expressed in the press. Politician and journalist Abdol Hafiz Mansur, for example, told *Payman*-e Melli newspaper: "The US's threats to Pakistan will have a lasting negative impact on the relationship between two neighboring countries that have many communalities. We need to legalize the presence of the foreign troops in Afghanistan to reassure our neighbors that Afghanistan will not become a base from where they'll face threats."

Mansur showed foresight when he said that the foreign troops were bound to leave Afghanistan at some point while the local population had no choice but to stay. For this reason, Kabul had to get along with its neighboring countries.

All the Afghan commentators were in agreement that Pakistan needed to be put under pressure to take a clear stance against terrorism. But some, like Mansur, doubted that "sending pilotless planes" and using military means alone would be the right approach.

Needless to say, on the other side of the border, the shift in US strategy was met with anger in tribal areas. At a news conference, Pakistani tribal leaders said if the US continued to take military action, the tribes would attack Kabul. The Afghan government seemed unfazed by this threat. The foreign ministry spokesman told a press conference: "I am fully confident that the people in the tribal areas on the other side of the border [i.e. Pakistan] are supporting the US strategy against terrorism."

But the journalists pressed him. What if Islamabad attacks us? Is the government prepared? To this the spokesman replied that "Afghanistan has always been a victim of terrorism and security forces are trying to prevent any terrorist attack in Kabul." In brief he meant, we're used to attacks and we can deal with them.

Not really, said a *Payman-e Melli* editorial. It posed a rhetorical question: "How can a government that is incapable of ensuring the security of its citizens within the limits of the capital city defend the country's borders?" The paper added that Karzai's insistence that Pakistan was the sole reason for the continuation of violence aimed to distract from his administration's shortcomings. The editorial's caption put it neatly: "The new US strategy is not going to save the Afghan government."

An article in *Daily Afghanistan* had a different take on the tribal leaders' threat. It said the threat was in fact a sign of weakness of those who were using tribal elders as a "tool" to threaten the US. The bottom line was that tribal leaders had lost both their economic power and social prestige. This was the result of the jihadi wars of the last thirty years which had created a new class of leaders, with the no-longer-humble mullahs of the past competing with historically privileged tribal elders. This change, the article said, was irrevocable. It meant that those who relied on tribal leaders for support must be seriously desperate.

The view that Pakistani tribal elders were not acting independently was widespread in the Afghan media. Mohammad Asam, an MP from Baghlan, said: "Pakistan has equipped the tribes to wage a war against Afghanistan. This is part of its warmongering policy." Are the tribes a threat? "Only if Afghanistan descends into chaos," he said.

Sayed Mohammad Golabzoy, former interior minister and currently an MP for Urozgan province, said that "when the Pakistani tribes make a threat like this, it's clear that they are not talking for themselves. They are speaking for the Pakistani army." Did he think the tribes were a threat? Not for the international forces in the country, said Golabzoy, but for Afghanistan, yes. He explained, "Unfortunately, our army is incapable of reacting to anything that might happen. In reality, we do not have a national army or national police to defend our territorial integrity."

The press reaction was diverse and this itself was testimony that Afghans were making use of one of the more solid spin-offs of the 2001 intervention: freedom of speech and media.

Cheap Talk: Obama and the Taliban

If you are a nation whose future is decided on the other side of the planet, you are obviously in a pickle. You have to wait until the other side of the world makes up its mind about you, weighing up its options. And so, Afghans kept waiting for Obama to finally deliver his highly anticipated speech about his Afghan strategy. He was elected president in 2008 but we had to wait until December 2009 to hear him talk. His speech had his trade-mark message of hope. But unfortunately this message of hope was directed at the Taliban and not the people of Afghanistan. In the words of a friend and fellow Afghan, Obama basically told the Taliban to go home and rest for eighteen months and then return to a no-man's land up for grabs.

Or, as an editorial in the Hasht-Sobh newspaper put it, the new American strategy was basically tantamount to "surrender before defeat."

"I'm feeling cheap and used for someone else's political agenda," said Fahim Khairy, an Afghan activist who had made fighting for the rights of disabled people in Afghanistan his mission. Like many other Afghans, Khairy had made the mistake of taking politicians of democratically elected governments of western Europe and the US at face value when they promised in 2001 that they were not going to abandon Afghanistan as they did after the Soviet withdrawal.

The promise turned out to be what is locally known as *gap-e moft*, or cheap talk. But as always, there was a positive side to this realization. Afghans understood that politicians were basically politicians, be they Afghan, American or British, and cheap talk was a universal currency, not an exclusively Afghan privilege. Some Afghans started to miss George Bush, pointing out that Bush had guts and was generous, whereas Obama sounded like a concerned father talking to teenage kids about a war led by the Taliban who are fully grown men of strong conviction. More optimistic Afghans hoped that Obama's message was simply a strategy to shake the Afghan leadership, waking them from their slumber and forcing them into action.

Be that as it may, the thought of even an initial withdrawal in such a short time took many by surprise. In the words of a fellow Afghan, "it's not that Afghans are in love with the foreign troops but they expect them not to leave the country in a mess." In other words, they expected the US to act responsibly, and not withdraw before the Afghan army was in a position to protect the people against the Taliban. Exactly how this goal could be reached in eighteen months was a mystery to everyone apart from Obama himself. As an article in Hasht-e Sobh put it: "The army has only two airplanes, presents from the US, and every time there is a public ceremony, the whole capital comes to a standstill." In other words, the government was far from being in a position to defend itself.

Many asked themselves what happened to the Afghans' famous sense of *ghairat*, or honor, as the "nation" began to realize just how dependent it had become on foreign aid. An equally eerie sensation was the idea of being left to one's own devices. After all, the only years in recent history in which Afghans were left to themselves were among the worst years of their recent history—the civil war years of the 1990s and the subsequent Taliban era.

Obama's message might have appeared as a complex speech to the rest of the world but to rural Afghanistan it meant only one thing: the return of the Taliban. For rural Afghans this meant that they had no option but to co-operate with the Taliban because the insurgents' ruthlessness was still fresh in public memory. The people of Kabul had worse to fear from Obama's message. After all, many Kabulis happily rounded up the Taliban and handed them over to the foreign troops in 2001. The likelihood of encountering a vengeful Taliban was a scary thought, especially since Afghans became aware that few people would be ready to take up arms and die fighting against the Taliban.

What became clear in Afghans' reactions to Obama's withdrawal speech was that thirty years of armed conflict had left behind a war-weary population that had been given a false sense of international importance in 2001. Judging by Kabul's record, the leadership itself had been living with the illusion that the country was going to be perceived as a serious international threat if left to its own devices and this fear was going to prevent the international community from abandoning it. The Afghans had put all their hopes into playing this card but they were not taken seriously. The Taliban, after all, were not exactly a threat to the US and had hardly ever engaged in international terrorist operations. They were not al-Qaida, they were the al-Qaida's hangers on, powerful locally but not internationally.

Exactly how Obama expected Afghans to overcome insurgency without a nation-building project was a mystery even to those Afghans who had kept an open mind about the American president. Obama's speech was contradictory at best. As Afghan blogger Dawood Siawash put it, "Bearing in mind that militias are being created in the south, what guarantee is there that the militias themselves will not try to bring down Kabul?"

Obama avoided going into detail about how the training of a viable Afghan army was possible in eighteen months, given that only a fraction of the fresh US troops would be tasked with training. Afghans understood that a withdrawal was ultimately inevitable but they had not expected it to happen so suddenly and under such adverse circumstances when, unlike in 2004, parts of the country were already under Taliban control.

Obama's message was a wake-up call not only to the Kabul administration but all those Afghans trusting of the international community's commitment to Afghanistan. The mission had created a people with a false sense of international importance and a brief but intense taste of what it was like to be part of the global community. A return to chaos and violence would obviously be hard for everyone apart from the hyphenated Afghans in possession of foreign passports. As to the Taliban, needless to say, time is what they always had in abundance.

Operation Moshtarak: "Fighting Together" or Not Really?

From the onset, the 2001 military mission was carried out on two fronts, on the ground with soldiers and war planes and on paper and internet through words and images. When we reached 2010, it was all but clear that the US army had failed to defeat the Taliban. The Afghan president was by then already jokingly referred to as Obama's son-in-law, a passive aggressive remark referring to the humiliating realization that Karzai was not the boss and Washington was calling the shots in the war against the Taliban. Afghans felt humiliated for not really being part of the war while the Americans were losing interest in dying in Afghanistan. In came the perfect solution: Operation Moshtarak. The word *moshtarak* means "together" in Dari-Persian. It went down in history as the first major operation conducted in Afghanistan since President Barack Obama came to power. It was the launch of Obama as a military commander-in-chief and the prominence it was given in world media was deliberate.

There are always multiple perspectives to each story and comparing Afghan and international coverage of the operation, I found striking differences. On the ground in Afghanistan, Operation Moshtarak was viewed through the prism of ethnic paranoia, national self-doubt and conspiracy theories. Reading between the lines of editorials in Afghanistan's opposition press, one could not help but sense that the opposition was not interested in the successful completion of the operation. After all, military success in Helmand province would amount to the Kabul government regaining the legitimacy that it had lost as a result of the fraud-ridden 2009 presidential election. The opposition had little interest in such victory, so media outlets critical of the government published editorials that belittled the operation, casting doubt over its strategic importance while highlighting the issue of civilian casualties.

Operation Moshtarak was launched to symbolize a new spirit of co-operation and Afghan ownership of the war against the Taliban. But on the ground in Afghanistan, it became the embodiment of Afghans' internal ethnic struggles. Karzai being Pashtun by ethnicity, his non-Pashtun opponents were not keen

PART THREE

on his government coming out victorious in Operation Moshtarak. Ironically, *moshtarak*—a spirit of togetherness—was exactly what was missing in the local media coverage of the operation.

The Daily Mandagar, a paper which had previously been banned after allegations of blasphemy, put its criticism in a characteristically blunt manner. It posed the question: are Marjah and Nade Ali (where the operation took place) really such strategically important districts to merit this concentration of efforts? The paper added that the local population themselves were astounded by the significance given to their region and doubted that the deployment of 15,000 troops was necessary to force out the Taliban.

Perhaps anticipating such criticism, the pro-government paper *Anis* had a ready answer to this question. It said that even though Marjah and Nade Ali were of no obvious strategic importance, the operation was of symbolic value as it offered a chance to test the Afghan army's skills against the Taliban. The paper added that the operation's outcome could define the future of the war.

While both government and opposition papers denied that Marjah and Nade Ali had been chosen for clear, military and strategic reasons, the Taliban themselves had no such doubts. Judging by an interview with the Taliban commander in charge of Marjah, the movement regarded the operation as part of an international imperialist conspiracy which rendered Marjah and Nade Ali of special military and strategic importance. This interview with Mullah Abdul Rezaq Akhund, the Taliban commander in Marjah, was conducted in Pashto and posted on Cheragh, an opposition political website.

The interview showed that seen through the Taliban's conspiracy prism, Helmand's geographic location gave the province strategic importance. (Helmand is the province to which Marjah and Nade Ali belong). In the interview, Akhund listed four primary reasons which, according to the Taliban, explained why

Helmand was of great geo-strategic importance to Nato. The Taliban commander alleged that the US and the UK intended to set up surveillance centers along the Iranian border to collect Iranian military and intelligence data. Akhund further alleged that since Helmand was also close to Gwadar, a Pakistani port of economic significance to China, controlling Helmand allowed Washington to curb the influence of its main economic rival in the region.

He then went on to allege that the US and the UK were also interested in taking control of the drug production laboratories located in Helmand in a bid to profit from the international heroin business. The fourth reason, as alleged by Akhund, was Helmand's alleged uranium resources. In the Taliban commander's own words: "According to eyewitnesses, British forces are bringing a large amount of equipment to the area and have started extracting uranium there and British transport planes land and take off from this area several times every day."

Seen through the lens international conspiracy theory as expressed by Akhund, US rivalry with Iran and China, plus uranium and the heroin trade were the reasons why military operations were carried out in Marjah and Nade Ali districts of Helmand.

According to anecdotal evidence, Mullah Akhund's views reflected those of a majority in Afghanistan. The conspiracy theory came in variations but common to all versions was a denial of the fact that the violence had local roots and that the problem was self-created and self-perpetuated. It was this denial that was *moshtarak*, or shared, by all parties, from the government to the opposition and the Taliban.

Obama's Nocturnal Visit

It is not exactly a welcome, appreciated or fashionable view to claim that the key change in US-Afghan relations was of a personal nature. But there is no denial that Karzai's close relationship with ex-President Bush helped smooth the Afghano-American alliance. Theirs was an easy relationship that involved talking regularly via video conferencing, with Karzai sometimes having his son on his lap. The truth is that most Afghans have more in common with Republican Americans than their democrat counterpart. Both are religious, conservative and not keen on state-interference in family affairs or heavy taxation. But the situation changed radically when the democrats came to power, electing President Obama, a holier-than-thou sanctimonious figure, for whom Afghanistan represented everything that was despicable: lies and corruption, chaos and disorganization, not to speak of the pink elephant in the room, that fact that he was suspected of still being a Muslim by his opponents in the US and could not possibly appear overtly friendly to a zealously Muslim nation. And then there was the issue of a war that he had not instigated but inherited and needed to bring to an end. In terms of their new American benefactor-in-chief, the odds were against Afghans but they, as always, had no idea. Never happy with what they had, most Afghans welcomed Obama's coming to power, and, inevitably, stressed his Muslim background.

To distance himself from Bush's close friendship with Karzai, Obama decided to neglect Afghanistan for a while. Or maybe he was just dithering because between 2008 and 2010 he was chiefly becoming famous for his indecisiveness. It was another snub that was a serious blow to Kabul—it signaled that with Bush gone, the US was no longer committed to Afghanistan. Obama finally paid a (we presume, much-dreaded) official visit to Kabul in March 2010, nearly two years into office. His visit was in tune with local traditions of hospitality: the guest arrived late and unannounced. But unlike his first visit as a presidential campaigner in 2008, Obama's departure after his first official presidential visit did not leave behind a silence filled with hope. Instead, rumours began to circulate in a vain attempt to make sense of this unexpected nocturnal visit. The notion that President Karzai had been kept in the dark about the visit until a mere hour before Obama's arrival was particularly embarrassing for the Afghan public, and was immediately dismissed by the government spokesman who reassured Afghans that they had been given three full days to prepare for Obama.

Be that as it may, the exact words exchanged at the meeting were not made public, leaving local media outlets with little choice but to interpret the visit in the absence of confirmed facts. A striking interpretation that emerged in the media and blogosphere linked Obama's visit to President Karzai's shift in foreign policy, which had become more provocative. This policy was expressed through Karzai paying official visits to Tehran and Beijing, Washington's key rivals in the region. Karzai's trip to China resulted in the signing of three major trade and economic deals, putting Sino-Afghan relations on solid ground. His visit to Tehran, which coincided with the Persian and Afghan New Year celebrations, had little economic impact, but was loaded with the symbolic meaning of a shared culture and history, linking Kabul to Tehran.

Karzai's intention to forge new regional alliances in preference to relying solely on US patronage was clear, but this change of heart was in part also a result of Washington's own policy. After all, in its eagerness to distance itself from Bush's legacy of "US leniency towards corruption" in Afghanistan, the Obama administration had repeatedly humiliated President Karzai, treating him like a naughty schoolboy rather than the leader of an ally country. In theory, such pressure should have resulted in a more efficient, corruption-free administration in Kabul. In reality, the move drove the Afghan leader straight into the arms of US's rivals in the region. President Karzai's critics in the media labeled his provocative foreign policy "an act of adventurism, reeking of political immaturity," but the fact remained that by contrast to the US, regional powers such as India, China, and even Iran, were seen as capable of delivering more efficient and less costly reconstruction work in Afghanistan. More importantly, they could do reconstruction without the patronizing democracy and reform sermons that had accompanied US reconstruction efforts in Afghanistan since Obama came to power.

Obama's visit could have been triggered by Washington's realization that Kabul was in danger of slipping away from the US orbit of influence, and entering the sphere of influence occupied by US rivals. If this was true, then, the realization was quite likely to have had occurred too late. In the words of one newspaper, "there is little doubt that these days, Karzai is no longer a politician who measures himself against the benchmark of US priorities. He has gained sufficient political self-confidence to allow him to choose his government's direction by himself."

It appeared that the trendy theory making the rounds in Washington since Obama's presidency—a theory which assumed that a stick and carrot approach was bound to result in better government because it forced aid-dependent states to reform in order to please donor nations—had failed to yield the desired results in Kabul. Instead of opting for reform, and so winning over the Afghan public, Karzai decided to seek the patronage of regional powers. Washington's plan backfired, but not surprisingly so. After all, Afghan leaders had always been notorious for their unpredictability, and the country itself was known to be too complex to fit into neat theories—no matter how fashionable or valid they might have appeared in their time.

Fear, Hope and Loathing in Kabul

If ex-President Bush was seen as a simpleton, Obama, his serious, intellectual and complex replacement, turned out to be a mixed blessing for Afghans. His dithering was felt keenly among Afghans on the ground and abroad, who thought that he was sending Afghans mixed signals. In his campaign months, Obama had gained fame as an excellent communicator both in the US and at international meetings but in Afghanistan his clarity of thought had disappeared in the fog of war.

When he came to power, the people of Afghanistan wanted a clear stance from him. They wanted to know whether he was or was not serious about fighting terrorism. But three months into his presidency, the general feeling among Afghans was that he was not serious—at least not as serious as he appeared to be during his campaign for presidency. In the polite words of Afghan daily, *Hasht-e Sobh*, "The main concern felt in progressive and civil society circles is that the international community, the US in particular, might negotiate with terrorists and bargain the people's fundamental rights in the process."

In other words, Afghans feared that the US might offer the Taliban a role in the government in return for abandoning the pursuit of democracy and human rights in Afghanistan. This was a terrifying thought for all those Afghans who had risked their lives to fight for women's rights, freedom of speech and civil society. According to Hasht-e Sobh, if such suspicion turned out to be true, "the biggest loser in the deal would be the US itself." The paper continued: "This is because the US came here to spread and support democracy and to fight terrorists. The same terrorists who eight years earlier, on 11 September, created such widespread fear in America that the whole world became witness to their horror."

But who was negotiating with whom and where? As always, rumours abounded about this and were presented as reports in the Afghan media. According to the Afghan daily Nokhost, which in turn quoted anonymous sources, a representative of Gulboddin Hekmatyar (renegade jihadi leader and troublemaker par excellence) had visited Washington, having already handed over a letter from Hekmatyar to US authorities. The content of the letter? Fix a date for US troops' withdrawal and Hekmatyar would cooperate in establishing a coalition government in Kabul.

In an article published on the Russo-Afghan news website Afghan-Ru, Dr Shah Massoud, an Afghan expert in international relations, said that US special envoy Richard Holbrooke and his staff had already held meetings with Taliban representatives, some in Pakistan, some in Dubai and yet others in Kabul's Serena Hotel where an entire floor had been booked under the name of the ex-US envoy to the United Nations, Zalmay Khalilzad. The meetings discussed the possibility of drafting a new Afghan constitution, presumably to include more Taliban ideology and less democracy. This would also explain why Zalmay Khalilzad, ironically himself a chief architect of the present constitution, had announced that Afghanistan was in need of a new constitution.

In the words of Dr Shah Massoud, "We all know that there is neither friendship nor enmity in politics. The United States created the Taliban to begin with in order to reach its own goals in the region and even now, it is aware that making use of the Taliban is the only option for the US to avoid further American casualties and to achieve America's goals in an easy and financially affordable manner." According to Dr Massoud, in the near future, we were to expect to witness the establishment of new oppressive regimes, from military dictatorships to suffocating theocracies, in strategic regional areas such as Afghanistan and Pakistan, Iran and Iraq. All these regimes would be oppressive but they would all be allies of the US administration.

The fear of abandonment (once again the world was seeing us as a trap that they need to escape from) was somewhat eased when Washington finally took a clear stance regarding the regional powers surrounding Afghanistan. Afghan commentators welcomed US secretary of state Hillary Clinton's encouragement of Iran and Pakistan to play a positive role in the country's stabilization. This happened in The Hague during a conference called "Afghanistan's Future." While the world media was reporting friendly meetings between US and Iranian officials, the people of The Hague were flying kites in solidarity with the Afghan people. The colorful kites were an Oxfam initiative and a reminder to the world leaders not to forget ordinary Afghans on the ground during their high-level schmoozing.

President Karzai was quick to welcome the new approach towards the neighboring countries. He said: "There will be no success in the fight against terrorism without true cooperation on the part of the neighboring countries. Indeed, winning is impossible without them." *Nokhost* daily was equally positive about the new approach: "The US presence in Afghanistan has for a long time caused worry to some of the regional countries and Afghanistan's neighbors. Afghanistan needs to reassure its neighbors about the US presence in the country so that they can help Afghans with peace of mind."

Sayed Hossein Olomi Balkhi, an MP for Kabul province, was also supportive of the new regard for the country's neighbors. "The regional countries reacted positively to the proposal and did not try to take revenge from Nato and the US. If they wanted revenge, they could have said no and could have abandoned Nato in this swamp and this would have resulted in defeat— Nato's defeat in Afghanistan which in turn would have meant Nato's dissolution."

Olomi added that it was in the interests of the neighboring countries to fight against terrorism because if the struggle was lost in Afghanistan, the threat of terrorism would spill over to their countries. Dr Massoud expressed a similar warning but put it in much stronger words: "The neighboring countries should beware that if the foreign troops leave Afghanistan, a war will break out in the country and this in itself will be a serious threat to the whole region. The US's priority is security for its own people, but not security in Afghanistan. An example for this is George Bush's suggestion to the Taliban prior to 11 September to hand over Osama Bin Laden in return for US protection of the Taliban's regime. That's why the neighboring countries should no longer pin their hopes on the US to sort out Afghanistan."

Months after Obama's coming to power, it became clear that the future of Afghanistan chiefly depended on the goodwill of its neighbors, Iran and Pakistan.

The British Policy Shift

"Your hand is open from here all the way to London" is an Afghan saying that means "do whatever you have in your power, I don't care." The saying is a hangover from the nineteenth century when Britain controlled foreign policy in Afghanistan. Those days are gone but the saying has remained, though Afghans are no longer sure exactly how much say Britain has in Afghanistan by comparison to its US ally. From an Afghan perspective, the Anglo-American relationship as played out in Afghanistan was marked by a lack of harmony. What was becoming clear to Afghans over time was that the US was the real power in Afghanistan while the UK had little impact but still stubbornly refused to follow the US's line of policy.

This was the mood in Afghanistan when Gordon Brown paid a surprise visit to Afghans in 2009. If the local papers were excited about the visit, they managed to conceal it. Or maybe they just weren't excited. Either way, Brown had the same effect on both Afghans and the British. People just didn't get excited about him.

But the BBC's Afghan service took the visit seriously, and dedicated its weekly radio program *Your Voice* to Brown's visit. The British Prime Minister, after all, had a new Afghan strategy. The BBC summed up the main points of this new strategy as seen from an Afghan perspective. Firstly, the strategy appeared to be more in harmony with the plans of the US administration, and this was considered a positive development. Afghan experts had repeatedly pointed out that the lack of co-ordination in the policies of the various western countries involved in Afghanistan was a serious problem. The fact that it took Britain seven years to understand this did not surprise local experts: they were aware that the international community had landed in Kabul and Kandahar armed with unrealistic optimism and a limited understanding of the region's complexity.

In the opinion of Nasrullah Stanekzai, a political analyst and professor of law at Kabul University, there were two reasons why the international community had failed to come up with a unified approach towards Afghanistan. Stanekzai told the BBC: Firstly there has been a lack of knowledge of the country and the region. The various countries involved in Afghanistan initially did not expect to encounter a crisis. They assumed that they would be doing a straightforward security mission and then would be leaving the country. They assumed that stability could be ensured. Secondly, the countries involved are obviously pursuing their own, separate but specific interests while at the same time engaging in a common fight against terrorism.

The second crucial point of the new British strategy as seen from an Afghan perspective was Britain's changed view of Pakistan. Afghan diplomats and officials had been painfully aware of Pakistan's advantage in influencing London's views, analysis and approach to Afghanistan. A former British colony, with an Oxbridge-educated elite fluent in English and familiar with the workings of the British parliament, Pakistani diplomats and military advisers had been able to take advantage of their privileged position in influencing Britain's Afghan policy in a manner most useful to Pakistan. Afghanistan, by contrast, was just beginning to train its own class of western-educated citizens with degrees from top British and American universities. The country's established intelligentsia was largely made up of Russian speakers whose English lacked the power of persuasion. Even the foreign minister of the time, Dadfar-Spanta, a much-respected academic and polyglot, was fluent in German but not yet fully in English.

Having had the privilege of meeting Fulbright and other Afghan scholars in the US, I found the students intelligent, hard-working and more importantly, displaying the sort of positive patriotism that was largely missing among current Afghan politicians. Individually, the students had been taking matters into their own hands, giving public lectures, meeting US politicians and trying to help the American public understand Afghanistan better. This mammoth task was carried out with little support from the Afghan government, leaving students with the unsettling feeling that they were operating in a vacuum.

Equally disappointing was their experience of dealing with the US embassy in Kabul when applying for scholarships. In the words of one scholar I met, "in terms of efficiency, they are hardly any better than us [Afghans]. It takes them a year to work on your application and then they end up misspelling your name." Comparing the Afghan situation with its Pakistani equivalent, Islamabad's diplomatic advantage over Afghanistan was obvious. That was the main reason why Afghans mostly welcomed Brown's new strategy, because Britain no longer saw Pakistan as a strong and reliable ally, but rather a troubled country facing the same threat of violent extremism as Afghanistan. From an Afghan angle, this meant that the UK was no longer prone to Islamabad's manipulation and Afghanistan would no longer be seen through a Pakistani lens. In brief, the shift in strategy was seen as good news.

The strategy's two final aspects included the strengthening of indigenous democratic structures such as shuras and jirgas and improving the capacity of the Afghan army and police force. Needless to say, the goal of creating a strong army of 134,000 troops was just about the only policy that had comprehensive support from all political sides in Afghanistan.

The Price of Success

There were two words that summed up the international community's chief preoccupation with Afghanistan since Obama's coming to power. The magic words were: the impact! Everything depended on the impact and questions were thrown around in a panic. What exactly is our impact on Afghanistan? How do we measure our impact? Has our impact been a good or a bad one? The impact question was raised during the phase of "let's get the hell out of here." To be fair, the leftwing camp of anti-interventionists had done a fair bit of publicity work, convincing the public abroad that the only impact of the mission had been dead Afghans and more hatred towards the West. There was hardly ever good news from Afghanistan, even though plenty of good things had happened.

To give you just one example, I returned to my former school and found an institution that could in every way compete with European equivalents. Ten years earlier, the school had been turned into a Taliban madrasa for boys and books were burned for fire to make tea. Now, corporal punishment was banned by law; a nursery catered for teachers with kids; there was a fully stocked library and the gardens were looked after. The school hadn't had it this good since its foundation in the 1940s. The impact was positive but the view that something good could have come as a side-effect of the invasion was no longer acceptable in most media outlets abroad. When I wrote a positive article about the impact, the comments left underneath my article were full of accusations of selling out to cultural imperialism and the even more bizarre claim that I was a CIA agent. It was a lose-lose situation, the damage had been done and the world was getting tired of Afghanistan.

I used to turn my frustration into comedy, talking to my sources in Kabul. An impact that was always missed out of the debates, we decided, was just how many young Afghan males managed to lose their virginity abroad. Prior to 2001, a young man had to either get married or travel to Tajikistan and visit a sex worker in order to lose his virginity. With scholarships, workshop, conference and seminar trips, a whole new sexual world had opened up for Afghan men. The virgins lost their virginity and the rest learned new tricks, taught to them by kindhearted Western women. There was, we can safely assume, quite a bit of compassionate sex going on because everybody knew that the men were returning to a dry spell that could last for years.

But to return to the less frivolous side of the question, it was in 2009 when global media organizations asked Afghans if they had seen any improvement in their lives since 2001. The question, of course, made the dubious assumption that five years of Taliban rule was an appropriate benchmark against which to measure success. After all, the Taliban period was hardly typical of governance in Afghanistan: it was an exception to the traditional patterns of political leadership in which legitimacy was hereditary and restricted to members of tribes of royal ancestry. "Anyone can do better than the Taliban," my colleague used to say whenever the question arose.

He was right. The Taliban leader, Mullah Omar, was a village preacher from an obscure tribe. He would have had little chance of leading the country under normal circumstances. His rise to power was a direct consequence of the jihad against the Soviets, which resulted in the Afghan state's loss of an already tenuous monopoly of violence over its citizens and the political empowerment of ethnic minorities, minor tribes and lesser-known political figures.

Flanked by a pre-war system of tribal aristocracy and the wartime anarchy of weaponry and piety, the central government struggled to gain a monopoly of violence in the face of armed irregulars, of whom the Taliban was merely the best known. The rest was Afghan history as we knew it.

While the convenient label of "Taliban" suggested a coherent dichotomy of players, the real picture was more confused. Mullah Omar was only one example of the rise to power of ambitious men of obscure backgrounds from historically neglected regions. The ruthlessness of such strongmen earned them many critics, but the diffusion of power that they embodied represented a democratization of sorts, albeit of an anarchistic rather than parliamentary kind. In an officialization of the de facto empowerment of such figures, many were co-opted into the post-Taliban administration as a direct result of the 2001 invasion. This legitimised the strongmen's place in society, ensuring that the wartime diffusion of power carried through. In spite of the exclusion of Mullah Omar himself, the gun-and-scripture politics he represented did make the transition into "democratic" power, for better or worse.

Be that as it may, the 2001 military mission was to topple the Taliban. It was only natural that when the anniversary of the invasion arrived, the media asked Afghans about the changes in their lives since the Taliban's fall: the news does, after all, have a short memory. The answers given in blogs, editorials and BBC Farsi's *Your Voice* program revealed Afghans to be deeply divided when it came to measuring the mission's success. The views expressed ranged from, "at least we have a degree of freedom of expression and can decide whether or not to sport a beard," to "this government is so corrupt that people seek refuge in Taliban judges because they are known for refusing to accept bribes."

Omid, a caller from Kabul, put it bluntly: "Let's be fair. The military occupation has created jobs and there are Afghans who are doing well, buying homes in Kabul and Dubai. Besides, if the foreign troops were to leave, there would be a civil war."

The military mission created economic opportunities, from cooks and taxi drivers to consultants, interpreters and advisers. Those Afghans who had carved themselves a niche in this economy were doing well. Those involved in illegal activities, from the drugs trade to taking bribes, were building themselves "opium palaces". The money in circulation could be regarded as *haraam* by some but the fact that a reversal of the situation was hardly likely to lead to a more moral society or a better economy made it easier to live with unethical side-effects of an invasion economy.

The fact remained that not all Afghans wanted to see the back of the foreign troops even though this was the predominant view offered to readers abroad. But there was general consensus that the money poured into the country had not been distributed evenly and the gap between the rich and the poor, urban and rural Afghanistan, was a fundamental trigger of the present violence.

Afghan blogger Abdul Hakim Tamana shared this view. In his *Notes from the Villages* blog, Tamana described a trip he had made to the remote province of Farah, which was becoming notorious for criminality and security incidents. There he met a community leader, Malek Afghan, and asked him a simple question: "How can we improve the living conditions of the local people?" The community leader's answer sent a shiver down Tamana's spine. "The people here are not very demanding. Just a loaf of bread is enough to make them happy."

Put yourself in the shoes of a farmer in Farah, said Tamana in his blog. Imagine you lose your harvest to drought and your animals to disease. Wouldn't you pick up a gun and demand your share in society's wealth by stopping travellers and asking for ransom? Wouldn't you disguise your criminal activity as political opposition and support for the Taliban? After all, who is the bigger criminal? A farmer committing petty crimes together with the Taliban or the minister in Kabul who asks for a share in bribe for construction projects costing millions? Tamana concluded that for many Afghans the present war was not about ideology but "a loaf of bread," which was to say an internal struggle for limited resources.

The small well-to-do middle class of Afghans and their criminal/insurgent counterparts respectively represented the success and the failure of the 2001 invasion. The mission created job opportunities for some and an excuse to carry on fighting for others. If Tamana's interpretation was correct, it all depended on the flow of cash and opportunity through the mountains and valleys of a fractured society.

Opium is All We Have

If you are Afghan and feeling down because there is hardly anything your country can be proud of, there is always the little consolation of poppies. At least we are number one world exporters of opium, we tell ourselves. Better than nothing, right? But the opium, like much else in Afghanistan, is a mixed blessing. Abroad, one can be held into account for it even if one has never seen a poppy in one's entire life. This is what happened to me one day when I had started a new student job. It was years ago but I will never forget the confrontation.

"It's because of you people that our children are dying of heroin addiction," said my boss in that encounter. He had just found out that I was Afghan and this was his kneejerk reaction. I stood my ground but I never forgot his exact words. President Karzai must have had similar encounters. That's why when he tours the West, he apologizes on behalf of his people: sorry for the poppies! Then back home he tells Afghans that drugs have tarnished their reputation abroad.

The truth is that for the majority of Afghan poppy farmers, reputation is the least of their worries. One of them summed up the reason: "Do you think they give us visas to go abroad anyway?" Their concern is much more acute. There is a video on YouTube that sums up the other side of the suffering that is caused by drug addiction. The footage shows poppy eradication in action in Helmand province. A horrified boy, crying and pointing at noisy tractors that are mowing down the poppies, says to the camera, "They are destroying our poppies. How are we going to eat with no money?" This is what Afghans call *zolom*; injustice and oppression of biblical proportions, as embodied in the qur'anic stories of the pharaohs. The Taliban understood this, exploited the desperation and came to the farmers' rescue. Later on in the same footage, you'll hear the sound of Taliban machine guns attacking an eradication team in Urozgan. The Taliban also use suicide bombers to attack government eradication campaigns. This is the Afghan side of the story. The government is protecting serious drug smugglers, while small farmers are forced to seek Taliban protection. Little wonder, then, that Afghans compare their government to a bowl of thin soup, it's so watery and lacking in substance.

Now let's look at the story outside of Afghanistan. I learned about this aspect between early 2005 and end of 2007 when poppies entered my professional life. As part of my job I'd sift through hundreds of local and international reports on the Afghan drugs trade and compile a monthly summary. The first time I saw the pile of reports, my heart sank at the sheer number of them. But my trainer reassured me: "You'll get a feel for it. Look out for new trends, official policy announcements and arrests." It sounded exciting, but I ended up disappointed. There were very few arrests, most of them along the Tajik border where petty smugglers were either caught or injured in shootouts. There was clearly not much money involved in such little smuggling ventures because on the way back from Tajikistan, solitary smugglers often tried to steal some cows in the process to make up their profits. As to foreign countries' policies, such was their repetitive nature that I soon had them memorized. You can still wake me up from deep sleep at three in the morning and ask: "What's Russia's stance on Afghan drugs?" And I can easily shoot back: "Angry at Nato's failure to control the situation and a desire for greater involvement. And they keep talking about the need for a security belt to cut off southern Russia from Afghan drug-trafficking routes. They plan to open an office in Kabul and they offer training to Afghan officials." At some point, eighteen Afghan officials were invited to be trained in counter-narcotics in Russia but they didn't show up, much to Russian annoyance.

And the Iranians? Also angry with Nato for the same reason. They say they are losing soldiers in shoot-outs with drug traffickers. They have threatened to build a wall along the Afghan border. There are reports that underage Afghan drug smugglers are kept imprisoned in Iran until they turn eighteen when they can be hanged. Iranian officials always deny such reports. The US? Keep suggesting aerial spraying. In one village the population suspected secret overnight spraying when they woke up to find mysterious diseases had affected their crop and livestock. Kabul promised an investigation but nothing happened. The UK? Against spraying but otherwise dithering, with no clear plan. Incidentally, the Taliban is equally divided when it comes to drugs policy. Some Taliban believe that rolling a joint after a good day of fighting is fine since Islam only bans alcohol explicitly but not cannabis. Others believe that the ban includes alcohol and all drugs. There has been some serious theological hairsplitting on this among the Taliban in Pakistan's Waziristan.

In view of this chaotic situation, it's not surprising that when it comes to the relationship between the drugs trade and the west, the Afghan rumour bazaar is bustling. Let me introduce you to one of the more outlandish theories making rounds and gaining ground. The theory is that the foreign forces stationed in Afghanistan are themselves involved in drug smuggling. What kind of feverish mind could have come up with this surreal story, you are asking? The answer is simple: Hollywood. The guilty party seems to have been the Ridley Scott movie *American Gangster*, which has fuelled people's imagination in Afghanistan about the way the West gets its drugs. The theory is that the film is not fictional but draws inspiration from what is happening in Afghanistan right now. In other words, that US army planes leave Afghanistan carrying coffins empty of bodies but filled with drugs instead. The champions of this conspiracy theory say this explains why poppy production has increased in exactly the same provinces where foreign troops are stationed. The rumour later took on pan-Asian proportions. Iranian official Ali Larijani was quoted as saying in Geneva that, "The majority of Afghan drugs are transported to the west via three airports that are under Nato control." The quote was published in an Iranian report with the title: "Revealed: The role of Nato airbases in transporting Afghan drugs to Europe." Iranian websites endlessly reproduced it.

Against this background of mistrust, it was not surprising that when Nato announced that its troops were to directly target the drugs business, the news fell flat on Afghans. Zalmai Afzali, the spokesperson for the Afghan counter-narcotics ministry, told a local newspaper: "We are not overtly optimistic because in the past, too, Nato made many promises that never materialized." Hajji Hanif Hanifi, an MP from Uruzgan province, said: "I don't think they'll succeed because in the last seven years, despite huge amounts of money and the use of the police force, the government failed to stop drug smuggling. So they are not going to succeed in the future either."

The Afghan paper *Hasht-e Sobh* had a different angle. An editorial headlined "Yet another strategic change" said, "The main facilitators, the biggest drug smugglers, do not reside in Afghanistan. Hence, it's not going to be easy to catch or arrest them."

With no clear and coherent drug policy between the Afghan government, the neighboring countries and the wider international community, few Afghans on the ground believe that the drugs business can be curbed.

Killer Fungus: Poppies and Politics

"Listen to this new song, it's quite fun," said a source, sending me the link to what seemed like a regular, traditional folklore tune. In the video, a bunch of young men had gathered together, sitting on a carpet as if at an outdoor picnic. Some of them played instruments, others clapped while the singer was engaged in a daring venture. He was singing a song that was an ode to smoking hashish. The bottom line of the song was, "We might be lethargic, lazy, layabouts, but hey, at least we don't cause any trouble. We are content with hashish, our best friend, soother of our pain, companion of our loneliness." For many Afghans, drugs are all they are left with to sooth the pain of trauma. For many others, it's their only source of income, the sole way to make quick money so you can marry, have a wife and children. The view on Afghan drugs on the ground is strikingly different to the way it's regarded abroad.

It was in this vein that when reports of a "mysterious" fungus damaging opium poppy crops in Afghanistan hit international headlines in 2010, on the ground the "mystery" was seen as an open secret. Helmand farmers interviewed by BBC Pashto service for the early-morning news program, for example, were convinced that "they" had deliberately destroyed the crops.

The pronoun "they" is a euphemism for US secret agents, whom farmers suspect of having sprayed the crops with the fungus. Afghan farmers have been cultivating opium poppies for a considerable period of time. This allowed them to distinguish between natural causes and artificially induced problems.

The accusations of Afghan farmers were bound to be ignored. The government lacked the necessary equipment to conduct proper research. The United Nations Drugs Office in Afghanistan was conducting research but the institution was no longer widely trusted. As with all other mysterious incidents in Afghanistan, this story too was bound to be lost and forgotten in the fog of war.

When the report of the fungus was first published, a reliable source directed me to the Sunshine Project, a now-suspended non-profit organization. In 2000, this international NGO had published a report about "dangerous US fungus experiments," warning against the potentially harmful impact of the fungus on biodiversity in the target drug-producing regions. The report said: "The strains of the fungi *fusarium oxysporum* and *pleospora papveracae* might infect and kill plants other than coca, poppy and cannabis in ecologically sensitive areas of Asia and the Americas."

An indication of the potential risks caused by the use of such fungi, tailored to affect drug-producing plants, was the fact that their use was banned in the United States itself. Further investigation into the fungi showed that their production and use was bordering on illegal. According to the Sunshine Project report, the US had created genetically modified strands of the fungus, and this, in turn, meant that the product could be classified as a biological weapon.

Farmers in Afghanistan regarded the disease affecting their crops as artificially induced but they were probably unaware of the manner in which the crop samples were in all likelihood collected. To trace the probable route of sample collection would lead us to a BBC Panorama program entitled *Britain's Secret War on Drugs*, broadcast in 2000.

The report took viewers to Uzbekistan, to a Soviet laboratory that was set up to conduct research into biological weapons. The laboratory was abandoned after the collapse of the Soviet Union but resumed operation with funding provided by US and British governments. It was in this laboratory that *pleospora papaveracea*, the fungus that affects opium poppies, was discovered, becoming the Soviet Union's first biological weapon.

Professor Abdusattar, a scientist working at the laboratory, explained to the BBC Panorama reporter, Tom Mangold, that samples from Afghanistan were provided with help from the US embassy.

Scientists working on the fungus back in 2000 said that the fungus was safe, affecting opium poppies only and that it represented no danger to the environment and was unlikely to spread to other regions. In a manner that was typical of scientists, it was pointed out that this assessment was to the best of scientific knowledge. A reasonable disclaimer but hardly reassuring. An interesting aspect of the fungus research was the fact that leading fungus researchers joined the UN's Drugs Control Programme and their endorsement helped to ensure British and American governments' funding of the project.

Research for a product bordering on illegality, funded with taxpayers' money from the United States and the United Kingdom, had led to the creation of a lethal weapon against opium poppy crops in Afghanistan.

Whether the fungus that affected the crops in Afghanistan was in fact *pleospora papaveracea* was far from clear. The UN Office on Drugs and Crime in Kabul was conducting sample research and turned out to be unable to confirm the identity of the disease.

But farmers in Afghanistan were convinced that the disease had been artificially induced. They suspected that Kabul's allies in London and Washington were involved. The loss of the crop was bound to subject small farmers to financial hardship and the consequences were bound to be felt by entire families. Young girls were likely to become the first victims of the situation as small farmers would not be able to pay their debts and offer the family's young girls for marriage in substitution for the missing cash.

The resentment felt among farmers was also bound to further drive them into the sphere of influence of the Taliban insurgents who present themselves as friends and protectors. Environmentalist activists in Afghanistan were equally likely to feel disenchanted as the contradictions between official policy of environmentalism advocated by London and Washington and the realities on the ground failed to make sense. If women's rights groups in the US and the UK were outraged by the fact that young Afghan girls were traded for debt, the fact that their own governments might have implicitly supported policies that increased risks for young girls was even more puzzling to Afghan women activists on the ground.

Perhaps the most pertinent aspect of debates about the Afghan drugs trade is the lack of discussion of the other side: the consumer markets in the urban centers of the western world which have turned opium poppy into a lucrative cash crop in a country in persistent threat of famine. To discuss the Afghan drugs trade in isolation from the markets that it supplies is not only morally questionable, it is also a denial of the social problems that lead to addiction from Moscow, to Paris and London. The small farmers of Afghanistan may not be entirely innocent but they certainly are as vulnerable as the addicts they supply.

The Devils, Dogs and Drama of Democracy

The polite word to use for describing Afghanistan would be the euphemism "interesting." Politically-speaking, it is a strange country. Here is why: Afghanistan is officially a democracy. It is also an Islamic Republic. In some parts of the country, it is an Islamic Republic by day and a Taliban-run Emirate by night. Depending on the situation, a contested district can switch "regimes," going back and forth between an Islamic Republic and a Taliban-run Emirate sometimes for weeks on end. In addition, there are independent shadow fiefdoms under war-lord command—they do not exist officially on paper but are real. The fiefdoms, just like the Taliban's Emirate, are ghost governments because their existence is not officially recognized. As is the nature of any authoritarian regime, these mini-kingdoms' policies depend on the tastes and predilections of the self-appointed dictator in charge. Some fiefdoms famously support women's rights, while others have gone back to the sixteenth century, turning provincial headquarters into Mughal courts, complete with musical soirees, court jesters and an entourage of sycophants. Depending on exactly in which part of Afghanistan you are, you are bound to encounter a different political system in action.

The official government and its ghost mini-rival regimes co-exist in a geographical space where presidential elections are held every five years. Most Afghans are illiterate and rely on their audio-visual abilities to identify and recognize the candidates they support. The election period is inevitably a visually demanding time, with entire walls turning into collages of political imagery. Candidates who intend to project Islamic conservatism inevitably sport a turban and a beard and have pompously pious names. To give you a taste, a name of this category would translate as, "Slave to Allah and Lover of Islam." The Islamists' rivals, by contrast, dress in suit and tie and have clean-shaven faces. Their last names are along the lines of "Cares for Humanity." The posters of pretty female candidates are particularly popular and usually end-up as pin-ups in markets, shops and teenaged boys' rooms.

If, in the past, aristocratic pedigree and personal reputation were keys to entering a successful political career, nowadays becoming famous through TV appearances can suffice to land a woman or man a seat in parliament. Let me repeat, ours is a largely illiterate society, so fame and reputation is a must for anyone who wants to have an impact as a politician, community leader, or businessman. As a result of having caught up with the rest of the world where media and politics are intertwined, there are at least two former entertainers in parliament in Afghanistan while some already established MPs are in danger of becoming more famous as entertainers than for their political views. There are regular bottle and shoe-throwing incidents in parliament and the culprits are often women MPs. The most notorious of such fighting scenes involved a female MP whose shoe attack and hair pulling resulted in one MP being sent to hospital for serious injury. The public reaction, "Oh yes, outside of parliament she's a famous gangster."

Be that as it may, elections are being held regularly in Afghanistan and like everything else in life the picture is neither white nor black. It's sort of grey.

Afghan Women and Politics: Family is King

Let's enter a time machine and speed back to 2001. We would find an unexpected new global cause for concern in the shape of the proverbial burqa-clad Afghan woman. When I was growing up in Kabul in the 1980s, I was used to women wearing all sorts of clothes. My school teachers' dresses stopped at just below their knees and their heads were bare. My art teacher was bottle blonde and with her stiffly sprayed coiffure, she contributed her fair share to damaging the ozone layer. In the poorer neighborhoods, women wore burqas but also hung their often massive bras to dry in public view. I am fairly confident that no-one even noticed those bras. People had more urgent problems to deal with. The issue of Afghan women's oppression was taken up by the communist regime, with publicity campaigns, television programs and women-only literacy classes. But it was only in 2001 that Afghan women became an international political concern. Let's go back to our time machine and enter the "negotiation with the Taliban era" that was officially launched with the Obama administration. The result for Afghan women was that they became increasingly concerned about their future. There was pressure on Kabul to negotiate with the Taliban so that the foreign troops could leave without losing face. Women feared that with the withdrawal of the foreign troops, the pursuit of their rights in Afghanistan would be altogether abandoned.

But even though this turn of events was alarming, the fact that it happened was not surprising. After all, the introduction of gender politics in Afghanistan was fraught with problems from the onset. It was a noble venture that meant well but it neglected the fact that individual rights were meaningless in a traditional

191

society where the place of both men and women was defined through their membership of a family and then, by extension, a clan. Given this context, Afghan women simply could not be liberated or empowered in isolation from their families. To empower the women, the whole society had to be empowered. But this reality was too complex to fit into the kind of neat, good-versus-evil moral binary that was needed to provide an ethical context to Operation Enduring Freedom of 2001.

As a result, Afghan society was presented to the world through the prism of gender politics as a nation divided between male aggressors and female victims. The campaign was initially successful and encouraged Afghans to wash their dirty linen in public, allowing the more outrageous cases of domestic violence to become the subject of international press stories. The loss of dignity and respect that accompanied the press revelations was the price Afghans had to pay if they wanted to sustain international interest in their country and ensure the continuous flow of aid.

But times changed and in 2010, when the mutilated face of Bibi Aisha (whose husband had cut off her nose) was put on the front cover of Time Magazine, the publicity campaign did little to stop London, Kabul and Washington from pursuing negotiations with the Taliban. The misogynist enemies of yesterday had become sought-after negotiating partners of an age of American and European austerity. The international community needed the Taliban's loyalty in order to leave the country without losing face. A vast majority of Afghan women anticipated this scenario early on and rather wisely decided not to get involved in gender politics.

Despite their widespread illiteracy, most Afghan women had the sense to realize that the international gender politics introduced to their country in 2001 were beyond Afghans' own control and because of this fact, it was not worth the risk of antagonizing their own families by allying themselves openly with the new politics of gender equality.

In three decades of war, regimes had come and gone and international politics had shifted beyond recognition. But the family had remained, allowing the survival of millions of people way before Afghan women were discovered as a worthy moral cause of international concern.

Afghan families were far from perfect but they had the advantage of resting on centuries of tradition (albeit of a flawed kind) rather than relying on whimsical policies formulated in the distant cities of London, New York and Washington. Weighing up the pros and cons of individual liberation in a traditional society versus the merits of sticking to tried and tested traditions, most women opted for the latter. This tactic was proven wise when Joe Biden blurted out that the US was to leave Afghanistan by 2014 "come hell or high water."

If a vast majority of Afghan women regarded the post-2001 gender politics with a healthy dose of suspicion, the Afghan political clans were quick to make use of the new opportunities, placing their own women in positions of power. The conflict of interest that affected ordinary Afghan women did not exist for the women of elite jihadi and technocrat clans currently in charge of the country. After all, by taking over political posts, far from antagonizing their families, these women further legitimised and expanded their family's scope of influence.

Having so extended the family's sphere of power, they also gained international accolade and fame, which was an added bonus. Few people outside Afghanistan realized that many of these women owed their rise to power not so much to personal merit but to the exalted position of their families. After all, politics in Afghanistan is often nothing more than thinly disguised private businesses run by elite families.

This is not to dismiss the small number of genuine grassroots women's rights activists who owe their prominence to their own effort, bravery and intelligence. But, as several crises surrounding women's shelters revealed, the women co-opted in the government ended up siding with the political establishment even at the cost of compromising the safety of their fellow Afghan women. Gender solidarity is something that has yet to emerge in a traditional society where women have internalized the male values of clan solidarity and political rivalry. That is why ordinary women and women of the ruling class alike tend to side with their families, even if their families stand for misogynist values or support the Taliban.

This truth, in turn, has allowed women's rights to be reduced to a mere smokescreen for the expansion of family-run, politico-financial ventures thinly disguised as politics. International politics, including in the guise of gender politics, might come and go in Afghanistan but the family is there to stay.

The First Presidential Debate

'We were a generation that had never known happiness, spending most of our lives on the run, knocking on door after door. Our shoes were hand-outs from our neighbors, our dreams secondhand. We watched others support their presidential candidates, and vote for them in terrifying excitement. But we didn't know what it felt like to elect your own president. We had become used to envying others for what they had. We had never owned anything.'

Written in Dari-Persian, these were the words of the poet Reza Mohammadi, summing up the feelings of an entire generation about the 2009 elections in Afghanistan. In July of 2009, Afghans had reason to be proud. The independent TV station *Tolo* aired live the country's first presidential debate. It ran smoothly. Regardless of the outcome, the debate marked a historic moment in the democratization of Afghanistan.

Links and information were shared rapidly via Facebook, allowing expatriates and locals alike to watch and listen no matter how far they were from Kabul. Comments rained in, but the common feeling was one of achievement. "I wished President Karzai had attended the debate; he could have had a share in our success," said observer Qasim Akhgar in a follow-up discussion program aired by *Tolo TV* and its sister stations *Lemar TV* and *Arman* radio.

Twenty-four hours before the broadcast, President Karzai pulled out of the debate. His campaign team came up with a contradictory set of explanations. The invitation had arrived too late; the TV station has violated media laws. And then the now banned Kabulpress website quoted Karzai's own bloke-in-the-bazaar words, a polemical style that he reserves for addressing ordinary Afghans: "Brothers, first I need to know whether the guy who I'll be up against and debating with is an Afghan or not? I mean, is he really an Afghan or has he been sent from abroad just to put me under pressure? Is he just some guy who's kept his foreign passport safe with the US embassy so he can do a disappearing act if he doesn't beat me?"

The jibe was intended for Ashraf Ghani, a World Bank economist and one of Karzai's two main rivals. Bearing in mind that Karzai himself for many years boasted of having the US's support as his main asset, the comment was somewhat ironic. Eager to downplay these old associations, Karzai banned a website for displaying a photograph of him looking disheveled and surrounded by a group of US special forces.

The photograph was taken in Urozgan during the early days of his career as Afghanistan's US-backed interim president. To be fair to Karzai, he is not the first Afghan leader to land in Afghanistan in a foreign helicopter and surrounded by foreign soldiers. The mujahedin leaders landed at Bagram air base in a Pakistani helicopter in the 1990s and before them, the Soviets flew in their candidate, President Babrak Karmal, in their Sikorsky.

Even if Karzai pulled out at the last minute, what did Afghans make of this first presidential debate which, in the absence of the president himself, was held between the two other candidates, Ashraf Ghani and former foreign minister, Abdullah Abdullah? Ghani stood out for his clear and specific economic policies but his understanding of Afghan politics was generally viewed as unsatisfactory. Abdullah, by contrast, was vague on economic questions but displayed a superior grasp of the working of Afghan politics and society. The candidates were civil to each other and shared a common criticism of Karzai's administration, even though both had a role in shaping it early on. Some Karzai opponents believe that the two rivals should join hands and campaign against Karzai as a team.

Their skills complement each other and their belonging to the two main ethnic groups, Abdullah a Tajik and Ghani a Pashtun, is seen as an added electoral asset. But there's one problem: their egos. Afghan leaders are famous for their reluctance to share power. They would rather preside over a smaller faction than abdicate power for the cause of the greater good and in doing so, become a mere deputy. As an Afghan saying has it, no one wants to be a dime; everyone wants to be a dollar. In any case, Karzai was the clear loser in this first presidential debate. His opponents accused him of cowardice while his supporters wished he had joined in even if only to prove his rivals wrong.

Be that as it may and despite the initial enthusiasm, not all Afghans are hopeful about this election. For some critics, the race between Karzai and Ghani is no mark of progress and only a continuation of the old tribal rivalry of Durrani versus Ghilzai Pashtuns for the leadership of Afghanistan. Karzai is a Durrani; Ghani, like Mullah Omar, is a Ghilzai which is why Ghani has reportedly claimed that unlike Karzai, he is capable of persuading the Taliban to negotiate peace. Accusations of ethnic nationalism and discrimination against non-Pashtuns have been leveled against Ghani though his main weakness appears to be his short fuse and his over-reliance on Western support. His choice of an American campaign advisor, James Carville, has not helped his cause.

By contrast to Ghani, Abdullah has been accused of keeping his head down for the sake of political expediency and not speaking up for any clear policy so as to keep his options open. Abdullah's critics claim his term as foreign minister from 2001 to 2006 allowed corruption to thrive, pointing out that his staff turned the Afghan embassy in the crucial neighboring capital of Tehran into a lucrative business, trading national assets such as precious stones and historical artifacts.

Such accusations are serious but then again, hardly any Afghan politician is free of allegations of corruption, racism or even espionage. Afghans have no choice but to make do with who is on offer and even those who were unimpressed by the candidates couldn't help but be impressed by the debate itself. Karzai or no Karzai, with the studio lights, debates and make-up, Afghan politics had come a long way from the Loya Jirga held in a borrowed Bavarian beer tent in 2001.

Afghans Discredit Their Own Elections

There is a time in every child's life when you turn into a tape-recorder, repeating everything you hear your parents and other adults say around you. I was in that tape-recorder phase of development when one day I found myself with my family in a restaurant. The era was one of high intensity paranoia, with the communist regime's spies lurking in every corner. It just happened that I was very hungry and the food was late and behind our table was seated one such spy. My parents noticed him immediately and they also became alarmed at my increased irritation. They knew that I was in my tape-recorder phase and was likely to repeat the words I had heard them say frequently whenever they felt angry. Something along the lines of "fuck this regime." Alarmed, they first tried to distract me with silly questions and then just grabbed me, put me in the car and told me bluntly, "You nearly got us all killed."

Given this history of living under brutal regimes, it would be reasonable to expect that Afghans would have welcomed democracy with joyous celebrations. No-one, after all, loses his head for insulting the government or laughing at the president. But we are a strange people and democracy is sort of taken for granted. Perhaps it's because it was a gift rather than a right that Afghans had fought for. It certainly didn't help that Afghan Mooj leaders destroyed the former parliament building in their civil war and were then rewarded with a brand new building. The truth is that Afghans didn't shed a drop of blood for democracy and didn't pay a cent for it. It's something that happened to them and they deal with it in their own eccentric way.

And so, when the Afghan 2009 election campaign officially opened, the people of Kabul woke up to a city covered in images of presidential hopefuls. "We are not in love with your faces," said an editorial in *Hasht-e Sobh* newspaper, pointing out that none of the candidates had come up with a solid plan for the country's future. "One of them is wearing a Pakol hat, the other a tie, and another a home-spun woolly. Are they taking us for a ride?" it said.

The following day, at least half of the posters were torn, triggering speculation in the local media. Who was tearing the posters and why? Karzai's rivals? Angry Afghans? Or a bunch of trouble-makers paid to vandalize the city? Pajhwok news agency sent out a journalist to investigate and discovered that the culprits were children. To be more precise, schoolboys between the ages of seven and fourteen who vandalized the posters on their way home after school. One of them explained his action with "I don't like them." He was asked "why" and he said: "Why not? I don't have to like them."

Even those posters with Obama campaign copycat "support change" messages were obviously not enough. The people wanted public debates between candidates, proper plans and solid strategies. Responding to this pressure, Karzai agreed on holding a public debate with key rival candidates. The president's nervous eye-twitching and increasingly incomprehensible speech had been causing alarm in the local media, raising doubts over Karzai's mental wellbeing. His agreeing to a debate was perhaps an attempt at dismissing such concerns.

But despite all its flaws—including voter registration cards distributed to newly-born babies (one of them was yet to be born, the birth year on the card was 2010); a candidate who was banned because he had smuggled drugs into the US in the 1990s; and the fact that twelve districts were under Taliban control and hence barred from voting—the 2009 presidential election was in some ways more interesting than the one of 2004.

The world had changed since 2004 and so had Afghanistan. Regionally, the US's magic spell as the global police force had broken due to its failure to curb the Taliban insurgency. This, in turn, had given Afghanistan's neighbors a new burst of energy, and fresh hopes of influencing the country's future. Iran, in particular, had grown in confidence because of its successful bullying of the US in Iraq and elsewhere in the Middle East. Russia's interest had equally intensified, especially after the conflict in Georgia, which had given Russia's southern borders new strategic significance. Let's not forget India and Pakistan, whose proxy border conflict was in part being played out in Afghanistan via the Taliban insurgency.

On the ground in Afghanistan, nothing was the same. Ethnic minority leaders had lost their momentum largely because of their eagerness to trade their constituents' interests for favors from Karzai. The Hazara leadership was a prime example of this, having failed to solve the recurrent nomad versus settled Hazara population's conflict in Behsud. The conflict resulted in bloodshed last year and bloodshed was likely to reoccur as a solution was yet to be found. But more importantly, Karzai himself was no longer the same. He had started off as a hapless *gomnaam* or nobody, in constant need of direction from Zalmay

Khalilzad. But in 2009, Karzai had successfully managed to broker deals behind closed doors with potential presidential rivals, and so gained the endorsement of a powerful group of individuals which included leaders of Tajiks and Hazaras.

His magic trick? Offering ministerial and other lucrative government posts in return for endorsement or promising to turn districts into provinces and in doing so, artificially enhancing the power of provincial strongmen. For example, rumour had it that the Wahdat party's leadership, which has a mainly Hazara support base, was allegedly offered five ministries in return for endorsing Karzai's presidency. Karzai was successfully following the divide-and-rule principle in his own country.

Endorsement for Karzai at times took extraordinary forms. The head of the Afghan peace commission, Sebghatullah Mojaddedi, for example, told the nation that he had been given instructions from Allah to support Karzai. The divine intervention in the presidential campaign raised many eyebrows, leading to satire and mockery in the local media. Yet Mojaddedi's public pronouncement was only one example of how Afghan politicians were trying to adjust to democracy without radically departing from Afghan traditions.

The Mojaddedis had for long been Afghanistan's kingmakers, with the tradition of Sufi endorsement of political leadership going back to Ahmad Shah Abdali and the country's foundation. Yet a new generation of Afghan voters was increasingly demanding for a line to be drawn between the past and the present and for Afghanistan to become a proper democracy with democratic institutions, political parties and a federally-run government. They argued that the ad-hoc mixing of tradition with modern democratic structures was doomed to failure as Afghan traditions often resulted in ethnicized politics and personality cults, both of which undermined long-term stability.

Be this as it may, and judging by the local media reactions, Afghans were watching the election campaign with little enthusiasm. The US's reluctance to identify its favorite candidate had added to the confusion, as most Afghans found it hard to believe that Washington could be truly neutral in this game. The suspicion was justified, bearing in mind that the US was heavily involved in all aspects of Afghan life, from military operations to reconstruction, to the fight against the drugs trade. A pragmatic people, Afghans wanted to know who the US's favorite candidate was and support him rather than vote for Karzai and then watch the US resurrect local power-holders in an attempt to counter-balance a re-elected Karzai's weak and corrupt administration. But rightly or wrongly, the Obama administration was feigning neutrality.

The mood on the ground was best summed up by a friend and fellow Afghan who announced on his Facebook page, "No need to wait for election results. Karzai has already elected himself."

Empty Slogans of Change

Politics in Afghanistan is so complex that, dealing with it, one often feels like pulling one's hair out and shouting: "Can you please explain this craziness to me? Because as far as I am concerned, you guys just don't make sense." Needless to say, to Afghans who unlike me have not lived for many years in genuine democratic societies, their politics makes perfect sense and that's why they do what they do the way they do. And what they do sometimes appears to me as seriously crazy. So when the 2009 Afghan presidential election arrived, I paid close attention to the way Afghans were handling democracy. The word itself had by then already become seedy-sounding. In Pashto, it sounded similar to a word that described the private parts of one's mother and people often used the Pashto version as a passive-aggressive joke.

A day before the 2009 presidential election Afghans were basking in the global media spotlight. The Taliban were staging spectacular attacks, aware that the violence would make international headlines and provide them with free publicity. Campaigners were driving up and down the country in vehicles covered in posters, courting the population with the promise of a better future. Free lunches, a rare concept in Afghanistan, became the rule in those days as campaigners fed the poor in the hope of getting votes in return for pilau rice. The poor, in turn, wished that every day would be a campaign day. Such charity, after all, was a rarity in the Islamic Republic of Afghanistan.

Democracy was apparently working small wonders in Afghanistan in 2009. Local newspapers quoted the Qur'an as evidence that there was no contradiction between Islam and the principles of democracy. Presidential candidates invoked early Muslim history to show that the rule of the people was rooted in Muslim tradition. Debate instead of violence; citizenship instead of clientelism; nationhood instead of tribalism; all these noble principles were recurrent phrases in articles revealing the desires of progressive Afghans for their country. The second presidential debate was aired live on national TV and included Hamid Karzai. It was broadly interpreted as a sign that democracy was slowly taking root in Afghanistan. The cost of the election process: US$221m. Democracy didn't come cheap but in a country where humans were forced to live in caves for want of a roof over their heads, the electoral pomp did seem morally questionable to some.

After all, once the ballot was cast and a new government elected, the daily routine of struggling for the next meal would resume for the majority of Afghans and not much was likely to change. But still, slogans of change were on everyone's lips and President Karzai was adamant that if re-elected, he was going to bring peace to Afghanistan by holding negotiations with the Taliban. "Peace and security are an absolute must in Afghanistan," Karzai told the BBC's Afghan service hours before the presidential palace came under a rocket attack. No one was hurt in the attack but the Taliban managed to get their message across: even the president was not safe from the Taliban.

The Taliban made their presence felt in Kabul with suicide and rocket attacks targeting the supposedly safe diplomatic neighborhood. Elsewhere they told people not to vote—threatening to cut off the thumbs of those found with voting ink on their hands.

The fear of the Taliban was real, justified and expressed openly. The Taliban, after all, believed in the power of sheer force rather than debate and peaceful negotiation. But reading between the lines of editorials published in media outlets loyal to Karzai's rivals, it appeared that democracy was also likely to lead to violence in Afghanistan. Judging by the articles' carefully crafted arguments, Karzai's opponents were anticipating widespread fraud and were ready to contest the election results if Karzai were to win again.

Needless to say, such protests had to be staged in the name of democracy, giving Karzai's rivals a legitimate cause. Protests could easily lead to violence and violence, in turn, could easily get out of control. After all, the Afghan army and police force were notorious for their inadequacy, which was why President Karzai reportedly decided to put tribal militia groups in charge of ensuring security at polling stations. The decision was soon deemed an act of provocation. Karzai's opponents believed that the militia were bound to intimidate voters, forcing them to vote for Karzai instead of their candidate of choice.

Between the Taliban's open threat and the peril of civil war disguised as a struggle for democracy, Afghans were casting their votes in a country where some of the most fundamental questions were regularly brushed aside and dismissed on the part of its politicians. While presidential candidates happily declared that they were ready to welcome back into the nation's arms "our disappointed brethrens," a euphemism used for the Taliban, few asked themselves the following question: what if the Taliban refuse the hug?

After all, the Taliban were waging a war not only against the foreign troops but also the mujahedin leaders who had been defeated by the Taliban in 1996 only to return to office triumphantly with the help of Nato in 2001. In other words, the Taliban were likely to carry on fighting even after the foreign troops left the country.

But if Taliban violence was likely to continue, what was the point of spending US$221m for a democratically elected government that was incapable of protecting democracy from the threat of the Taliban? What was the point of investing US$221m for democracy in a country where politicians themselves were the first to break the law and trade constituents' rights in return for personal privileges?

The Karzai administration, a democratically elected body, was itself becoming a threat to democracy in 2009. It curbed media freedom and increased the power of ethnic and religious community leaders notorious for their lack of respect for democracy and human rights. This is not to say that Afghans' enthusiasm for democracy was not real in the days before the vote casting. The enthusiasm was genuine but few Afghans believed that their vote would solve their country's bigger problems.

Voting With Your Genes

"You have to learn to read between the lines," said my colleague when I asked him to help me make sense of a report from Kabul. He was a disillusioned Afghan, with over twenty years of experience in observing Afghan politics. I followed his advice and understood that there was an omnipresent, big pink elephant in my ancestral homeland that everybody pretended not to notice. Talking about it was a taboo almost on a par with discussing sex in public. Blasphemy was the only more powerful taboo than this elephant. The beast was called ethnic hatred. If there was one clear revelation in the 2009 election, it was the fact that the people's vote revealed that they identified themselves with an ethnic groups rather than the abstract concept of Afghan nationhood.

The BBC's Afghan desk as always took the task of reporting the election thoroughly and asked the three leading candidates of 2009 the following question: "What would you do, if you were to lose the election?" All three—Hamid Karzai, Abdullah Abdullah and Ashraf Ghani—came up with the standard response: "We would respect the people's verdict." In other words, Afghanistan was a democracy ruled by the will of the people. Such humble words were just what was expected from politicians of developing countries whose survival relied chiefly on foreign aid. In the motto of the benevolent international community: no ballot, no aid. Or in the case of Afghanistan, no pots of paint flown specially from Dubai to decorate the president's office.

The truth was that in 2009 not all Afghans were able to deliver their verdict in the election. The Taliban, who in contrast to the mavericks in Kabul, were sticking to the traditional bullet-not-ballot style of governance, successfully managed to frighten the people in the south into non-participation. Although small voter turnout was expected in the restive south, the people were not free from threat even in relatively calmer regions. In Herat, the now dead local strongman Yahya Akbari reportedly had threatened to fire rockets if the people dared to venture out and greet Karzai on his campaign trip to their city. In sum, the security that is an absolute must for a fair election was not felt even in relatively calmer regions of Afghanistan. It was this condition of high risk for questionable reward that made many Afghans wonder whether the 2009 election was an exercise in true democracy.

Be that as it may, Afghan and international observers were quick to point out that at least 35 per cent of the population ventured out to cast their votes, in spite of threats of violence, and that this showed that ordinary Afghans had matured politically and a democratic culture was taking root in the country. At first glance, there seems little reason why this should not have been the case. In contrast to 2004 (when the public mood was optimistic, the Taliban on the run and the neighboring countries Iran and Pakistan well-disposed towards Kabul) voters in 2009 had little reason to believe in democracy, let alone risk their lives to cast their votes. After all, 2009 was a much more violent year, with Taliban attacks reaching the heart of the capital and the Kabul administration and its international allies losing credibility both in terms of delivering peace or improving the people's living conditions. And yet millions of Afghans risked their lives, ventured out and cast their votes fully aware that voting meant taking a serious risk and knowing very well that the election would be fraudulent and the candidates most probably either lying or making empty promises. Afghan and international observers celebrated this as evidence that Afghanistan had moved forward and was no longer an essentially tribal society upon whom the West had imposed democracy by sheer force of military. In brief, a success story. But there is another, more compelling reason.

Preliminary results based on a random sample of one million votes were published and they told a different story. According to the sample, the people's verdict had given rise to two leaders: Karzai closely followed by Abdullah Abdullah. In other words, a Pashtun leader followed closely by a half-Tajik leader with a majority Tajik support base. This was what analysts called "identity voting." The preliminary results showed that Karzai's attempt at nation-building had failed and most Afghans' loyalty lay first with their ethnic group, and then the nation as a whole. Karzai's critics had repeatedly pointed out that his nation-building attempts had been largely superficial, consisting of throwing dinner parties for discredited leaders of ethnic and religious minority groups. In the words of presidential candidate Ramazan Bashardost, making a Hazara leader sit next to nomadic

Pashtun leader at dinner is not exactly nation-building. The many mass graves scattered around the country bore witness to the ethnic rivalries that followed the Soviet army's withdrawal from Afghanistan and led to the civil wars of the early 1990s. During the presidential election campaign, ex-Taliban commander turned candidate Mullah Rocketi was the only contender to openly admit that ethnic mistrust was the only reason why Afghans so easily became tools in the service of foreign powers and hence carried on fighting. Nation-building had a long way to go in Afghanistan but as economist Paul Collier argues, leaders must build a nation before they can build a state.

This pattern of identity voting was the natural outcome of the ethnicized politics that had thrived over the last three decades. And ethnicized politics create lazy politicians who are automatically given support by members of their ethnic communities regardless of their performance, personal integrity or even education. The fact that voters in Afghanistan had opted for identity voting showed that the idea of the state as a service provider had still not taken root in Afghanistan and ethnic loyalties overrode loyalty to Afghanistan as a whole. To put it bluntly, apart from a small group of educated young people, most Afghans hadn't moved on from the ethnicized politics that had led to the civil wars of the early 1990s. The only difference between then and now was that ballots were used instead of bullets. But this, in itself, was a kind of progress.

Elections: Paranoids, Agitators and the Indifferent

"Have a look at this fax, it's from Mullah Omar," said my favorite colleague, closing his bag and leaving for home. The fax had been sitting there for four hours but my colleague just couldn't be bothered to read it. He had spent most of his professional career observing Afghan politics and had reached a point when even Mullah Omar's fax failed to excite him. I wanted to be like him, easy-going and laid back and not be taken by surprise by anything Afghan-related. To reach this goal was easy, our politics was repetitive and always basically boiled down to God, paranoia, and ethnic rivalry. So it came as no surprise to me when news broke that the 2009 election had ended in a runoff. There were serious allegations of fraud that needed to be explored. I investigated the Afghan media reactions, already knowing the answers. This is what I found.

Afghans were divided into three camps after the run-off news: the angry, the enthusiasts, and the disenchanted. The angry regarded the runoff as a foreign conspiracy and were suspicious. The enthusiasts welcomed it as a step towards greater democracy. The third camp—the disenchanted—couldn't care less. For this group, President Hamid Karzai and his opponent, Dr Abdullah Abdullah, were both discredited politicians and, as such, interchangeable. The disenchanted didn't vote the first time around and were likely to stay at home for the runoff, too. They were sick and tired of politics and didn't feel like getting involved.

I searched for representatives of the enthusiast camp. Professor Arafat of Kabul University was one of them. In his own words: "The runoff has shown Afghans that their vote does matter after all, and that there are institutions in the country that take fraud seriously and do something about it." In his view, the mistakes of the first round were part of the country's learning process. "What matters now is that the country has been given a chance to correct the mistakes. There's willingness in the government to reform and this should be supported."

Calling BBC Farsi from Kabul, Abdullah Jawed was equally optimistic. He said: "Despite much negative publicity, there's still optimism. The runoff shows that democracy is taking root in Afghanistan. The people are hopeful and are going to take the runoff seriously."

Jawed said that his entire family, including people in their seventies, had voted in the first round and were planning to vote again for the run-off. Judging from the locations given by the enthusiasts contacting the BBC, supporters of the runoff were mainly from Kabul and the north and the west of the country. In other words, from the relatively calm, better-off parts of Afghanistan where the Pashtuns are a minority. We can safely assume that supporters of the runoff were essentially composed of Tajiks whose identity voting originally brought Dr Abdullah into close competition with President Karzai. The runoff had given them a second chance in their struggle for political supremacy of the Tajik ethnic group.

Against this background of ethnic competition, it was not surprising that the angry camp was essentially made up of Afghans who lived in the south and the east of the country. The Pashtuns, in other words. Shafaq, a caller to the BBC from Helmand province, summarized their views in his comment: "The foreigners exaggerated the extent of fraud, blowing it out of proportion. The Obama administration is against President Karzai because Karzai was close to the Republicans. The foreigners have forced Karzai to agree to a runoff. They have their own plans."

In the view of people like Shafaq, far from representing a step towards greater democracy, the runoff was a political show orchestrated by foreigners with the goal of installing a puppet regime in Kabul. This bleak interpretation was part of a larger conspiracy theory that suspected Washington of trying to push the Afghan insurgency towards the north of the country, in an attempt to destabilize central Asia and so put Russia under pressure by encouraging a proxy war on its southern border. Hence, for this group, the runoff represented the start of a new cold war front in the Tajik-populated north, making the support of the Tajik candidate, Dr Abdullah, an essential part of the game for Washington.

This camp believed that deals had already taken place behind closed doors, ensuring that the future government was in tune with Washington's interests in the region. For this camp, the runoff was not a sign of authentic democratization but the loss of already fragile Afghan self-determination.

Drowned out in the shouting match between the angry and the enthusiasts was the voice of the disenchanted. Given that only a third of the population chose to exercise their right to vote in the first round, there were strong grounds to believe that the disenchanted represented a majority of the Afghan population. Sarfraz, a caller from Jalalabad, summed up their disappointment in his comment. He said: "Five years ago, Afghan votes brought to power a legitimate government which turned out to be utterly corrupt. What's the point of ensuring a transparent election when all we do is help establish another corrupt regime?"

This was a fair point, and yet a point that got easily lost in the obsession with vote-counting and fraud. For the disenchanted, even a perfectly transparent election leading to a solidly legitimate government offered little hope. This was because the mechanisms to ensure good governance and curb corruption were not in place in Afghanistan, so in the five-year term between elections, the government was left to its own devices, unchecked and unsupervised. People like Sarfarz feared that by casting their vote all they achieved was to help corrupt officials loot the country in the name of democracy. Hence they decided to stay at home, watching Indian soap operas instead of casting their vote.

Democratization in Afghanistan had thus far failed to convince most Afghans that it actually leads to good governance. Since promises of policy were widely seen as a smokescreen for the favoritism and profiteering that constitutes governance in practice, the Afghans who remained enthusiastic for the democratic project were mostly those who regarded it as a means of either maintaining or toppling traditional Pashtun dominance. In the absence of politics based on policy, the only kind of politics that remained was ethnic block voting.

Despite all the debates and the excitement, the run-off was cancelled and President Karzai announced as winner of the 2009 presidential elections.

The Afghan Political Comedy Show

President Karzai was re-elected leader of Afghanistan after a strange election marked by ethnic paranoia, near chaos, the announcement and subsequent cancellation of a run-off owing to security concerns. But the news that the people of Afghanistan would be treated to another five years of Hamid Karzai's eccentric rule was covered in all Afghan media outlets apart from Karzai's own mouthpiece, the state-run RTA television. Instead of reporting Karzai's re-election, the TV station ran a *Tom and Jerry* cartoon.

Given the ridiculous nature of the August 2009 elections, *Tom and Jerry* was a fitting response to Karzai's victory. After all, what was Afghan politics in the run up to 2009 but an international comedy show, making fun of its people and future? The comedy started in 2001, when Afghans were promised peace, justice and disarmament only to see warlords and local strongmen elevated to positions of power, complete with democratic titles, fancy cars and bodyguards. In the words of a source: "It was like expecting Genghis Khan and his entourage to run a peaceful democracy."

Beards were shaved off and local attire replaced with western suits and ties, but the turf-war mentality of many Afghan power-holders had not changed. It was the same inability to compromise for the sake of Afghanistan and prioritize the people's future over a personal and ethnic agenda that resulted in the civil wars of 1990s and the rise to power of the Taliban. Then as now, the Taliban were the sole winners of such crisis. The losers were the people and the country's fragile democracy.

An editorial in *Hasht-e Sobh* newspaper summarized the consequences of the inadequate handling of this election for the country's future. The paper said the hasty declaration of Karzai's "victory" amounted to saying no to democracy and democratic elections. "Besides, it has given the Taliban and their allies an opportunity to claim that the people of Afghanistan are not ready for democracy and that a return to traditional forms of leadership is the sole viable solution." The paper said that cancelling the runoff on the grounds of security and other problems had set a dangerous precedent. "Who can guarantee that the same reasons of saving costs and other problems will not be used as an excuse in the future to disregard democracy altogether?"

Hasht-e Sobh reflected the views of those Afghans who believed that no cost should have been considered too high, no challenge too overwhelming to ensure a decent election because democracy was the only viable solution for Afghanistan. In other words, dismissing democratic principles for the sake of short-term expediency was not going to work out in the long term because all it did was to prepare the ground for a return of totalitarianism. And yet this was exactly what happened in 2009, though this time with the support of the international community. One could go a step further and claim that the international community had become Afghanized. After all, mutiny inside the United Nations Assistance Mission in Afghanistan and constant bickering between various Nato countries and a dithering Washington were all but a mirror image of Afghan politics.

Be that as it may, the 2009 election was a historical event in that it revealed just how profoundly inadequate the country's leadership was in handling a crisis. Hence, disappointment set in even among those who displayed unwavering support for the two main candidates. Karzai's supporters had no choice but to admit that by agreeing to the runoff, the president had further compromised his independence and was left with little choice but to make concessions to the country's international allies.

As a result, many Afghans believed that foreigners were now officially running the show in Afghanistan. Given the growing anti-western sentiment in the country, this was not an enviable position for the president to be in. The Taliban had already declared him a western puppet, the rest of the country was beginning to agree with them. Abdullah Abdullah's supporters were equally let down. They had to face the following question: given that everybody, including Abdullah, knew that fraud was bound to happen during the 2009 elections, why did he decide to run a campaign to begin with? Why did he not retreat, giving a chance to other candidates who would have faced up to a run-off? In other words, why kick up a massive fuss only to chicken out in the last minute?

As it turned out, in the historical 2009 election the people of Afghanistan voted for a cheat and a chicken respectively and the only reasonable explanation for this irrational decision is the country's obsession with ethnicized politics. As long as politicians are supported in return for the sole quality of representing this or that ethnicity, Afghans would be fools to expect any other outcome but a ridiculous comedy show plunging the country into further crisis. To build a decent state and run a democracy, the Afghan leadership must work on nation-building so that the people vote for qualities other than ethnicity. After all, Afghanistan's core problem is that it's a country without a nation.

A New Cabinet

Afghans did the 2009 presidential elections in their unique, eccentric way. The poor were thrilled to be offered free lunches of rice and kebab, a cheap kind of buying votes. The Taliban did their usual violence, terrifying the population, throwing tantrums and altogether getting themselves noticed. The ethno-nationalists voted for the representatives of their gene pool and the rest of the country decided to watch TV. It came to a run-off and Karzai was elected president. The city was left looking ugly, with torn campaign posters sticking to the walls, while Karzai was faced with the unpleasant task of choosing his ministers.

What happened next was not surprising, given the conflict-ridden nature of the election. Karzai delayed announcing the new cabinet for the 2009 term. Local media sources said that Afghanistan's president was being ground between two political millstones, caught in a predicament of his own making. After all, he was believed to have had offered ministerial posts to various political heavyweights in return for their support for his presidential campaign. Those supporters now expected the president to fulfill his promise and put them in ministerial seats.

But Karzai found that his hands were tied. Washington was expecting him to come up with a clean, competent and capable cabinet. This, after all, was Obama's world, a corruption-free, happy and fair planet. The individuals who allegedly were offered ministerial posts were not chosen for these qualities. So what was Karzai to do? Please his internal supporters or his international critics? The former were bullies, the latter were paying the bills. The public was kept waiting; the president was delaying; and as always, there were rumours and speculation as to the outcome.

But what did Afghans expect of their new cabinet? The BBC's *Your Turn* program put this question to a diverse group of people in Afghanistan and abroad. They all came up with a standard response, "We expect our ministers to be honest, professional and patriotic," implying that the cabinet in power was none of the three. A similar view came to the fore at around the same time in parliamentary debate over the issue of dual nationality of some ministers. Even though the constitution does not explicitly ban ministers from holding dual nationality, many Afghans view some ministers' holding on to their foreign passports as problematic.

To put it bluntly, many Afghans believed that ministers who held two passports were likely to flee the country as soon as there was a serious crisis. Kabul's famous "surrender of the ties" urban legend neatly summarized this view. According to this story, during the June 2006 Kabul riots, a ministry official approached the minister and his entourage, telling them that their ties would identify them to the rioters as western lackeys. The frightened technocrats quickly handed over their ties as they prepared to flee. But the riots came under control, making an imminent departure unnecessary. The resourceful tie collector, though, refused to return the ties and so became a hero in Afghan political folklore.

Whether a true tale or an urban legend, the story was illustrative of the gap that divided the cabinet from both parliament and the public. The cabinet in charge pre-2009 election was mainly composed of the bourgeoisie who had left for the West in the 1980s, and so had no part in the jihad against the Red Army. The people who stayed behind, those who fought or moved to Iran and Pakistan, referred to such Afghans by derogatory terms including "dog washer" or "westoxicated." The phrase "dog washer" was in reference to the fact that most Afghans living in the West were unskilled, working in the service sector, which in the vivid imagination of Afghans back home included washing domestic pets of wealthy European or Americans. The term "westoxicated" referred to those Afghans who returned to the country with exaggerated western affectations.

This clash of cultures played out between a largely Islamist parliament and a westernized cabinet made up of the old bourgeoisie was a recurrent source of political stalemate. To be fair to the old bourgeoisie, the radicalized politics of the 1980s and 90s had no room for the moderate, nationalistic views of the westernized elite. They left the country because they supported neither the communist regime in Kabul nor their nemesis, the mujahideen. In the heat of thirty years of battle, the bourgeoisie was forgotten, representing as it did an irrelevant leftover of the past, too far away from home to merit consideration. Their return to the country since 2001 turned out to be as surprising as the rise of the Taliban five years earlier.

Yet the consequences of decades spent away from Afghanistan were plain for all to see. The dual passport-holders were accused of lacking in loyalty to their country. The public viewed them as arrogant and out-of-touch. Their image of Afghanistan was equally believed to have been frozen in a distant, idealized past, the country they knew in their peak years of life, in the 1960s and 70s.

But if the cabinet was accused of lacking in common touch, its critics in parliament had their own, particular shortcomings. Perhaps the tragedy of Afghanistan was that it was run by a cabinet that was alienated and a parliament that was largely composed of former warriors. Neither of the two had a chance to learn the craft of politics under what would be deemed normal circumstances: in a sovereign and peaceful country they can call home.

Some critics argue that in the results-driven age of the noughties, both the Afghan public and the international community were expecting too much, too soon. Given that Afghanistan had emerged out of thirty years of turmoil, not to mention many more decades of under-development, the critics may well have had a point and the president might well have been right to take his time choosing his new cabinet.

Too Many Cooks in the Afghan Cabinet

Nothing is simple in Afghanistan because we live under the illusion that we have all the time in the world. And so it was that after his election in 2009, President Karzai first took his time to announce his list of cabinet and then, when he presented the list to parliament, the result was a disaster. Parliament gave seventeen ministers a vote of no confidence. The public regarded the rejection as a sign of genuine democratic progress. After all, there was widespread suspicion that some proposed ministers were stand-ins for the jihadi leader who had backed Karzai's election campaign, while others had been favorites of the international community.

President Karzai then presented Afghanistan's parliament with a revised list of cabinet members eight days after the original list was rejected. But since Afghan politics was no longer a purely domestic affair, the international community was quick to interfere. The then UN chief in Kabul, Kai Eide, said that parliament's decision was a setback. The international community's contradictory visions for Afghanistan were growing in distance from Afghans' own aspirations.

Many Afghans were becoming increasingly unhappy about such open interference in their affairs but since the international community was paying the bills, Afghans had little ground for objection. Those who paid the bills also wanted to a have a say and it was also this latter group of foreign financiers that Karzai took into consideration while drafting his first list. But parliament said no.

Yet this was Afghan politics and as a local saying goes, there's always a bowl underneath the bowl. Soon after parliament's rejection was announced, it was leaked to Afghan journalists that the president had deliberately offered parliament a "death list." To put it bluntly, the president had anticipated the rejection. He wanted a vote of no confidence because it offered him a legitimate way to dismiss unwanted figures proposed to him in secret deals with the strongmen who lent him support during the presidential election. According to the leak, the real list was kept hidden in the president's drawer, ready to be presented to parliament as soon it offered its rejection. The revised list was allegedly the real list.

So what did Afghans think of the new list? "Zalmay Rasool as foreign minister? What a joke!" answered a respondent to my question. But why? I probed. "He's been following the president closely since 2001 and if there's a press conference, you'd always find him sitting right next to Karzai. But he has never uttered a word. No one knows what he thinks. He doesn't speak." A positive spin-off of the silent man might be that he is unlikely to indulge in cheap talk, a favorite pastime of Afghan politicians. What do you think of the new list? I asked a fellow Afghan journalist. "At least it's new," was his response. No enthusiasm there. The local press's reception of the revised list was equally lukewarm. The president has drafted the new list in haste, lamented an editorial in Hasht-e Sobh, contradicting the leak. The paper speculated that the president probably hadn't met some of the people he had suggested. The list was indeed full of unfamiliar names belonging to unknown individuals. This was a problem in Afghanistan, where having a reputation is crucial for people in public positions because reputation allows for a judgment of character. According to Hasht-e Sobh, one name on the list stood out: Abdulhadi Arghandiwal. He was the head of the Islamic party, and known for his reluctance to speak out against renegade jihadi leader Gulboddin Hekmatyar. The latter's troops were fighting an armed struggle against the government. According to Hasht-e Sobh, Arghandiwal's appearance on the list signaled a shift in Karzai's policy towards extremists.

But the revised list also included three women, presumably to ease fears that Karzai had officially opened cabinet's doors to extremist fundamentalists. The policy of pleasing everyone is in character with Karzai and has dismayed those who wish to see Afghanistan run by a decisive leader with a clear vision. But since historically Afghan governments have been brought down due to internal rivalries rather than public revolts, the president was acting rationally by co-opting rivals, rather than alienating them. Hence, Karzai's spokesman was quick to clarify that the rejected individuals' skills would be put to use elsewhere. "Karzai is the most tolerant man in Afghanistan," said a supporter in a private conversation. Not all Afghans were happy with this tolerance.

Be that as it may, the seeds for the 2009 cabinet troubles were sown months earlier, during the presidential campaign. In an unwise move, the strongmen who rallied around Karzai boasted

PART THREE

that they had been offered ministerial seats in return for backing the president. The boasting made the news and was discussed with much distaste.

The motivation for these sorts of pronouncements might be that the strongmen's powers were diminishing, triggering a desire to impress the public by exaggerating their influence. The strategy backfired but luckily for the strongmen, their rivals were equally inept. Hence when the first list was rejected, MP Frahi, a member of the National Front, the opposition that lost the election, blurted out that the rejection was the Front's revenge, punishing Karzai for conducting a fraudulent election. This thoughtless outburst insinuated that the Front had influenced parliament's decision, and the rejection had been politically motivated. Frahi stands in a long line of Afghan politicians who have a talent for undermining their own cause.

But fortunately for the Front, other MPs dismissed Frahi's remarks. "MPs gave their vote on the basis of merit or lack thereof. No one, neither a front nor a political grouping, can claim this victory for themselves and pronounce that they have influence over parliament's decisions," said Abdul Satar Khawasi, the deputy parliamentary leader.

However, it seemed that the Afghan cabinet was simply not large enough to accommodate the candidates of all interested parties. "Maybe we should set up three cabinets: one for the international community, one for the jihadi leaders and one for the people," said a source, summarizing the view of all those tired of foreign interference and internal machinations. The old cliché that too many cooks spoil the broth certainly was true when it came to Afghanistan.

Progress and Stagnation in Afghan Elections

Readers, just imagine what life would be like if you weren't able to read or write? You would feel impaired, having to rely on

219

your eyes, ears and memory alone to process and maintain information. This is what life is like for most Afghans and their introduction to such a complex political system as democracy means that they have to remember many names and faces in order to vote for the right candidate. To be fair to the electoral commission and all other bodies involved in elections, this key problem was taken into account and inventive minds worked out ways to make it easier for Afghans to take part in the parliamentary elections of 2010.

With an electorate that was largely illiterate, the campaign—like its predecessors—was a highly visual affair, with faces of numerous candidates staring down at the people from the heights of billboards. Among the many promises of a better future there was a "Yes We Can" message, looking oddly out of place in Kabul's dusty environment. Given Obama's lack of faith in Afghans, the copycat message was unintentionally ironic.

But how did voting work in a place where most people were acutely politically aware but unable to even read their candidates' names let alone page through their manifestos (though I doubt such manifestos exist)? I perused the lists of candidates to get a sense of what voters held in their hands when casting their ballots.

Judging by the lists, the vast majority of candidates were independent, with no party affiliation. In a conformist society such as Afghanistan, this display of individualism was rather odd. Cynics would argue that independent candidates were easier to bribe, hence candidates' reluctance to appear linked to a larger organization. But it was equally true that political parties were chiefly known for their war atrocities and so, being associated with them reduced candidates' chances of success. This, too, explained the appeal of independent candidacy.

Given the sheer number of candidates, making a choice was a daunting task for many voters. With little indication of candidates' political orientation, voters were left to draw upon visual clues, and titles carried in names. Those unable to read had to rely solely on photographs and symbols—but what sort of politics were voters supposed to associate with images of shovels, envelopes, and airplanes? Democracy and illiteracy didn't seem to go smoothly together.

Candidates' photographs were equally unhelpful. The only candidates that stood out were the attractive ones and those sporting striking beards or interesting headgear. A few stood out because they were smiling. Other than that, the lists were a fair cross-section of largely anonymous-looking, average Afghans. The sheer length of the lists was disorientating, perhaps explaining why some electoral officials allegedly felt tempted to interfere and manipulate voters. Mistakes were bound to be made, so why not give voters a little help?

Aside from the bewildering lists of nearly identical-seeming candidates, the election bore signs of both positive and negative trends. Positive change chiefly manifested itself in the candidacy of women and members of religious minorities, including Sikhs and Hindus. But even such encouraging trends were often testimony to the courage of candidates rather than reflecting a more open society.

In the words of Partapal Singh, a candidate of the Sikh community, despite having lived in the city for centuries, Sikhs were treated merely as guests in Kabul. Kabul is a city of immigrant returnees and in Partapal Singh's experience, most of its inhabitants had little idea of Kabul's history of religious diversity. Like most candidates, Singh found that his campaign posters had been torn. But unlike most candidates, his defaced posters had threatening messages written on them: "You are an infidel. How dare you stand as a candidate?" Yet the fact that Partapal Singh's supporters were not exclusively Sikh and also included young Muslims showed that democracy was indeed taking root in Afghanistan.

While international media outlets focused on Taliban threats of violence, internal tensions unrelated to the Taliban that appeared in the election were largely ignored outside Afghanistan. The most regrettable tension was ethnic distrust chiefly felt in the Hazara community.

As with other traditionally-sidelined groups in Afghanistan, exile and jihad equipped the community with an acute sense of historical injustice and desire for equality. Given this background, voting arrangements should have been planned very carefully in Hazara-occupied places but, judging by early reports, in some neighborhoods and districts polling stations had either closed prematurely or simply did not open at all. Voters also complained of a shortage of ballot papers.

The reason for these shortcomings seemed unclear but some Hazaras regarded it as a deliberate attempt to exclude their community from the country's power structure. The fact that because of Taliban threats, large numbers of Pashtuns had also been excluded failed to persuade some Hazaras that their suspicion might have been exaggerated.

Interestingly, similar accusations of deliberate manipulation of democracy were raised against the Hazara community itself, chiefly in the city of Herat. In the absence of proper investigation, such inter-ethnic disputes are usually left unsolved, allowing resentment to turn into hatred, further damaging the process of democratization. This is exactly what happened in Herat.

Judging by initial reports, the most enthusiastic voters were the traditionally excluded entities, ethnic and religious minorities and women in calmer urban centers of the north and west. But even in these regions, rural voting patterns had all the hallmarks of block voting, and sometimes fraud.

Observers also noted the conspicuous presence of a new class of wealthy Afghans who owed their wealth to reconstruction projects and contracts with the US army. Members of this new business class were observed trying to buy votes, either by paying henchmen to stuff ballot boxes or by entering into deals with community leaders.

It was highly ironic that the same class that was the greatest financial beneficiary of the US mission was also the one that was undermining democracy through corruption and in doing so, damaging the US's reputation in Afghanistan. But then again, historically Afghan elites have always caused their own downfall and this, too, represented continuity—albeit of a regrettable kind.

The Illusion of Change

As a nation, Afghans have disappointed themselves and their allies so frequently that they lap up every opportunity for hope. This is particularly true of hope for better politics. In the words of a source, "It's like a mule stuck in the mud. Just imagine the villagers pushing and shoving the mule from all sides but the stubborn mule would not move an inch. This is Afghan politics for you." So when a series of protests against the Iranian government took place in various cities in Afghanistan, they made so many headlines that they threatened to damage diplomatic relations between Kabul and Tehran. It felt like something was happening, something dangerous but exciting was in the air.

Judging by the banners and protesters' comments, the gatherings were in response to the hanging of Afghan citizens, arrested and imprisoned in Iran for drug smuggling. The Afghan leader, Hamid Karzai, disagreed with the protests. He told a press conference: "In my view, protesting against a country that is friendly and fraternal is wrong."

The president's concern made sense, given that Kabul was trying to consolidate its relations with Tehran in an attempt to counterbalance Afghanistan's heavy reliance on the United States with new regional partners. But since the Afghan constitution granted citizens freedom of protest, Kabul had little choice but to tolerate them.

The protests, which were widely reported on the ground in Afghanistan, had some eye-catching features. The slogans were supranational in character, demanding justice not only for the hanged Afghans but also for a group of Kurdish political activists, among them a woman. But the call for solidarity beyond national borders did not stop there. Protesters made a public show of their solidarity with the Iranian opposition movement, carrying posters of Neda Agha Soltan, the young woman whose killing triggered international outrage against Tehran. A banner prominently carried in front of the rally said "Death to Oppression—in Kabul or Tehran."

To untrained eyes, the hallmarks of a new progressive movement were all there. Women, men and even schoolboys were marching alongside each other, condemning political oppression, demanding justice regardless of gender, ethnicity or even the category of crime that had led to imprisonment to begin with. They were curious protests, creating the impression that a reformist movement similar to the one in Iran was emerging in Afghanistan. The party that had officially organized the protests was, appropriately, named the Afghanistan Solidarity party.

A well-organized, grassroots movement seemed to have emerged in Afghanistan. But an objective assessment of the protests told a different story. In spite of their humanitarian message, the protests used means associated with rallies that have the potential to trigger violence. Effigies of Iranian officials were set on fire, and the phrase "death to" was not only shouted but was displayed on banners in large letters. This type of aggressive slogan was a hangover from the radical politics of the 1970s and 1980s, and had little room in progressive political movements of the twenty-first century.

Then there was the conspicuous presence of uniformed schoolboys, who in Afghanistan have a reputation for attending any protest as long as they are offered pocket money. Their marching alongside adults somewhat undermined the authenticity of the protests in a country where such dubious means of increasing rally numbers were well known. Was this really a new, authentic and progressive grassroots movement?

Afghan politics is rarely what it appears to be on the surface. Digging deeper into such seemingly new political movements, what usually resurfaces is old political rivalries—and even older ideologues reinventing themselves in tune with the demands of time.

The anti-Iranian protests were no exception. Research into the organizing party revealed that its leader was a seasoned political player, with a background in the Maoist Afghan political party established in 1968. The party's subsequent history mirrored that of its Islamist counterparts. Conflict set in soon after the party's establishment, creating splinter groups that operated clandestinely, often in exile. A number of important leaders were then killed under mysterious circumstances, and the true cause of their deaths was never revealed. The fog of war offered plenty of opportunities to blame the deaths on political rivals, Islamists led by Gulbuddin Hekmatyar, or foreign intelligence services, the ISI, the KGB or the CIA.

It was this murky world of politics in exile and on the ground that created the widespread paranoia in Afghanistan, a prism through which most Afghans today tend to interpret reality.

The leader behind the scenes also had a reputation among people familiar with his history and political circle for harboring strong sentiments against Iran. And so, what seemed a new and exciting Afghan grassroots movement turned out to be an extension of an old activist's personal feelings of resentment towards Iran. Afghans were briefly given the illusion that there was something new, and perhaps hopeful, on the horizon. But as it turned out, the protests were simply a confirmation of the old adage that everything must change so that everything can remain the same.

Malalai Joya: The Darling of Western Liberal Left

Malalai Joya is the undisputed darling of the liberal left in Europe and North America. Her devotees include wealthy liberals, idealist students, anarchists and the occasional intellectual star—Noam Chomsky, for example. To her fans, Joya represents the Afghan face of leftist anti-militarism. There are many people in the world who hate the United States but few of them have carved a career for themselves out of their contempt for Washington. Joya has made anti-Americanism her profession and her products range from ghost-written biographies to posters to lecture shows conspicuous for the use of crude language and display of photographs of injured Afghan babies. In sum, she is best-known for her categorical rejection of the US intervention in Afghanistan and it is this wholesale nature of her repudiation that is unfair. After all, without US intervention, Joya would not have been able to own a passport, let alone travel abroad. Equally, without the international community's interference, there would not have been the 2003 Loya Jerga where she first gained international fame. Joya's anti-US military rhetoric resonates with the leftist circles of the West who are her chief audience, and Joya's celebrity status reached a climax when she appeared alongside Noam Chomsky in Boston. Back home in Afghanistan, though, she has become irrelevant.

But to understand Joya's contradictory views, we need to look at how her career began and developed. Let's go back to the constitutional Loya Jerga of 2003 when Joya first became famous. At the time, she was an independent voice and had the audacity to make a relevant, but politically explosive comment. She said that the inclusion of war criminals threatened to undermine the assembly's legitimacy, that Afghans risked missing out on a historical chance for justice. Morally, she was absolutely right; but the truth was that, after two decades of violence, it was inevitable that the leaders that had emerged owed their power to war.

The international community had to work with what was there—and what was there was war leaders with dubious human rights records. To exclude them from the assembly was unreasonable because it would have driven them to start a new war front. Including them in the assembly meant that the Taliban remained the sole insurgents while the former mujahedin stopped fighting and began a new government. It was a morally flawed but pragmatic solution. Joya was driven by a burning desire for justice—pragmatism has never been her strength.

Joya's outspoken comment took the assembly by surprise. It was up to the assembly leader, Sebghatullah Mojaddedi, to diffuse the situation because he was older and more experienced. But Mojaddedi took offence and ordered Joya to leave the assembly. He then changed his mind and struck a gentler note, "Come back, child, you owe us an apology." But it was too late: the old man had lost the young woman. And with that, Joya lost a chance to fully develop her potential and work on the kind of constructive and reconciliatory politics that Afghanistan needed.

Since then, Joya's career as MP has been marked by repeats of that crucial early scene of her, a young woman, confronting old jihadi men. The location shifted from the Loya Jerga tent to parliament, but Joya and her jihadi nemesis remained stuck in an endless cycle of accusation and counter-accusation. The Afghan audiences found the confrontations first interesting, then amusing and finally lost interest in them altogether. By then, Joya was ousted from parliament, but her career abroad was beginning to flourish. Her book tour of the US, where she met Chomsky, was part of this development.

The tragedy of Joya is that she was spotted by the international media and a clandestine radical leftist Afghan organization at a time when Afghan democracy was in its infancy. At the time, Afghan human rights groups had not yet developed fully to give Joya the kind of support she needed. Isolated and vulnerable, she became an easy prey and was picked up by a group whose politics were steeped in the anti-imperialist revolutionary world of the 1960s and 70s ideological battles. Joya has served as a respectable front for a group that otherwise has little backing in Afghanistan. Joya's recurrent reference to "warlords in the pay of the US" are all about the group's bitterness that Washington allied itself with the group's Islamists rivals in the 1980s, enabling them to defeat the left. The alliance was abandoned between 1992 and 2001, but resumed fully with the 2001 intervention. Little wonder, then, that the group felt doubly betrayed by Washington.

But Joya's sudden fame in the West offered the group an unexpected chance to turn the tables and use Joya's popularity abroad to give her legitimacy to attack the group's jihadi nemesis in parliament. Joya's confrontations often came out of the blue. During a session about trade, Joya raised her hand but instead of asking questions about trade, she questioned the mujahedin's legitimacy. The speaker cautioned her that her comments were irrelevant because the session was about trade, but the damage was done and the session disrupted. Joya's disruptions of parliament eerily resembled similar incidents of leftwing versus rightwing fights that interrupted parliament in the 1960s. The resemblance is natural because the parties involved were the same old leftist comrades versus rightwing Islamist brothers. Joya has become simply a new player in an old political dynamic.

This also explained the intensity of the jihadis' reaction to Joya. After all, criticizing warlords was nothing unusual by 2007. But Joya was re-opening old wounds. Her repeated reference to the internal wars of the 1990s was the group's message that the jihadi victory was not complete since they had failed to cement it through establishing a solid state.

Needless to say, such nuances have been lost on the western media who presented Joya's provocations as a woman's struggle for rights and democracy. The thought that her disruption of parliament was evidence of an anti-democratic attitude on her part did not occur to them. After all, in the simplistic world of western politics, a young woman fighting bearded old men simply cannot be wrong.

EPILOGUE

Afghan Sufi tales tend to end with something along the lines of, "and the Sheikh's devotees were joyous that the problem was thus solved wisely and peacefully and no harm had come to anybody." No animal or human was harmed in the making of this book but I did neglect myself and my cat, revising the manuscript. My cat had food but not much entertainment. She became a bit bored and tried in vain to engage me in conversation. Cats look very serious when they miaw, as if they have something terribly urgent to say. I do admit that it was hard to ignore her while writing about the Taliban. They, too, are attention-seekers but of a much more dangerous variety. In Afghanistan, there is something that we got wrong. We reward bullies, spending all our energy on appeasing them, understanding them, offering them seats in the government, while we neglect the good people. The international community over time became Afghanized, focusing on trouble-makers while neglecting its natural allies, progressive Afghans who actually believe in democracy, diversity, and human rights. They may be a small section of society, but to be fair, in every other country the makers of change started off small, facing up and challenging the majority. Exactly why Afghanistan should be any different is not clear to me. But it has something to do with the dogma of cultural relativism, the idea that progressive Afghans do not represent authentic Afghanistan and should not be taken seriously.

If you read this book and found your head spinning, then don't worry. This is exactly how Afghans feel most of the time. For us, too, our country, culture and society are too bewildering to comprehend. If you ended up thinking that after this book, you are now more than ever uncertain what kind of country Afghanistan is, then, rest assured that we feel the same. We don't understand ourselves and are often tapping in the dark, searching for something to hold on to. I'd go even further and claim that we are yet to become. We are a nation in transition whose past is just as unknown as its future. It is the price we pay for having served first as an isolated buffer state and then the battlefield of proxy wars. Much was lost in the process, our past as well as our potential for a happy future.

But still, when individual Afghans are taken out of their unhealthy environment, they often show remarkable talent, revealing Afghanistan as a place of considerable potential. Despite thirty years of constant war, we have Olympic medal winners and beauty queens; internationally famous writers, a host of talented female journalists and writers as well as staunch young feminists who make Simone de Beauvoir look rather harmless. It's not a bad record for a desperately poor, war-torn country. So don't give up on us, please, even after we disappear from the news.

Nushin Arbabzadah
Los Angeles, June 2012

INDEX

Abdul-Ahad, Ghaith: writings of, 10

Abdullah, Abdullah: 197, 205, 208–9, 213; background of, 196; former Afghan Foreign Minister, 196–7; presidential election campaign of (2009), 100; supporters of, 212–13

Abdullah, King: 143–4

Afghan Civil War (1992–6): 142, 164, 207, 211

Afghan Pajhwok: 198; report on gay pride movement in Afghanistan, 75

Afghanistan: xi–xiii, 16, 20, 22, 26, 28–9, 65, 72, 76, 85, 93, 133, 139, 149–50, 152, 159, 190, 210, 216, 230; Badakhshan Province, 124; Badghis Province, 135; Baghlan Province, 99, 162; Bagram air base, 103, 107, 195; borders of, 38, 129, 132, 146; Buddhist monastery discovered in (2010), 42–3, 45; Christian population of, 26, 28, 40; culture focussing on women, 13, 21–3, 25, 29, 67, 88, 159; economy of, 19; Ghazni, 34; government of, 39, 51, 87, 134, 136, 140, 142, 145, 152, 165–6, 168, 177, 183, 193–4, 206; Helmand Province, 125, 128, 141, 147–8, 166–8, 182, 186; Herat, 7, 34, 59, 99, 119, 127, 222; Hindu population of, 59; homosexual community of, 73; Jalalabad, 210; Japanese embassy in, 5; Jewish population of, 58–60; Kabul, xvi, 2–3, 6, 8, 10, 16–20, 22, 24–7, 30–1, 34–5, 38–40, 42, 45, 48–50, 53, 55, 57–9, 64–5, 67, 69, 71, 73–5, 78, 84–5, 87, 99, 101, 107–13, 117, 120, 123–4, 126, 129–30, 134–9, 148–9, 152–3, 156, 159–61, 164–5, 169–71, 177–8, 180–1, 188, 191–2, 194, 198, 203–4, 206, 209, 214–15, 217, 220–1, 223–4; Kandahar, 34, 52, 86, 123, 127, 138–9, 146, 148, 153; Konar Province, 83; martyrdom culture in, 7, 40, 48; Mazar-i-Sharif, 153; media image of, 11; mercenaries in, 19; military of, 2, 157, 164; Ministry of Interior, 99; Ministry of Islamic Endowment, 104; Muslim population of, 48; Nangarhar Province, 124; NATO presence in, 55, 168,

INDEX

ground of, 196; invitation to mujahedin to join Taliban, 142; leader of Taliban, 134, 148, 179
opium: cultivation in Afghanistan, 182, 186–9; means for prevention of cultivation, 186–8; smuggling of, 184; Taliban's relationship with farmers of, 183
orientalism: 80

Pakistan: 37–8, 54–5, 72, 128, 142, 157, 161, 173, 175–6, 206; Afghan refugee population of, 215; borders of, 56, 129, 132, 146; conflict with India, 124–5, 199; government of, 160; Gwadar, 168; Inter-Services Intelligence (ISI), 78, 225; Islamabad, 53, 129, 144, 158–9, 161, 177; Peshawar, 53, 84; support for Tablighi Jama'at in, 42; Waziristan, 184
Palestine: Hamas, 135
Pashtun: 59, 100, 125–7, 159, 166, 196; code of honour, 141; Durrani, 196; Ghilzai, 196; Pashto (language), 54, 57, 66, 94–5, 100, 167, 201; self-determination, 128–9; territory inhabited by, 53, 100
Pashtunistan: concept of, 159
Payman: articles of, 36–7, 39; closure of (2009), 36; political ideology of, 37–8; 'Prediction of the Third World War', 36–7
Pazhwak, Abdur Rahman: poetry of, 15
People's Democratic Party of Afghanistan (PDPA): Central Committee of, 130
Persian (language): 30–1, 33, 61, 71, 89; Afghan, 94; Dari-, 31, 41,

47, 55, 57, 115–16, 143, 145, 158, 194; Iranian, 94–5; Judeo-, 60; poetry, 31, 93
Poland: 16
Porshor, Jalil: memoirs of, 130

Qaderi, Homira: writings of, 117
Qizilbash: 53

Rabbani, Burhanuddin: 141
Rabia: legend of, 88–93
Radio France International: Dari-Persian service, 145
al-Rahman, Qari Ziya: bounty placed on, 83
Rafat, Azita: 98
Rasool, Zalmay: 217
Republic of Ireland: 19
Republic of Vietnam: Saigon, 118
Rocketi, Mullah: 207
Rushdie, Salman: fatwa issued against (1989), 56
Russian Empire: military of, 43
Russian Federation: 142, 183–4, 199, 209; Moscow, 189

Sadat, Olga: *Yak, Do, Seh*, 118–19
Samanian, Shorab: 64–5, 67; blog of, 66
Saudi Arabia: 143; Al-Watan, 144
Saur Revolution (1978): 156; bombarding of presidential palace, 130
Saudi Arabia: 40, 128; Mecca, 29
Schwarzenbach, Annemarie: 70
Scott, Ridley: *American Gangster*, 184
Second World War (1939–45): 70
self-immolation: examples of, 118–19; of women, 118–19
Shah, King Zahir: family of, 128
shalagi: 26; concept of, 24

INDEX

Drugs and Crime (UNODC), 186, 188; personnel of, 86, 217
United States of America (USA): xvi, 9, 111, 141, 155, 175, 223; 9/11 attacks, 55, 102, 125, 141, 172, 174; Central Intelligence Agency (CIA), 178, 225; Los Angeles, 27, 80; military of, 83, 103, 166, 184, 222; New York, 5, 25, 27, 60, 80, 85, 125, 160, 193; use of fungi on opium crops by, 186–8; Washington DC, 71, 104, 133, 135, 157, 160, 166, 168, 170–2, 188, 192–3, 201, 209, 228
Uzbeks: 100

Vanga, Baba: story of, 36, 38

Wahhabism: spread of, 36
War on Terror: 160; development of, 38, 159
Wilson, Christy: *More to Be Desire Than Gold*, 39

women: 7–8, 13, 63, 85, 115, 193; Afghan culture of, 13, 21–3, 25, 29, 67, 88, 159; assigned value of in polygamous marriages, 29; *bacha posh*, 96–9; forced marriages of, 119; impact of social restrictions on, 61–2; maltreatment of, 119–20; mandate for in Qur'an, 64; *namoos* culture, 121–2; self-immolation of, 118; warrior legends, 86
World Bank: personnel of, 195

YouTube: 83, 99, 149, 182

zabaan: culture based on, 93
Zaeef, Mullah: background of, 140
Zaid, Mullah: former Taliban ambassador to Pakistan, 140
Zaki, Jan Ali: writings of, 84
Zalmay, Ghows: 57; arrest of (2007), 56; translation of Qur'an (2007), 55–6
Zoroastrianism: 34